WORLD CONGRESS ON COMMUNICATION FOR DEVELOPMENT

WORLD CONGRESS ON COMMUNICATION FOR DEVELOPMENT

Lessons, Challenges, and the Way Forward

The Communication Initiative

Food and Agriculture Organization of the United Nations (FAO)

The World Bank

1818 H Street NW
Washington DC 20433
Telephone: 202-473-1000
Internet: www.worldbank.org
E-mail: feedback@worldbank.org

1 2 3 4 10 09 08 07

ISBN-13: 978-0-8213-7137-4
eISBN-13: 978-0-8213-7138-1
DOI: 10.1596/978-0-8213-7137-4

Cover illustration: Cyrus Tafty, Incentive SPA.
Cover design: Circle Graphics.

Library of Congress Cataloging-in-Publication Data

World Congress on Communication for Development (1st : 2006 : Rome, Italy)
World Congress on Communication for Development : lessons, challenges, and the way forward / The Communication Initiative, Food and Agriculture Organization of the United Nations, The World Bank.
p. cm.
"The first World Congress on Communication for Development was held between October 25 and 27, [2006] at the Food and Agriculture Organization (FAO) in Rome, Italy. It was organized by the World Bank, the FAO and The Communication Initiative"—Executive summary.
Includes bibliographical references.
ISBN-13: 978-0-8213-7137-4
ISBN-10: 0-8213-7137-1
ISBN-13: 978-0-8213-7138-1 (electronic 13)
ISBN-10: 0-8213-7138-X (electronic 10)
1. Communication in economic development—Congresses. 2. Communication in public health—Congresses. 3. Communication in public administration—Congresses. I. Communication Initiative (Organization) II. Food and Agriculture Organization of the United Nations. III. World Bank. IV. Title.
HD76.W67 2006
338.9001'4—dc22

2007019880

Contents

Foreword ix

Preface xiii

Acknowledgments xv

Executive Summary xxvii

The Rome Consensus xxxi

Abbreviations xxxvii

1 *The First World Congress on Communication for Development* 1

Organization of the Congress 5

Participants in the Congress 6

2 *Communication and Health* 11

Sex, Lies, and Stories of AIDS 13

The Race to Immunize Every Child: Communication for Polio Eradication and Immunization 18

Of Birds and Humans: Communication Aspects of Avian Influenza 22

Message and Voice 26

Of Rubber and Road: Impact and Evidence 29

Key and Emerging Issues for the Health Strand 31

Papers Used in the Health Sessions 32

3 *Communication and Governance* 33
Securing Political Will: The Prerequisite for Public Sector Reform 36
Strengthening Voice and Accountability: The End-Goal of Communication for Development. 40
Building Media Systems: Enabling an Effective Fourth Estate 43
Fighting Corruption: Beyond Technocratic Solutions 47
Making Public Institutions Transparent: The Cornerstone of an Open Society 49
Good Governance in Practice: The Example of Infrastructure Projects 53
Key and Emerging Issues for the Governance Strand. 58
Papers Used in the Governance Sessions 58

4 *Communication and Sustainable Development*. 61
The Regional Meetings 61
The Plenary and Workshops on Communication for Sustainable Development 64
Communication for Food Security, Rural Development, and Livelihood Strategies 65
Poverty Reduction and Equity Issues. 67
Communication and Sustainable Natural Resource Management. 69
Communication for Development and Global Environmental Issues 73
Mainstreaming Communication in Sustainable Development Policies: Local Perspectives and Priorities 77
Sustaining the Process: Local Appropriations of Communication for Sustainable Development 81
Key and Emerging Issues for the Sustainable Development Strand 83
Papers Used in the Sustainable Development Sessions 85

5 *Communication Labs* 87
News Media as a Pro-Development Tool 88
Fighting Poverty: Community Media and Communication for Development in the Digital Age. . . 90
Implementing Communication for Development Thinking in Southern Realities: Negotiating Politics, Profit, and Poverty toward Social Inclusion 93
Impact and Assessment: Innovative Ways to Determine Communication Effectiveness 97
The Rationale, Value, and Challenges for Adopting Participatory Communication in Development Programs 99
Which Kind of Development Communication Does Attract Media?. 102
Communication for Development and ICTs: Where Do They Meet? 104
Communication and Disabilities 106
Indigenous Peoples 107

6 *Overall Recommendations* 111
Recommendations from the Health Strand 111
Recommendations from the Governance Strand 113
Recommendations from the Sustainable Development Strand 115
Recommendations from the Cross-Cutting Themes 117
Key Recommendations from the Policy Makers' Forum . . 119

APPENDIXES

1 *Congress Participants* 123
Plenary Session Speakers 124
Full List of Participants 127

2 *Media Attendees* 201

3 *Communication for Development: Making a Difference—A WCCD Background Study* 209

4 *Papers Selected by the Scientific Committee for the World Congress on Communication for Development* 293

References 305

Foreword

The first World Congress on Communication for Development sought to provide the evidence and make the arguments for placing Communication for Development much closer to the center of development policy and practice. The Congress did so by creating a space for practitioners, academicians, and decision makers to come together formally and informally to review impact data, share experiences on processes and approaches, listen to stories, learn from new research, and strengthen the networks that will carry the work of the Congress beyond Rome. The presentations and discussions underlined the importance of Communication for Development and distinguished it from communication per se for an influential audience not steeped in the lessons and experiences of the field.

The United Nations defines Communication for Development as a process that "allows communities to speak out, express their aspirations and concerns, and participate in the decisions that relate to their development" (General Assembly resolution 51/172, article 6). This definition contrasts sharply with the tendency to associate the word "communication" with concepts such as dissemination, information, messages, media, and persuasion. The term "Communication for Development" encompasses these concepts but embraces a much broader vision. While it certainly draws on many years of experience developing methods to facilitate dialogue, investigate risks and opportunities, compare perceptions, and define priorities for messages and information, it is also and most fundamentally a social process to involve people in their own development. The real difference between communication and Communication for Development lies in this broader vision that views the people most affected by development change as being active participants in a social process, not only as receivers of messages. If development is something done "with" people, not "to" them, Communication for Development must be central to any development initiative from the very beginning.

Communication for Development allows stakeholders to take part in development projects and programs at the initial planning stage, ensuring a better design and the required buy-in by those most affected by development change. Furthermore, it is key in fostering communities' participation by reflecting their views and priorities and strengthening local communication processes. The application of communication to development is not simply a matter of acquiring better information. Communication processes and techniques need to be used for better negotiation, risk management, project design, and active engagement of those most affected if we are to make development initiatives more successful and sustainable.

The Congress dealt with these issues at great length. Debate among the participating practitioners, academicians, and decision makers offered a rare occasion for such broad interaction. The long road leading to the Congress also provided a space where organizations with different mandates, size, and geographical origins joined in the planning and decision-making process. The positive results, and we believe there were many, must be attributed to those diverse individuals and organizations that helped make this Congress a reality. The shortcomings, and we are humbly aware of them, stem at least partially from the difficulties of putting together an event without precedent or blueprint, combined with high and varied expectations.

The Congress was a milestone for Communication for Development, but like all milestones it was only a marker on a longer road. We believe it moved the field forward and helped bring together not only evidence and stories but also people and ideas. Many have told us that it created momentum, and if the legacy of papers, proceedings, contacts, and networks strengthens our ability as a field to argue for and gain a more central role in development, then the Congress has achieved its central goal. The one thing we heard time and again (and unanimously) was that Communication for Development as a field, as a process, and as an approach to development is essential to achieve the Millennium Development Goals (MDGs) and to meet the many development challenges and decisions that await us over the coming years.

We hope you will find these proceedings useful as you move down the road toward other milestones.

Alexander Müller
Assistant Director-General
Natural Resources Management and Environment Department
FAO

Paul Mitchell
Manager
Development Communication Division
The World Bank

Warren Feek
Executive Director
The Communication Initiative Network

Preface

The first World Congress on Communication for Development (WCCD) took place in Rome, Italy, on October 25–27, 2006. The main goal of the WCCD was to position and promote the field of Communication for Development in the overall agenda of development and international cooperation.

Toward this end, three types of stakeholders, who rarely interact, gathered in Rome: academics, practitioners, and policy and decision makers. The interaction and exchange of perspectives among these three groups served to enhance the overall understanding of the field of Communication for Development by a broader audience.

These proceedings contain the wealth of knowledge included in the presentations, panel sessions, and plenary discussions that took place in Rome. The organization of the proceedings reflects the structure of the Congress, where three thematic areas were selected to guide the main discussions: health, governance, and sustainable development. A fourth area, named Communication Labs, dealt with cross-cutting methodological issues in the field of Communication for Development.

The book also includes other important contributions:

- A background paper titled "Communication for Development: Making a Difference," which was prepared by a group of top scholars and practitioners who actively participated in the preparation of the Congress as members of the Scientific Committee

- The "Rome Consensus," a declaration that was agreed upon by the WCCD participants and that summarizes key recommendations for mainstreaming Communication for Development in relevant policies and practices
- A multimedia DVD that includes all the papers accepted through a call for papers, as well as some videos presented during the Congress

Finally, the proceedings include a broader treatment of the historical trajectory and current practices of Communication for Development. This approach is intended to further promote the understanding of the scope of this field, which has broadened well beyond the original idea of diffusion and persuasion aimed at changing individuals' behavior and now encompasses also the idea of communication as a two-way process for (a) engaging stakeholders in the assessment and prioritization of development needs, and (b) providing the inputs that will lead to more effective and sustainable design of development initiatives.

It is our hope that at the end of this book, readers will have a much better understanding of the value and role of Communication for Development.

Acknowledgments

It is not easy to properly identify and acknowledge the different roles played by so many individuals and institutions that made the first World Congress on Communication for Development (WCCD) possible and successful. We have tried our best, hoping to be forgiven in case of any unintentional omission.

First of all, we would like to thank the Ministry of Foreign Affairs of Italy, represented by the Directorate General for Development Cooperation, for their vision and generous support. The WCCD never would have happened without them.

But even with the support of the Italian government and the hard work of many people from the Secretariat, an event such as this Congress still would have not been possible without the dedicated efforts of many other people, as well as the commitment of institutions from around the world. It took more than two years to get to the WCCD. There were many issues to take into consideration, many things to do, and, as we all know, many different perspectives and scenarios to include. To ensure that the WCCD would embrace the geographic, institutional, cultural, and theoretical richness of the Communication for Development experience and scenario, several ad hoc committees provided strategic inputs and expertise. We would like to acknowledge the work of these organizations and individuals for their essential role in making the WCCD a success. We give an additional thanks to all those actively involved in the process for their patience and passion in the long and winding road to the WCCD. Despite animated discussions and a few intense moments, everyone worked passionately and cohesively for the achievement of the intended results and deserves due credit. The following list acknowledges the major actors involved in this process.

The Steering Committee

The Steering Committee provided guidance and direction to the planning and implementation of the WCCD. It played a significant role in setting the strategies and goals and in establishing the broad framework for the agenda. The committee was composed of representatives from organizations active in the field of Communication for Development around the world, and it helped ensure that the WCCD was as representative as possible of all the different groups that took part in it.

AMARC
Marcelo Solervicens, Secretary General

AMIC—Asian Media Information and Communication Centre
Indrajit Banerjee, Secretary General

Calandria
Rosa Maria Alfaro, President

CECIP—Centre for the Creation of People's Image
Claudius Ceccon, Executive Director

CFSCC—Communication for Social Change Consortium
Denise Gray-Felder, President and CEO

DFID—UK Department for International Development
Sina Odugbemi, Former Program Manager and Adviser

GCRA—Global Communication Research Association
Basyouni Ibrahim Hamada, Secretary General

Healthlink Worldwide
Andrew Chetley, Director of Programs

Italian Development Cooperation
Claudio Glaentzer, Former Head of Financial Department
Antonio Morabito, Former Head of Communication
Stefano Cacciaguerra, Information and Communication Technology for Development Adviser

SADC-CCD—Southern Africa Development Community, Centre of Communication for Development
Chris Kamlongera, Director

SDC—Swiss Agency for Development and Cooperation
Gerolf Weigel, Head, ICT for Development Office

Soul City-IHDC—Institute for Health and Development Communication
Sue Goldstein, Senior Manager, Research, Resource Centre

UNDP—UN Development Programme
Jean Fabre, Deputy Director

UNESCO—UN Educational, Scientific and Cultural Organization
Kwame Boafo, Chief, Executive Office

UNICEF—UN Children's Fund
Rina Gill, Senior Program Officer

USAID—U.S. Agency for International Development
Elizabeth Fox, Deputy Director, Office of Health, Infectious Diseases, and Nutrition
Roberta Hilbruner, Chair, Sustainable Tourism Working Group

The Advisory Body

The Advisory Body worked along with the Steering Committee and Secretariat to ensure the widest possible participation of organizations and individuals working in the field of Communication for Development; to help identify the most appropriate policy and decision makers to participate in the Policy Makers' Forum; to contribute to the pre-WCCD study on mainstreaming communication ("Communication for Development: Making a Difference"—see appendix 3); and to advise on the post-WCCD advocacy strategy and mainstreaming agenda.

AFD—Agence Française de Développement
Jean-Michel Severino, Director General
Henry de Cazotte, Director of Communication

African Development Bank
Eric Chinje, Manager, Internal and External Communication Division
Felix Njoku, Internal and External Communication Division

ALER—Latin American Association for Radio Education
Nelsy Lizarazo, Executive Director
Florencia Cremona, Director of Training and Research
Luis Dávila Loor, Former Executive Director

American University
Dr. Shalini Venturelli, Director, International Communication Division

ANDI—News Agency for Children's Rights
Veet Vivarta, Director

Asian Development Bank
Jeffrey Hiday, Director General, Department of External Relations
Sue Hooper, External Relations Department

Association of Italian NGOs
Sergio Marelli, President
Mario Grieco, Responsible for International Agencies

BBC World Service Trust
Stephen King, Director
Gerry Power, Director, Research and Learning
Sophie Garnham, Director, Strategy and Development

Bernard van Leer Foundation
Patricia Light-Borsellini, Communication Director

Communication Publique
Pierre Zemor, President

CTA—Technical Centre for Agriculture and Rural Cooperation
Oumy N'diaye, Manager, Communication Channels and Services Department

FELAFACS—Latin American Federation of Communication Faculties
Maria Teresa Quiroz, President

FNPI—Fundación para un Nuevo Periodismo Iberoamericano
Gabriel García Marquez, President
Jaime José Abello, Executive Director

Fondazione Pubblicità Progresso
Alberto Contri, President

Global Alliance for Public Relations and Communication Management
Sejamothopo Motau, Chairman
John Paluszek, Ambassador at Large
Toni Muzi Falcón, Past Chair

IAMCR—International Association of Media and Communication Research
Robin Mansell, President

ICA—International Communication Association
Jon Nussbaum, President
Michael Haley, Executive Director

IDB—Inter-American Development Bank
Luis Alberto Moreno, President
Elena Suarez, Chief, Special Programs Section

IDRC—International Development Research Centre
Maureen O'Neil, President
Guy Bessette, Senior Program Specialist

IFAD—International Fund for Agricultural Development
Lennart Båge, President
Helen Gillman, Manager, Editorial Services

IFPRI—International Food Policy Research Institute
Klaus von Grebmer, Director, Communications Division

IICD—International Institute for Communication and Development
Jac Stienen, Managing Director
Stijn van der Krogt, Head of Country Programs

Interaction
Sam Worthington, President and CEO
Nasserie Carew, Director of Communications

IPS—Inter Press Service
Mario Lubetkin, President
Sabina Zaccaro, Program Manager

IUCN—The World Conservation Union
Mohammed Valli Moosa, President
Elroy Bos, Acting Head, Global Communications Unit

Johns Hopkins University, Center for Communication Programs
Jane Bertrand, Executive Director
Jose Rimon, Senior Deputy Director

MISA—Media Institute of Southern Africa
Kaitira E. Kandjii, Regional Director

NORAD—Norwegian Agency for Development Cooperation
Jackob S. Thompson, Adviser, ICT in Development Cooperation
Tone Bratteli, Media
Hem Thore, Senior Adviser, Knowledge Management

PAHO—Pan-American Health Organization
Mirta Roses Periago, Director
Richard Van West-Charles, Area Manager, Information and Knowledge Management

Panos
Mark Wilson, Executive Director
Kitty Warnock, Communication for Development Senior Adviser
Teresa Hanley, Director of Programs

Plan International
Nigel Chapman, Chair
Amanda Barnes, Communications Manager

SAfAIDS—Southern Africa HIV/AIDS Information Dissemination Service
Lois Lunga, Executive Director

Sesame Workshop
Lewis Bernstein, Executive Vice President of Education and Research
Charlotte Cole, Vice President of Education and Research

SIDA—Swedish International Development Cooperation Agency
Maria Stridsman, Head, Department for Democracy and Social Affairs
Peter Erichs, Media Program Officer

Transparency International
David Nussbaum, Chief Executive
Barbara Ann Clay, Communication Director
Donal O'Leary, Senior Adviser

UNCTAD—UN Conference on Trade and Development
Habib Ouane, Director, Special Program on the Least Developed Countries, Land-locked Developing Countries, and Small Island Developing States
Michael Herrmann, Economic Affairs Officer, Special Program for Least Developed Countries

UNDP Oslo Governance Centre
Bjoern Foerde, Director
Elizabeth McCall, Civil Society and Access to Information Policy Adviser

UNECA—UN Economic Commission for Africa
Aida Opoku-Mensah, Officer in Charge, Development Information Services Division

UNEP—UN Environment Programme
Klaus Toepfer, Executive Director
Kilaparti Ramakrishna, Deputy Director, Division of Policy Development and Law

UNFPA—UN Population Fund
Kristin Hetle, Chief, Media Services Branch
Omar Gharzeddine, Information Officer

University of the Philippines Los Baños, College of Development Communication
Maria Celeste Cadiz, Dean
Dr. Cleofe S. Torres, Associate Professor and Dean

The Scientific Committee

The Scientific Committee was composed of 23 academicians and practitioners in the field of Communication for Development, selected on the basis of their contribution to the theory and practice of the discipline. The members were responsible for selecting the papers and presentations for the WCCD and for compiling papers and presentations for inclusion in the WCCD proceedings.

We give additional thanks to the members of the Committee who also wrote the WCCD background study (appendix 3).

Chair:
Jan Servaes, PhD (Belgium/Australia), Professor and Head
School of Journalism and Communication, University of Queensland, Australia

Members:
Silvia Balit (Italy), Consultant

Guy Bessette (Canada), Senior Program Officer
International Development Research Centre (IDRC)

Maria Celeste H. Cadiz (Philippines), Dean
College of Development Communication, University of the Philippines Los Baños

Nabil H. Dajani (Lebanon), Professor
Department of Social and Behavioral Sciences, American University of Beirut

Cees J. Hamelink (Netherlands), Professor
Amsterdam School of Communications, University of Amsterdam

Robert Huesca (Bolivia/United States), Professor
Department of Communication, Trinity University

Thomas Jacobson (United States), Professor
Temple University

Ullamaija Kivikuru (Finland), Professor
University of Helsinki

Rico Lie (Netherlands), Professor
Wageningen University

Shuang Liu (China/Australia), Professor
School of Journalism and Communication, University of Queensland

Eric Louw (South Africa/Australia), Professor
School of Journalism and Communication, University of Queensland

John Mayo (United States), Dean and Professor
Florida State University

Francis B. Nyamnjoh (Cameroon/Senegal), Associate Professor
Head of Publications and Dissemination, CODESRIA

Levi Obijiofor (Nigeria/Australia), Professor
School of Journalism and Communication, University of Queensland

Rafael Obregón (United States/Colombia), Associate Professor
Ohio University

Charles Okigbo (United States), Professor
North Dakota State University

Ricardo Ramírez (Mexico/Canada), Assistant Professor
School of Environmental Design and Rural Development, University of Guelph

Douglas Storey (United States), Associate Director
Communication Science and Research, Johns Hopkins University Bloomberg School of Public Health

Pradip Thomas (India/Australia), Associate Professor
School of Journalism and Communication, University of Queensland

Thomas Tufte (Denmark), Professor
Roskilde University

Robert White (Tanzania), Professor
University of Tanzania

Karin Gwinn Wilkins (United States), Graduate Adviser and Associate Professor
Department of Radio-TV-Film, University of Texas at Austin

Finally, special thanks go to those individuals in the three organizations that joined forces to organize this event. The following paragraphs highlight the scope and mission of the three organizations that composed the Secretariat of the WCCD.

The subsequent Credits section highlights the organizers of the Congress and contributors to this publication.

The Communication Initiative

The Communication Initiative supports people and organizations engaging in development communication action. It works with a wide range of groups, whether they be small, local, rural organizations using traditional drama to address HIV/AIDS, script writers for popular TV entertainment with an environmental theme, editors and journalists, policy makers, or funders. The purpose of The Communication Initiative is to create a place and space where these groups can quickly and easily identify, choose, and engage with the information, knowledge, ideas, and networks that they deem necessary to improve the impact and value of their work on the major concerns in their communities, organizations, and countries. The process is supported by three Web sites: The Communication Initiative, http://www.comminit.com/; La Iniciativa de Comunicación, http://www.comminit.com/la/; and Soul Beat Africa, http://www.comminit.com/africa/. Together they offer more than 35,000 pages of summarized information and a variety of interactive features, coupled with a series of electronic publications. More than 68,000 people from more than 200 countries have already subscribed, with the numbers growing every day. The Communication Initiative is led strategically and supported financially by a group of 29 partners (http://www.comminit.com/partners.html) representing some of the leading Communication for Development organizations in the world today.

The Food and Agriculture Organization of the United Nations—FAO

Since the early 1970s FAO has pioneered Communication for Development. In the past 30 years, hundreds of such programs, projects, and systems have been implemented in developing countries under FAO's leadership to achieve food security, sustainable natural resources management, and rural development. FAO's Communication for Development Group (ComDev@fao.org), presently located in the Research and Extension Unit, Natural Resources and Environment Department, focuses on strengthening the capacities of rural people and institutions in managing participatory communication processes to share knowledge and information and to enhance participation and dialogue for sustained rural development. Within this framework, FAO assists governments, institutions, and organizations to apply the tenets of Communication for Development to such key development issues as national programs for food security; sustainable natural resources management; national agricultural research and extension systems; rural information and communication systems; and sustainable livelihoods of vulnerable groups. Over the last years FAO has activated a series of regional platforms for Communication for Development to improve knowledge exchange and cooperation among institutions and practitioners and to advance Communication for Development at the policy level as well as in the field.

The World Bank

The World Bank recognized the importance of the discipline fairly recently, and in 1999 created a division devoted specifically to mainstreaming communication in Bank operations and upstreaming it in the development agenda. The Development Communication Division grew from only four professional staff members to more than 20. It was created mainly to provide communication support and analysis of nonfinancial risks (political, cultural, and social), in order to achieve more effective and sustainable projects. Donors have seen the importance of this work, and the Sustainable Development Operations Unit was created with financial support from the government of Italy, a long-time champion of the discipline. Recently the UK Department for International Development has also provided substantial assistance in communication and governance.

The Division's work in Bank operations and analyses soon revealed that, for the field to advance, it is of paramount importance to take stock of all the work already done, and also to reach out to other development partners to create a solid community of practice. In particular, Lucia Grenna, Head of the Sustainable Development Operations Unit recognized the momentum to create institutional synergies and partnerships. When she envisioned the organization of an event of global magnitude that would connect for the first time academia, practitioners, and policy makers, she found a partner in the Ministry of Foreign Affairs of Italy, which generously supported and hosted the event, and also in FAO, the natural organization to approach given its extensive body of knowledge and experience garnered over 30 years. It was also important to engage the wider community of practice and The Communication Initiative clearly stood out with an extensive worldwide network of practitioners.

Credits

Our most sincere appreciation is due to the following:

The Secretariat

The Communication Initiative: Warren Feek, Executive Director; Chris Morry, Director, Special Projects and Coordination

FAO: Mario Acunzo, Communication for Development Officer; Jean Pierre Ilboudo, Communication for Development Officer; Marcela Villareal, Director of Gender and Population Division

World Bank: Daniele Calabrese, Communication Officer and project coordinator for this publication; Diana Chung, Communication Officer; Lucia Grenna, Senior Communication Officer and task manager for the Congress; Piotr Mazurkiewicz, Communication Officer; Paolo Mefalopulos, Senior Communication Officer and project coordinator for this publication

In addition, at the World Bank, special thanks are due to Manuela Faria, Eliana Esposito, and Serena Cavicchi for taking care of the overall logistics and support for all aspects of the WCCD; Christian Hofer for the media contacts; Ricardo Torrado for his contribution to the graphic design of the WCCD material; and Michele Bruni for being the "everywhere man" in the final stages of the WCCD preparation.

At The Communication Initiative (CI), thanks are due to Adelaida Trujillo for the coordination and communication role she played leading up to the WCCD and throughout the event; Anja Venth for volunteering as rapporteur; all of the others who filled in gaps to make the WCCD possible; and, of course, to all CI partners who supported the WCCD in many ways, especially by recognizing the strategic importance of CI being involved. In particular, the Panos team supervised by Nikki van der Gaag deserves special mention for their work as rapporteurs.

On the FAO side, there are too many people to thank individually for their participation in the preparation and during the WCCD. A collective thank-you goes to all of them.

For their work on the publication and the DVD-ROM, acknowledgments are due to the following:

Publication—Eliana Esposito, Manuela Faria, Barbara Catherwood, Publications Professionals, Circle Graphics, Grammarians, and Goodway Graphics

DVD—Eliana Esposito at the World Bank, Pavan Arora and Rakesh Kumar at BNK Infotech, and Evatone

The publication of this book and the replication of the DVD were managed by the World Bank's Office of the Publisher.

Executive Summary

The first World Congress on Communication for Development was held between October 25 and 27, 2006 at the Food and Agriculture Organization of the United Nations (FAO) in Rome, Italy. It was organized by the World Bank, FAO, and The Communication Initiative. In the run-up to the Congress, a series of regional meetings with a specific focus on sustainable development fed into the discussions and debates.

In addition to about 200 journalists and representatives of media outlets, the Congress attracted more than 900 participants from all over the world. They attended workshops and special events on three broad themes: communication for health, governance, and sustainable development, as well as an additional cross-cutting theme labeled "Communication Labs." The participants brought a wealth of knowledge and experience, which they shared in a series of plenaries and two debates televised by Radiotelevisione Italiana (RAI) and the British Broadcasting Corporation (BBC). At the end of the Congress, proposed recommendations were discussed with participants and with a panel of policy makers.

During the course of the debates, there were points of difference but also consensus on many issues. There was agreement that communication is integral to development and to achieving the Millennium Development Goals. For this reason, it must be built into development planning and embedded in strategies for poverty reduction, health planning, and governance.

There was also understanding that Communication for Development is not a quick fix: it requires long-term consistency of engagement. Involving people actively from the start takes time and resources, but it pays off in terms of results and sustainability. All participants recognized the need to foster partnerships among government agencies, donors, academia, international organizations, nongovernmental organizations (NGOs), and the people affected.

Participants noted that Communication for Development is about listening, as well as talking. It is a two-way dialogue that is horizontal rather than vertical. Debates must be inclusive—the rights of those most affected must be guaranteed. This approach was underlined in sessions involving disabled people and indigenous peoples.

Participants also noted that giving information is not the same as communicating—it does not address the structural issues that maintain poverty. There is also a place for the crucial and complementary role of purposeful communication programs (including communication campaigns) aimed at such goals as reducing the burden of disease and increasing women's control over their own health.

The importance of culture was recognized in a number of workshops. Culture is part of everyone's reality and can be both an enabling factor and a barrier to communication. People are more ready to change cultural practices or adapt them than many assume when they think of culture as static or traditional.

Communication was also seen as having a role in holding people to account—including donors. For example, community involvement in monitoring the work of Poverty Reduction Strategy Papers (PRSPs) included bringing service providers and district-level officials together in Rwanda to discuss progress. It is, however, clear that methods must be found to help decision makers understand the benefits of Communication for Development.

There was much discussion about the need for building professional communication capacity—particularly for developing-country practitioners—because at the moment there is too much reliance on international experts. Understanding and knowledge of Communication for Development are key but are often missing. For example, natural resource management experts are sometimes scientists who often do not have a mind-set oriented toward social development and participation or skills in Communication for Development.

The Congress noted the importance of ensuring that processes are valued as much as outputs or technologies. New technologies provide many new possibilities but are not the only answer. Communication for Development needs a range of tools.

For communication to take place, there must be public spaces for debate: most people stressed the importance of diverse media. Access to information is important, but the means and space to communicate are even more so. But Communication for Development cannot just be done through the media—people-to-people communication and community media are just as important. A responsive community media provides a way of making governance, education, and health initiatives more effective.

Congress participants recognized a need to think further about what successful change looks like, in terms of both what is seen to be a success and what is considered to be good change. Reconsidering the nature of change is an increasingly pressing need in a development context that is increasingly driven by top-down global indicators of success and uniform measures of development. Communication for Development is not the miracle cure. It must not overlook the real politics and structural and power issues, which need to be addressed.

The Congress showcased many examples of successful Communication for Development but recognized that there is inadequate documentation of these successes. The many voices at the Congress were evidence of just how far Communication for Development has come in 40 years and of the variety of people now working in this field from all over the world. "This Congress has given us confidence that we are not alone in our profession," said one participant. The words of some of its original founders still ring true: "The core of all development is empowerment, and the key to empowerment is communication" (Donald Snowden, Fogo Process activist). The next stage is for Congress participants to use the ideas gleaned during the three days to make this a reality in the world in which they work.

The Rome Consensus

Communication for Development—A Major Pillar for Development and Change

Communication is essential to human, social, and economic development. At the heart of Communication for Development is participation and ownership by communities and individuals most affected by poverty and other development issues. There is a large and growing body of evidence demonstrating the value of Communication for Development.

Below are a few examples of that body of evidence presented at the WCCD:

- In 1959 a study of 145 rural radio fora in India found that forum members learned much more about the topics under discussion than non-forum members. In the words of the researcher, "Radio farm forum as an agent for transmission of knowledge has proved to be a success beyond expectation. Increase in knowledge in the forum villages between pre- and post-broadcasts was spectacular, whereas in the non-forum villages it was negligible. What little gain there was in non-forum villages, occurred mostly in those with radio" [Data presented by Dr. Bella Mody from Neurath, P. (1959), "Part Two: Evaluation and Results," in J. C. Mathur and P. Neurath (Eds.), *An Indian Experiment in Farm Radio Forums* (pp. 59–121), Paris: UNESCO].

- The participatory communication approach adopted in Senegal led to significant reductions in the practice of female genital cutting (FGC). Since 1997, 1,748 communities in Senegal have abandoned FGC. These represent 33 percent of the 5,000 communities that practiced FGC at that time [Tostan data, presented at the WCCD, 2006—http://www.tostan.org].

- In Uganda a national and local communication process related to the corruption of centrally allocated public funds for education at the local level in schools resulted in a very significant decrease in the level of funds that did not reach that local level—from 80 percent "lost" to only 20 percent lost [Reinikka, R., and J. Svensson, "The Power of Information," Policy Research Working Paper # 3239, 2004].

- Communication programs are linked to significant reductions in Acute Respiratory Infection—ARI—in Cambodia. Since the communication campaign started in 2004, awareness of ARI grew from 20 percent to 80 percent and the reported incidence of ARI halved [BBC World Service Trust, Film on Health Communication, presented at the WCCD, 2006—http://www.bbc.co.uk/mediaselector/check/worldservice/meta/dps/2006/10/061027_health_wst?size= 16x9&bgc=003399&lang=en-ws&nbram=1&nbwm=1].

- Use of mobile phones and other communication techniques for farmers to obtain information on market prices in Tanzania resulted in farmers increasing the price they receive per ton of rice from US$100 to US$600. A $200,000 investment resulted in $1.8 million of gross income [The First Mile Project, presented at the WCCD, 2006—http://www.ifad.org/rural/firstmile/FM_2.pdf].

Development Challenges

As of 2006, it is estimated that 1.3 billion people worldwide still live in absolute poverty. Even though many countries have experienced considerable economic development, far too many remain worse off in economic and social terms.

Nelson Mandela reminds us that "Poverty is not natural—it is man-made and it can be overcome and eradicated by the actions of human beings."

People's rights to equality and to communicate are protected and advanced in the Universal Declaration on Human Rights.

Related to poverty and rights there are other very considerable and related challenges. These are delineated in the Millennium Development Goals (MDGs), which are often the benchmark for decision making in civil society, national governments, and the international development community.

Achieving improved progress on these issues requires addressing some very sensitive and difficult challenges: respect for cultural diversity, self-determination of people, economic pressures, environment, gender relations, and political dynamics—among others. It also highlights the need to harmonize communication strategies and approaches, as indicated by the 9th UN Roundtable on Communication for Development and in other international fora.

These factors often complicate and threaten the success of overall development efforts in the local, national, and international arenas. It is the people-related issues that are the focus of Communication for Development.

Communication for Development

Communication for Development is a social process based on dialogue using a broad range of tools and methods. It is also about seeking change at different levels including listening, building trust, sharing knowledge and skills, building policies, debating and learning for sustained and meaningful change. It is not public relations or corporate communication.

Strategic Requirements

Development organizations must assign a much higher priority to the essential elements of Communication for Development process, as shown by research and practice:

- The right and opportunity people have to participate in the decision-making processes that affect their lives
- Creating opportunities for sharing knowledge and skills
- Ensuring that people have access to communication tools so that they can themselves communicate within their communities and with the people making the decisions that affect them—for example community radio and other community media
- The process of dialogue, debate, and engagement that builds public policies that are relevant, helpful and which have committed constituencies willing to implement them—for example on responding to preserving the environment
- Recognizing and harnessing the communication trends that are taking place at local, national, and international levels for improved development action—from new media regulations and ICT trends to popular and traditional music
- Adopting an approach that is contextualized within cultures
- Related to all of the above, assigning priority to supporting the people most affected by the development issues in their communities and countries to have their say, to voice their perspectives, and to contribute and act on their ideas for improving their situation—for example indigenous peoples and people living with HIV/AIDS

In order to be more effective in fighting poverty and meeting the other MDGs, the Communication for Development processes just outlined are required in greater scale and at more depth, making sure that the value-added of such initiatives is always properly monitored and evaluated.

Long-Term Foundation

These processes are not just about increasing the effectiveness of overall development efforts. They are also about creating sustainable social and economic processes. In particular:

- Strengthening Citizenship and Good Governance

- Deepening the communication links and processes within communities and societies

Those are essential pillars for any development issue.

Recommendations

Based on the arguments above, in order to make much more significant progress on the very difficult development challenges that we all face, we recommend that policy makers and funders do the following:

1. Overall national development policies should include specific Communication for Development components.
2. Development organizations should include Communication for Development as a central element at the inception of programs.
3. Strengthen the Communication for Development capacity within countries and organizations at all levels. This includes people in their communities, Communication for Development specialists, and other staff, including through the further development of training courses and academic programs.
4. Expand the level of financial investment to ensure adequate, coordinated financing of the core elements of Communication for Development as outlined under Strategic Requirements above. This includes budget line[s] for development communication.
5. Adopt and implement policies and legislation that provide an enabling environment for Communication for Development—including free and pluralistic media and the right to information and to communicate.
6. Development communication programs should be required to identify and include appropriate monitoring and evaluation indicators and methodologies throughout the process.
7. Strengthen partnerships and networks at international, national, and local levels to advance Communication for Development and improve development outcomes.

8. Move toward a rights-based approach to Communication for Development.

Conclusion

As Nelson Mandela highlighted, it is people that make the difference. Communication is about people. Communication for Development is essential to making the difference happen.

The Participants
World Congress on Communication for Development
Rome, Italy
October 27, 2006

Abbreviations

ACC	Administrative Committee on Coordination
ALER	*Asociación Latinoamerica de Educación Radiofónica*
AMARC	World Association of Community Radio Broadcasters
ANDA	National Association of Advertisers
ARH	adolescent reproductive health
BBC	British Broadcasting Corporation
CAC	Community Action Cycle
CADRE	Centre for AIDS Development Research and Evaluation
CLIC	Community Learning and Information Center
CRHP	Comprehensive Rural Health Project
CSO	civil society organization
DFID	UK Department for International Development
DSC	development support communication
EE	edutainment
EPI	Expanded Program on Immunization
FAO	Food and Agriculture Organization of the United Nations
FGC	female genital cutting
FNPI	*Fundación para un Nuevo Periodismo Iberoamericano*
ICT	information and communication technology
IEC	information, education, and communication
IFAD	International Fund for Agricultural Development
ITDG	Intermediate Technology Development Group

KAP	knowledge, attitudes, and practices
LDCs	least developed countries
MDG	Millennium Development Goal
MENA	Middle East and North Africa
MSC	Most Significant Change
NGO	nongovernmental organization
PAHO	Pan American Health Organization
PLWHA	people living with HIV/AIDS
PRODERITH	*Programa de Desarrollo Rural Integrado del Trópico Húmedo*
PRSP	Poverty Reduction Strategy Paper
RAI	Radiotelevisione Italiana
RAPID	recommended, agree, purpose, input, decisions
SIS	State Information Services
SMS	Short Message Service
TCO	total cost of ownership
UN	United Nations
UNEP	United Nations Environment Programme
UNICEF	United Nations Children's Fund
UNO	United Nations Organization
USAID	U.S. Agency for International Development
WCCD	World Congress on Communication for Development
WCED	World Commission on Environment and Development
YEAH	Young, Empowered, and Healthy

1

The First World Congress on Communication for Development

The first World Congress on Communication for Development (WCCD) took place at the headquarters of the Food and Agriculture Organization of the United Nations (FAO) in Rome, Italy, October 25–27, 2006. It was organized by the World Bank, FAO, and The Communication Initiative. About 900 participants came from all over the world to share ideas, presentations, and projects and to make recommendations for future practice. Almost 200 journalists and media representatives, from the international, national, and local levels, provided wide coverage of the event in many places around the world.

The Congress built on the work of Communication for Development pioneers, practitioners, academicians, and far-sighted policy makers going back nearly 50 years. The idea of organizing the first global event on Communication for Development arose in 2003 in the World Bank's Development Communication Division within the Communication for Sustainable Development in Operations unit, headed by Lucia Grenna. The original concept had one very distinctive trait: to bring together, for the first time, the three main groups with a stake in Communication for Development—that is, practitioners, academicians, and policy and decision makers. The government of Italy championed the initiative by providing the financial support and hosting the event. But this institutional support provided more than the financial means to carry out the event; it testified to the fact that the Italian government (and, by extension, many in the donor community) recognized the important role that Communication for Development plays and the need to deepen and expand this role.

The World Bank then reached out to key development partners able to undertake the endeavor jointly. Given its extensive body of knowledge and experience, FAO was the natural partner to approach. The Communication Initiative, with its worldwide network of communication practitioners, offered the link to the wider community of practice.

After almost a year of discussions, the Congress was announced in September 2004 at the ninth United Nations (UN) Roundtable on Communication for Development. The Roundtable focused on sustainable development, and it provided an overall framework for advancing communication in sustainable development policies.

In its final declaration, the Roundtable endorsed the idea of the first World Congress of Communication for Development and identified the following key challenges:

- How to fit communication into local and national development processes and policies
- How to demonstrate the added value and impact of Communication for Development and how to incorporate it in governmental, international, and donor policies
- How to adapt to the new and rapidly changing environment, resulting from globalization, privatization, ecological pressure, the decentralization of services, the explosion of media, and the emergence of new social actors
- How to balance the rapid expansion of information and communication technologies (ICTs) with the continuing gap between knowledge and information—and the related limited participation of the poorest in the development process

All these challenges have brought new opportunities but have also marginalized poverty-related issues. To counter this marginalization, collaboration and coordination among Communication for Development initiatives is a priority.

The main recommendations of the Roundtable emphasized the policy dimension of and the evidence on Communication for Development, in particular:

- *Scale*—Successful Communication for Development initiatives should be scaled up to improve practice and policy at every level.
- *Policies and resources*—Communication for Development initiatives should be properly enabled through concerted actions and adequate policies and resources, both human and material, with longer timelines.

- *Framework*—National governments should implement a legal and supportive framework favoring the right to free expression and the emergence of free and pluralistic information systems, including recognition of the specific and crucial role of community media in providing access to communication for the isolated and marginalized.
- *Research*—Research should address how to achieve and sustain processes and outcomes of Communication for Development. Undertaking this research requires a participatory approach, a framework shared between development agencies and local stakeholders, and community involvement in design, implementation, and dissemination.
- *Evaluation*—Evaluation and impact assessments should include participatory baselines and communication needs assessments. They should also include self-evaluation by the communities involved and should be of help to the communities themselves. Additionally, they should provide feedback at the policy level.
- *Training*—Training initiatives should focus on collaborative learning in Communication for Development, encouraging experiential, value-based, culturally sensitive training in participatory Communication for Development and fostering a community of practice across regions.
- *Coordination*—Information and consultation mechanisms should be set up to ensure coordinated action among UN agencies and other stakeholders at the international level.

Five cross-cutting issues emerged at the Roundtable as priority areas for collaboration among UN agencies, nongovernmental organizations (NGOs), and academicians:

- *Advocacy*—Stakeholders should foster the scaling up of Communication for Development initiatives and ensure that adequate attention and resources are devoted at the policy and field levels. Communication for Development must be recognized as a central component in all development initiatives.
- *Learning and capacity building*—Training and adult education activities should rely on a common instructional and methodological platform, which can facilitate partnership among different institutions and strengthen the consistency of the modus operandi.
- *Building alliances*—Effective links and joint communication initiatives need to give voices to the poorest and to influence

decision making on sustainable development issues. Special attention should be given to fostering national and regional strategies and initiatives for Communication for Development.

- *Research, monitoring, and evaluation*—Methodologies must be fostered for applied research and for monitoring and evaluation. An evidentiary base should be developed about the impacts of Communication for Development policies and projects and how to achieve and sustain them.
- *Information sharing*—Information sharing has a strategic role in advocacy, building alliances, and supporting capacity building. An information-sharing mechanism should facilitate partnerships; contribute to the definition of a common agenda on Communication for Development; and implement joint initiatives at the global, regional, and national levels.

This framework provided one of the major inputs for the first World Congress on Communication for Development.

The Congress focused on demonstrating that Communication for Development is an essential tool for meeting today's most pressing development challenges and that it should be more fully integrated into development policy and practices. The event brought together communication professionals engaged in development initiatives, policy makers, development practitioners, donor and civil society organization representatives, community representatives, and academicians from around the world to share experiences and best practices in this growing field. Discussions and presentations focused on what works, what does not work, and how Communication for Development contributes to more effective development.

The Congress showcased the wealth of innovative and creative work under way from around the world. Reaching beyond those working directly in Communication for Development, it included the broader development community and policy makers. To achieve a wider reach, the organizers structured the Congress around the most pressing development challenges confronting us today: Health, Governance, and Sustainable Development.

Presentations and discussions demonstrated the value added of Communication for Development; provided data on and evidence of the impact of communication in development projects and programs; and highlighted the most promising theoretical foundations and methodological approaches underpinning Communication for Development. The Congress included 24 workshops and a wide range of special events, exhibitions, and screenings. RAI (Radiotelevisione Italiana) and the BBC (British Broadcasting Corporation) recorded two of the plenary sessions, including a BBC World Debate on the question, "Is a free media essential for development?"

Organization of the Congress

Organizing the Congress was a particularly inclusive and participatory process that involved 4 bodies and 79 organizations; also it included a number of related preparatory events.

The host was the Ministry of Foreign Affairs of the government of Italy, represented by the Directorate General for Development Cooperation, which provided strategic guidance to the Secretariat. The Secretariat was responsible for the overall organization and coordination of the Congress. The members of the Secretariat also served on the Steering Committee. The Steering Committee consisted of 17 members, representing a balanced mix of bilateral and multilateral organizations, UN agencies, nongovernmental organizations (NGOs), and academia, who provided guidance on the planning and implementation of the Congress.

The Scientific Committee reviewed and recommended submissions for presentation at the Congress. It reviewed 559 abstracts and then 213 papers, of which 137 from 43 countries were considered acceptable and in line with the purposes and objectives of the Congress. The Scientific Committee included 23 leading scholars and experts in the theory and practice of Communication for Development, as well as mainstream development practitioners from 18 academic and research institutions. A core group of committee members produced a background study that reviewed the evidence and theoretical underpinnings for the core themes and rationale for the Congress.[1]

An advisory body formed by 41 representatives from the donor community, international and regional NGOs, bilateral and multilateral agencies active in development policy making, and practitioners in the field of Communication for Development provided strategic guidance to the organizers. This body further ensured the inclusiveness and plurality of the preparation process, as well as the engagement of policy and decision makers in the process.

In the run-up to the Congress, FAO and the World Bank implemented a series of regional studies and consultations around the world to obtain the views and proposals of local practitioners and institutions for mainstreaming Communication for Development into sustainable development policies. The studies and consultations delved into such topics as rural development and livelihoods, food security and natural resources management, information technologies, and indigenous peoples.

A number of e-conferences on Communication for Development facilitated a worldwide dialogue on key issues in preparation for the Congress. The topics discussed included sustainable tourism, measurement of the impact of communication, the role of media in corporate social responsibility, and rural development.

Participants in the Congress

Given how inclusive and participatory the organization of the Congress was, it involved an unequaled interagency effort. In addition to the considerable number of organizations and institutions that composed the organizational structure, several partners developed and coordinated each session and special event. The number of institutions involved in putting together the Congress agenda thus comes to a remarkable total of 200.

The Congress was opened by Jacques Diouf, the Director General of FAO. Paul Mitchell, Manager of the Development Communication Division, World Bank, delivered a message on behalf of Bank President Paul Wolfowitz. Patrizia Sentinelli, Vice Minister of Foreign Affairs, Italy; Alfonso Pecoraro Scanio, Minister of the Environment, Italy; and Rosa Maria Alfaro, The Communication Initiative Partnership, Founder and President of Calandria, also gave presentations. Opening plenary presentations followed by José Ramos Horta, Prime Minister of Timor Leste; Marta Maurás, Secretary, Economic Commission for Latin America and the Caribbean; Aram Aharonian, Director, Telesur, República Bolivariana de Venezuela; Garth Japhet, Executive Director, Soul City, and Chair of The Communication Initiative; Paul Mitchell, Manager, Development Communication Division, World Bank; and Marcela Villarreal, Director, Gender and Population Division, FAO.

Plenary moderators were Jorge Gestoso, Gestoso Television News, who moderated the opening ceremonies, the Policy Makers' Forum, and the closing ceremonies; Piero Di Pasquale, RAI NEWS 24, who moderated the opening plenary discussion; Duilio Giammaria,

RAI, who moderated the Governance plenary; Mario Lubetkin, Inter Press Service, who moderated the Sustainable Development plenary; Muthoni Wanyeki, a Nairobi-based political scientist working on Communication for Development, who moderated the Health plenary; and Stephen Sackur, BBC, who moderated the World Debate plenary.

Although there is no space here to list everyone who contributed to the plenaries and sessions, a few names provide some flavor of the diversity of organizations and perspectives represented. From government, Lyonpo Sangay Ngedup, Minister of Agriculture, Bhutan; Laurent Sedogo, Minister of the Environment, Burkina Faso; and Nonofo Molefhi, Member of Parliament (National Assembly), Botswana. From the United Nations, bilaterals, and international financial institutions, Kevin Kellems, Acting Vice President of External Affairs, World Bank; Elizabeth Fox, Deputy Director, Office of Health, Infectious Diseases, and Nutrition, U.S. Agency for International Development; and Bernard Petit, Deputy Director General, Directorate General for Development, European Commission. From academia, Joseph Stiglitz, Professor and Chair, Columbia Committee on Global Thought, Columbia University; Bella Mody, Professor, University of Colorado, Boulder; and Anwar Ibrahim, Visiting Distinguished Professor, Georgetown University. From NGOs and civil society, Peter da Costa, Coordinator, Strengthening Africa's Media Project; Alfonso Gumucio Dagron, Communication for Social Change Consortium; and Kumi Naidoo, Secretary General, CIVICUS: World Alliance for Citizen Participation. For a complete list of all the speakers and participants, see appendix 1.

The members of the Policy Makers' Forum were Jac Stienen, Managing Director, International Institute for Communication and Development; Gerolf Weigel, Head, ICT for Development Division, Swiss Agency for Development and Cooperation; Kilaparti Ramakrishna, Chief Policy Adviser, Office of the Executive Director, UN Environment Programme (UNEP); Matthew Wyatt, Assistant President for External Affairs Department, International Fund for Agricultural Development (IFAD); Mervat Tallawy, Executive Secretary, UN Economic and Social Commission for Western Asia; Alfredo Barnechea, External Relations Adviser, Inter-American Development Bank; Jeffrey J. Grieco, Senior Deputy Assistant Administrator for Public Affairs, U.S. Agency for International Development; Sandra Charles, Senior Economic Policy Adviser, Economic Development, Policy Branch, Canadian International Development Agency; Hu

Shuli, Editor in Chief, *Caijing*, China; Kumi Naidoo, Secretary General, CIVICUS: World Alliance for Citizen Participation; Tesfai Tecle, Assistant Director General, FAO; Marcela Villarreal, Director, Gender and Population Division, FAO; Paul Mitchell, Manager, Development Communication Division, World Bank; and Warren Feek, Executive Director, The Communication Initiative Network.

This report presents the proceedings of the Congress, with key issues and recommendations from each workshop and additional material from plenaries, special events, and some of the papers, presented in the form of case studies. It includes a summary of the recommendations from each strand—Health, Governance, Sustainable Development, and a fourth one discussing cross-cutting issues. The wealth of material here showcases the richness and variety of the Communication for Development field (box 1.1). We hope that this report will contribute to future debates so that the Congress will be, as one of the policy makers put it, "not the end of the story but the beginning of a new one."

Note

1. The final version of the study was reviewed and edited by three members of the Secretariat: Mario Acunzo, Chris Morry, and Paolo Mefalopulos.

Box 1.1 What Is Communication for Development?

Although Communication for Development is established as a discipline and there is recognition at many levels that communication is essential for development, the general public and policy makers are still less clear about what it entails. A perception study prepared in 2006, "What Do They Think? Policy-Makers and the Role of Communication for Development,"[1] noted that, among the decision makers interviewed, "there was widespread recognition of the general importance of communication in the development processes, but with a vague understanding of how it could actually be applied."

One of the purposes of the Congress was to demonstrate how and why Communication for Development should be mainstreamed into development policies and processes. To this end, the organizers of the WCCD and the members of the Steering Committee agreed on a basic set of seven principles describing the discipline of Communication for Development:

1. It is, first and foremost, about people and the process needed to facilitate their sharing of knowledge and perceptions in order to effect positive developmental change. Media and technology are tools to this end, but they are not ends in themselves.
2. It is based on dialogue, which is necessary to promote stakeholder participation. Such participation is needed in order to understand stakeholder perceptions, perspectives, values, attitudes, and practices so that they can be incorporated into the design and implementation of development initiatives.
3. It follows the two-way, horizontal model and not the traditional one-way, vertical model of Sender-Message-Channel-Receiver and increasingly makes use of emerging interactive forms of communication made possible through new technologies. Even when used along more unidirectional models (for example, campaigns), communication needs to facilitate understanding and take into account people's perceptions, priorities, and knowledge.
4. It gives voice to those most affected by the development issues at stake, allowing them to participate directly in defining and implementing solutions and identifying development directions.
5. It recognizes that reality is largely socially constructed. The implications are that there can be different realities (or different perceptions of the same reality) for the same situation, according to specific groups' perceptions and needs. Thus, the role of development—and by extension communication—is not to "impose" the correct reality, but rather to foster dialogue to facilitate mutual understanding among different perspectives. Communication for Development, therefore, respects and works with the different social, religious, and cultural foundations of the people, communities, and nations engaged in development processes.
6. Communication is contextual. There is no universal formula capable of addressing all situations; therefore, it should be applied according to the cultural, social, and economic context.
7. It uses a number of tools, techniques, media, and methods to facilitate mutual understanding and to define and bridge differences of perceptions. It takes action toward change, according to the particular needs of the development initiative. These tools and techniques should be used in an integrated way and are most effective when used at the beginning of development initiatives.

---

1. The study was commissioned by the Development Communication Division, External Affairs, Communications and United Nations Relations Vice Presidency of the World Bank. It was conducted under the leadership of Leonardo Mazzei of the Development Communication Division of the World Bank. The study was written by Colin Fraser, Leonardo Mazzei, and Sonia Restrepo Estrada, with the cooperation of Silvia Balit and Lucia Grenna.

2

Communication and Health

Health communication was chosen as a major thematic area for the Congress because communication has long been established as a core element of health care delivery and programming. Few would argue its substantial contribution to saving lives, preventing and containing the spread of disease, improving service access and delivery, increasing social involvement and cooperation, cutting health care costs, and reducing the impact of poverty on health by showing how simple measures can prevent diseases. An important aspect of the sessions at the Congress was to place this history and evolution of thought and practice in the context of seeking greater impact and more effective development outcomes.

For many years health communication focused on ways to deliver messages about good practice and policy to a variety of audiences: health workers, patients, community members, and policy makers. More recently the focus has begun to shift away from the channel or medium being used and the message or product being conveyed to the processes of dialogue and discussion that are fundamental to communication. As a result, practitioners are paying more attention to the social and political environments in which people live and earn a livelihood, and the influence those environments have on social and behavioral change. "The individual is no longer a target, but a critical participant in analyzing and adopting those messages most suited to her or his own circumstances" (Jacobson 1997). The plenary session, "Health in a Time of Poverty," looked at communication as a process, not merely a tool to apply or a technology to use.

This said, however, it must also be recognized that purposeful communication programs (including communication campaigns) play a crucial and complementary role when aimed at such targets as reducing the burden of disease and increasing women's control over their own health. Such programs helped create the very conditions that make it possible for women, men, and children to be healthy, active, and informed participants in civil society.

Health communication today takes a wide variety of forms, from the cutting edge of entertainment education to participation and dialogue approaches, to "outbreak communication," which just recently began to develop approaches that integrate participation and community engagement. There are also new approaches to immunization, long seen as a relatively well-understood, established, successful intervention but now responding to crises brought on by complex cultural and political contexts.

The health plenary made it clear that a body of well-documented evidence exists on different aspects of health communication. Less is known, however, about what evidence policy makers want or actually use—and they do not use evidence nearly as much as might be assumed. Research shows that to find information, policy makers go to informal, often closed networks, networks based on power and trust, but do not necessarily go to the people who are the best informed. People in the field clearly recognize that this body of evidence has not been communicated effectively in many cases, nor used as systematically as it could have been to underpin program design, implementation, and evaluation (Healthlink 2006).

Session organizers were asked to consider the following questions:

- What has experience shown to work well, on which we can continue to build?
- What has not been working? What approaches should we be moving away from?
- What new and interesting initiatives show promise for the future?
- Are there recent innovations that will have a real impact?

This section of the report draws on the background paper for the health strand, the workshop sessions on health, and some of the special events. It picks up some key and emerging issues and recommendations from the workshops, along with data and evidence from some of the papers presented.

The six workshop sessions focused on three topics currently important in health communication—HIV/AIDS, immunization, and avian influenza—as well as the importance of voice and democratic processes and measuring impact. The workshops had these titles:

1. Sex, Lies, and Stories of AIDS
2. The Race to Immunize Every Child: Communication for Polio Eradication and Immunization
3. Of Birds and Humans: Communication Aspects of Avian Influenza
4. From Patients to Citizens: Health Care, Communication, and Rights
5. Enabling the Voices of Those Most Affected by Ill Health to Be Heard and Acted Upon
6. Of Rubber and Road: Impact and Evidence

A number of special events focused or significantly touched on health communication, including "Where Do We Drop the Pebble? An Exploration of the Pathways to Effective Health Communication" and "Reframing the Avian Influenza Communication Discourse."

Sex, Lies, and Stories of AIDS

> *"There is more and more evidence showing that when mass media programs are developed with input from their audiences along each step of the way, they have an important role to play in impacting on HIV and AIDS preventative behavior."*
>
> —Susan Goldstein, Soul City

The background paper on health for the Congress, in the paragraph on HIV/AIDS, said,

> *HIV/AIDS remains one of the most profound and intractable public health crises in history. The world has increased its response over the past several years with the creation of large-scale new initiatives such as the Global Fund to Fight AIDS, Tuberculosis and Malaria, the establishment of coordinated country-level plans, and the provision of new (if still not sufficient) funding (Communication Initiative 2006: 3).*

The background paper notes that it is important to focus on what has worked in the past and to identify some principles to guide communication practice. For instance, successful approaches (such as the ongoing Treatment Action Campaign in South Africa, which campaigns for the rights of people with HIV/AIDS[1]) have moved from putting out messages to fostering an environment in which the voices of those most affected by the pandemic are heard and their needs moved to the center stage of dialogue and action. This change in focus from message to voice marks a potentially fundamental and radical shift in the response to AIDS. While accurate health information remains important in the struggle against HIV/AIDS, real progress must involve looking beyond the messages—no matter how empowering and context-sensitive they may be—to developing environments in which vibrant and internally legitimate dialogue can flourish and the needs and perspectives of the most affected can become central to the response.

This line of thought on HIV/AIDS ran from the workshop through discussions in the health plenary and special events and also a number of papers, from which the case studies are drawn (box 2.1).

KEY ISSUES

- The engagement process is as important as the media product. In the case of *Soul City* broadcast program and *Sexto Sentido*, it is important to recognize the process of thorough research and engagement with communities. Stories must be based on real-life issues and situations. Constant feedback on the programs to see what impact they have and how communities relate to them is key to their success.
- To enhance communication, it is important to use drama and easily accessible and interesting formats that are acceptable to people.
- *Sexto Sentido* was able to deal with controversial issues, such as male homosexuality, on prime-time television by using human drama people can relate to. But in keeping with the process, the producers remained responsive—for example, when some people commented that they presented only gay characters who could "pass" and did not deal with the intense stigma faced by transgendered characters, the producers responded by intro-

Box 2.1 Soul City, Puntos de Encuentro, and Ethiopia: Youth Dialogues

Soul City

South Africa is in the throes of a devastating AIDS epidemic. Over the years there has been a remarkable change in behavior and the incidence seems to be slowing down, though not fast enough. Goldstein and Scheepers (2006) presented detailed evidence of the impact of Communication for Development in South Africa, where *Soul City* is a dynamic and innovative multimedia project promoting health and social change. *Soul City* carries out regular evaluations showing that the *Soul City* edutainment vehicle has influenced the prevention of HIV infection through a positive impact on sexual behavior:

- Eighty percent of the total sample and 90 percent of the youth subsample reported any exposure to *Soul City;* 67 percent of the total sample and 71 percent of the youth subsample reported exposure to *Soul Buddyz.*
- *Soul City* was rated the highest of all interventions measured in assessing the usefulness of HIV/AIDS programs and campaigns: 91 percent of 12- to 14-year-olds, 95 percent of 15- to 24-year-olds, 93 percent of 25- to 49-year-olds, and 80 percent of respondents 50 and older mentioned *Soul City* as a useful HIV/AIDS program.
- Compared with respondents with no exposure, respondents with exposure to *Soul City* multimedia over six series were four times as likely to report always using a condom with a regular sexual partner.

Source: Goldstein and Scheepers 2006.

Puntos de Encuentro

> *"For us, possibly what marks Puntos de Encuentro as somewhat different from other organizations involved in social communication initiatives is the way in which we understand 'change' and what it is, means, and implies."*
>
> —Amy Bank

Amy Bank from Puntos de Encuentro, a Nicaraguan feminist NGO, presented evidence of the success of its weekly TV social soap *Sexto Sentido* (Sixth Sense) as a launching pad for a multimethod initiative on communication for social change called "Somos Diferentes, Somos Iguales" (We're Different, We're Equal). The initiative asks its young audience to challenge social norms. Rather than seeking to promote specific behavior change, it seeks to promote the right of young people to make decisions about their own behavior, to accept responsibility for those decisions, and to accept decisions made by others.

(*continued*)

CASE STUDIES

Box 2.1 Soul City, Puntos de Encuentro, and Ethiopia: Youth Dialogues (*Continued*)

So instead of presenting some forms of behavior as "good," such as preserving virginity until marriage, the initiative promotes the right of each individual to make informed decisions about when, with whom, and under what conditions to have sex. As a feminist organization, the issue of power and gendered power relations provides the focus for all of Puntos de Encuentro's work. It seeks to address not only power relations based on gender but also those based on age.

Source: Solórzano, Bradshaw, and Bank 2006.

Ethiopia: Youth Dialogues

Mirgissa Kaba from UNICEF Ethiopia described the success of the youth dialogues in that country, one of the four countries in the world with the highest number of HIV/AIDS-infected people. It is also one of only a few countries with a broad-based, self-organized youth movement. Four hundred dialogue sites in five regions involve more than 20,000 young people, who discuss issues twice a week at youth clubs. Youth dialogues have inspired individual and group action at local levels. As well as the benefits of participation itself, notable impacts include increased demand for and use of condoms, increased demand for youth-friendly services, and greater uptake of voluntary counseling and testing. With a variety of partners, hundreds of clubs are now engaged in a nationwide effort to have an impact on the norms governing HIV/AIDS behavior. As one of their partners puts it, "To change the dance, you must change the music."

> *"We talk forever about countries where the level of awareness of HIV/AIDS is very high, but behavior change is negligible. These community conversations have resulted in huge behavior change. Can the pattern be replicated elsewhere? Who knows, but it's certainly worth a try."*
>
> —Stephen Lewis, UNDP

Source: Gray-Felder and others 2006.

ducing a transgendered character and showing the stigma that character faced and that character's attempts to get beyond that stigma.

- Communication must be consistent over the years. Community conversations must be sustained over time and scope allowed for issues, problems, and solutions to be discussed thoroughly.

Such long-term investment and attention to the communication process is still not the norm.

- Social and political environments can constrain or enhance the likelihood of change. For example, in South Africa the political context in relation to HIV and AIDS has challenged and at times directly contradicted the information that people need to have to control the epidemic.
- It is possible to measure the change attributable to an intervention, albeit imperfectly. Consistency of results over many years and the increasing popularity of the *Soul City* and *Soul Buddyz* and *Sexto Sentido* series demonstrates that edutainment is a useful tool in communication.
- Not all the variance in behavior change can be attributed to communication interventions such as *Soul City* and *Soul Buddyz*. This confirms the Ottawa charter health promotion model, which emphasizes a holistic approach, using policy (such as condom distribution), services, and community action (such as that of the Treatment Action Campaign and the youth dialogues in Ethiopia), as well as improving an individual's knowledge and skills and creating supportive environments for change (such as *Soul City*).
- Good communication can bring about a shift in power—in Ethiopia, young women involved in the dialogues say their relationships with their husbands have changed as a consequence; in Nicaragua, the issue of power and gendered power relations provides the focus for all of Puntos de Encuentro's work.
- Puntos de Encuentro's experience highlights the need to think further about what successful change looks like, in terms of both what is seen as a success and what is considered good change.

RECOMMENDATIONS

1. Reconsidering the nature of change is increasingly urgent in a development context that is driven more and more by top-down global indicators of success and uniform measures of development.
2. Communication professionals need to do much more work on harm reduction and injecting-drug consumers, issues that

have been neglected by both Communication for Development practitioners and HIV/AIDS communicators.

3. More work needs to be done on concurrent sexual partnerships, which multiply the risk of HIV transmission.
4. People need more education about anal intercourse as a risky practice. Not only an issue for gay men, it can be viewed equally in the context of avoiding pregnancy and preserving virginity, because young women often are forced into it by male partners.
5. Consistent engagement on an issue over an extended period of time is necessary to see sustained changes in behavior.

The Race to Immunize Every Child: Communication for Polio Eradication and Immunization

The background note for the Congress, in the paragraph on immunization, gave the context for this workshop session:

> *Since the launch of the World Health Organization's Expanded Program on Immunization in 1974, vaccination programs have been one of the world's most cost-effective public health strategies. These programs reduce the burden of infectious diseases globally and serve as a key building block for health systems in the developing world (Communication Initiative 2006: 4–5).*

Immunization is a story of both successes and failures. With the push to universal immunization in the 1980s, the world accelerated immunization coverage in an unprecedented fashion, reaching more than 70 percent of children globally with the basic six vaccines by the end of 1990. Yet coverage has stagnated since then, leading to two million unnecessary deaths annually from vaccine-preventable diseases. In many countries immunization services disproportionately miss the poorest and most excluded populations.

The stagnation in vaccination coverage is due to a range of issues, from the infrastructural problems of health delivery systems to funding pressures that divert resources away from routine immunization. Immunization programs are also affected by the interplay of local and national politics. Challenges range from isolated episodes of nonacceptance in a population (owing to religious, ethical, and medical considerations) to active political mobilization of a population against immunization programs driven by political and conspiratorial arguments.

Persuading these populations to accept vaccination is not simply a matter of disseminating knowledge about vaccines. Knowledge about vaccination, although important, does not necessarily lead to acceptance of immunization. The impact of information on immunization behavior is mediated by sociocultural and political influences, a situation that calls for locally appropriate communication responses.

Immunization programs confront a number of challenges, not least a global communication environment filled with contradictory information about vaccine safety. Addressing these communication challenges requires drawing out the lessons of past successes and failures, while adapting these lessons to new and changing communication environments in which communication to change sociopolitical contexts becomes at least as important as communication to change individual behavior.

The workshop session that dealt directly with immunization was "The Race to Immunize Every Child: Communication for Polio Eradication and Immunization," but the issue was also mentioned in a number of other health sessions at the Congress. The workshop presented case studies on the issues of immunization, two of which are briefly outlined in box 2.2.

KEY ISSUES

- For polio there is an effective vaccine, but rumors and misinformation—driven by religious, cultural, and ultimately political factors—hamper effective response. This issue is all about communication and diverse ways of depicting vaccination.
- The media have an important role to play in informing and encouraging discussion about polio vaccination. However, examples from Uttar Pradesh and Nigeria show that the media sometimes report inaccurately and conflictingly on polio, and they also stigmatize certain groups in society (though this may also reflect broader political and underlying issues).

CASE STUDIES

Box 2.2 Nigeria and India

Nigeria: Lessons from a Boycott

Lora Shimp, Senior Technical Officer, JSI, on the Immunization Basics project with the U.S. Agency for International Development (USAID), talked about the lessons learned from the vaccination boycott in Nigeria:

> *Until late 2004 polio had been virtually eradicated from most of the world; Nigeria and Niger were among a small number of focus countries left. In August 2003, it was reported that local traditional and religious leaders in the north of Nigeria were voicing objections to polio vaccines. Subsequently, the governors of two northern Nigerian states announced that the polio eradication initiative would be officially suspended until answers could be found about vaccine safety. Rumors and distrust spread throughout northern Nigeria. By the time the boycott ended 11 months later, several hundred new cases of polio had occurred among unvaccinated children within the region. From India and Pakistan to Indonesia and parts of West Africa, pockets of resistance to polio immunization sprang up along with new cases of polio. While the suspension resulted in new cases of polio and its expansion across a number of countries, it also served as a catalyst for more positive dialogue within Nigeria and within the global health community. Urgency in meeting eradication targets had forced heavy reliance on top-down dissemination of information or horizontal dissemination of information. The communication work now under way in Nigeria more heavily involves traditional leaders and more effectively focuses on ways in which average people can understand the issue through direct conversations.*

Source: Presentation at the WCCD by Lora Shrimp, Senior Technical Officer, JSI.

India: A Targeted Strategy

Michael Galway, Chief of Program Communication for UNICEF India, described a successful polio immunization strategy in that country that targeted children in high-risk areas. To assist with the strategy, a nationwide mass media campaign was implemented over three years. Media reach and recall surveys show that polio immunization is the most widely recalled social marketing campaign in India. Seventy-seven percent of people surveyed in Uttar Pradesh, West Bengal, and Madhya Pradesh in November 2004 cited polio immunization as the campaign they most remembered in the past month. In Uttar Pradesh, one of the states with the highest concentration of wild poliovirus remaining, a major social mobilization campaign was implemented in 2004–2005. As a result, there was an absolute reduction in the number of families who refused to allow children to be immunized. The difference in immunization status between Muslim and Hindu children shrank considerably between 2003 and 2005, following intensive operational and communication activities to reach out to Muslim families and communities.

Source: Presentation at the WCCD by Michael Galway.

- Civil society has an important role to play in polio eradication. In Angola, for example, people can take part in microplanning, surveillance, polio campaigns, monitoring, and evaluation. These opportunities enable tailored communication interventions that address myths and rumors, and work with community activists and volunteers.
- The experience in Nigeria offered two key communication lessons. First, involve people early. People representing the affected groups can be critical in planning effective communication and in formulating responses during crises. Second, communication must be two-way. Communicators must be equipped and inclined to listen as well as talk or teach, particularly in volatile environments rife with rumor, misunderstanding, and conflicting political agendas.

RECOMMENDATIONS

1. Communication should be considered from the start in planning, implementation, and monitoring of impacts. It should be included in health program design. The contribution of the communication component should be explicitly evaluated and then lessons learned should be applied in future programming.
2. In epidemics or disease outbreaks, communication experts should be part of any outbreak investigation and response team.
3. Advocacy, social mobilization, and interpersonal communication are all needed in an effective disease control communication strategy.
4. Measurement of the achievement and impact of communication activities, through key indicators and a data collection system, also needs to be integrated within the health strategy.
5. Although many positive behaviors and practices can be reinforced through mass media, more targeted messaging provided by trusted health workers or community influencers has greater impact, especially with marginalized populations.
6. Sustaining fresh messages and motivation for a program such as polio eradication is difficult; it requires a multidisciplinary approach and the active involvement of communication experts, epidemiologists, and civil society.

Flexibility to react to a rapidly changing environment is paramount.

7. It is important for donors and policy makers to factor in the communication needs of immunization and disease control programs.

Of Birds and Humans: Communication Aspects of Avian Influenza

In regard to avian influenza, the background paper stated, "Clear and well-planned communication during a health emergency can save lives, avoid panic, and shorten its duration" (Communication Initiative 2006: 6). But as noted in a recent article in *Perspectives on Health* (Sandman and Lanard 2005: 1),

> *Public health officials have a pandemic-size communication problem. Experts believe a deadly human influenza pandemic is quite likely to be launched by the H5N1 avian virus that has killed millions of birds and dozens of people in Asia. They are more anxious than they have been in decades. But infectious diseases are unpredictable. So it's hard for officials to know how aggressively to sound the alarm. They don't want to be accused of needlessly frightening the public. They also don't want to be accused—later—of leaving the public underprepared for a disaster.*

The background paper continues,

> *The potential risk posed by the avian influenza is so high and global in nature that it requires a coordinated global communication strategy with national and local variations appropriate to different groups such as health care workers, poultry producers, policy makers, and the general public. Preparing for it will require strong communication strategies at many levels and in many places to make sure decisions are made based on the best available information, panic is avoided, and appropriate steps are taken, but not too many or too few.*
>
> *Preparing communication plans for the avian influenza will require the development of communication strategies at a global, national, and local level. Risk communication strategies will need*

> *to start with raising awareness and reducing apathy toward the potential danger and then be prepared to move quickly to crisis communication focused on providing the information required to make it through the crisis quickly and in a way that minimizes its impact. However, we will also need to have communication strategies for prevention. Approaching this will require the entire communication toolbox and all its approaches and methods. But to be successful this will require trust and acceptance—things that cannot be relied upon just because the situation is urgent. Communication approaches that build trust through local dialogue and input will be as important as the design and dissemination of accurate information (Communication Initiative 2006: 7).*

This workshop and a special event that also focused on avian influenza offered a number of examples of data and evidence of impact. The cases from Egypt and Vietnam are presented in box 2.3.

KEY ISSUES

- Finding appropriate ways to address and engage with cultural practices is vital. In Vietnam, birds have ritual importance and people express a need to look them in the eye when buying them in the market (militating against both easy ritual substitution and frozen or packaged birds). In West Africa, bird rearing is one way that young people are socialized into adult responsibilities. Both the Egyptian and Vietnamese examples also illustrate the importance of responding to cultural needs.
- Partnerships and a multifaceted communication approach are crucial in tackling avian influenza.
- Communication strategies need to deal with the confusion about avian influenza and how it affects humans and the possible pandemic among humans.
- Responses are not always consistent with the level of threat—for example, the radical drop in poultry consumption in several countries was unjustified. Thailand's well-developed industry had to change manufacturing processes totally to respond to the perception of a threat. At the same time, responses to avian influenza—which is only a potential threat—compete with responses to other pressing priorities, such as malaria and HIV.

Box 2.3 Egypt and Vietnam

Egypt: National Communication Strategy

Between 2003 and 2006 Egypt had 14 human cases of avian influenza and 6 deaths, all of them women involved in raising poultry in small, backyard, cottage industries. The development of Egypt's national communication strategy for avian flu involved many partners, including the government, NGOs, UN organizations, and the commercial sector. Egypt anticipated the outbreak before it happened and used an integrated communication program that was ready to go when there was an outbreak. This program was launched within 24 hours of the outbreak. All national, state-owned media aired television spots and an estimated 86 percent of adults (36 million people) saw them within 24 hours. A subsequent national survey showed that 70 percent reported initiating at least one new protective behavior as a result of the messages they received.

This campaign seemed highly successful but in the debate that ensued, an audience member representing commercial producers in the poultry industry claimed that the campaign provoked panic and massive overreaction, as people reduced their intake of chicken and 60 percent of poultry birds were destroyed.

Two key points emerged. First, partnerships and issues of coordination, division of responsibility, and timing are critically important. Second, mass communication can have an impact—but the process is as important as dissemination or behavioral motivation.

Source: Presentation at the WCCD by Doug Storey, Associate Director for Communication Science and Research, Johns Hopkins Bloomberg School of Public Health, Center for Communication Programs.

Vietnam: Reflections

Vietnam saw its first human cases of avian influenza in late 2003 and its first recognized poultry cases in January 2004. In 2004 it responded mainly by killing infected flocks and flocks located in a zone around infected birds. That was not sufficient: by late 2004 the country was leading the world in human cases of the disease. In 2005 the response began reaching out to people. The government launched a comprehensive set of strategies that paired aggressive animal prevention and control with communication initiatives. This appears to have worked: Vietnam's last human case was diagnosed on November 14, 2005, and its last poultry case in December 2005.

However, the country still faces a very tough set of communication challenges, because to keep avian influenza under control the national government plans to ask for a whole additional set of changes in behavior. Government officials are resolute that the changes will happen. Ordinary people agree that control of the virus is vital but also agree there is almost no chance that the populace will honor these measures. The purchase of live ducks and poultry is simply not going to disappear, because buying a live bird says so much about its value as food, as well as its significance in religious observance. People appear to have decided that the importance of following cultural practices and honoring both their understanding of nutritious food and their concept of small agriculture far outweighs the more remote (for them) and theoretical risk of bird flu.

Source: Presentation at the WCCD by Maryn McKenna.

- New media and bloggers influence the pandemic story in a very important way: a large community talking in this way affects public understanding. But so far no health communication seems to address this audience.
- For measures to be effective, compensation issues must be communicated clearly. Rates vary from minimal to half or even market rates, but communication about rates is likely to affect the willingness of many farmers and rearers, commercial and small-scale alike, to take effective measures.

PROPOSED RECOMMENDATIONS

These recommendations were prepared in advance for presentation but because of time factors were not discussed during the session. Nevertheless, they seemed important enough for us to share them in the proceedings.

Broadly, the strategic advocacy and communication goals for the global, regional, national, and subnational levels can be articulated as follows:

- Catalyzing greater societal ownership and public participation in regional and national responses to avian influenza, including the wide-scale adoption of safe poultry practices and preventive behavior, to reduce the risk of virus transmission and spread.
- Instilling a sense of urgency in policy makers to ensure full preparedness and to strengthen communication capacities at all levels for the rapid rollout of response interventions in the short as well as longer term, including the mobilization of adequate resources.
- Protecting livelihoods and mitigating poultry market shocks and negative consumer reactions, as well as minimizing market recovery time following any announcements of avian influenza outbreaks.

Toward achieving these goals, the panelists proposed the following recommendations as expected outcomes from this special session:

1. A comprehensive, systematic, and multidisciplinary meta-analysis of the avian influenza communication interventions to date and their effectiveness should be conducted soon, within three months of the Congress. Findings from this meta-analysis should

form an authoritative basis for the design of future communication strategies and interventions, with strong theoretical and empirical underpinnings.

2. A mechanism—with adequate resources and agreed procedures—needs to be established for the systematic sharing and management of knowledge and information generated about communication interventions.
3. A unified approach, backed by the establishment of decentralized resource centers, needs to be developed for providing technical assistance in rapidly building and strengthening avian influenza communication capacities within countries and across institutions.
4. There is a need to establish indicators, baselines, and benchmarks to assess the progress and contribution of communication in the prevention and control of avian influenza. There is also a strong need to develop guidance on adequate resource allocations for communication activities. Communication experts and practitioners need to adopt a unified approach and engage with donors through a common platform to agree on measures of progress and how to fill resource gaps, through a unified approach.
5. Practical mechanisms for greater policy engagement of and dialogue between national authorities, the private poultry sector, and community poultry keepers and producers need to be advocated for and established, to ensure a common understanding and vision with regard to rural livelihoods, nutritional and food security, biosecurity, and poultry sector organization.
6. Multisectoral and multistakeholder partnerships at the global and national levels, along the lines of successful models (such as the Stop TB Partnership, the Polio Eradication Initiative, and the Global Environment Facility), should be encouraged to ensure broader participation from civil society, community networks, the media, and the private sector.

Message and Voice

The two workshop sessions on message and voice were called "From Patients to Citizens: Health Care, Communication, and Rights" and "Enabling the Voices of Those Most Affected by Ill Health to Be

Heard and Acted Upon." Both dealt with the importance of voice and are therefore considered together for the purposes of this report. One of the key questions in both workshops was "Why to encourage voice in health communication?"

The workshop on enabling voices was an innovative interactive session in the form of a radio show with a host—WCCD FM. Participants were given phones and told that some did not have access, others did not have credit, some shared phones with other people, and some were not English speakers. Discussions focused on the enhanced impact if those most affected by ill health participate and can express their needs. Examples were given from HIV/AIDS programs.

KEY ISSUES

- How groups and individuals can be supported in realizing their rights to health and in using communication to strengthen their awareness and entitlements.
- Many people, especially women, children, and those most affected, often do not believe in their own power and are not used to being heard. To include their voices would constitute a real paradigm shift for which training and capacity building may be necessary.
- Voice is only part of the equation: a person might have a voice but still not be listened to. Often agencies and programmers would rather speak with representatives than with those most affected.
- There is a difference between having a voice, using it, and being heard. Even if people speak out, it is not easy to get policy makers to listen to the voices of those affected. Those implementing policies may also need to be trained to listen.

A number of issues emerged from the special events:

- Communication is power—who's talking to whom and about what? This is the issue with which we as communicators should be engaged.
- Ordinary people do not feel they have influence, so they hold back on communicating the issues that concern them; however, health issues are a link into Communication for Development—everyone likes to talk about their health.

- Those who have the answers cannot communicate them and those who have the power and influence cannot get the answers to the problems for which they are responsible.
- People cannot articulate their needs in ways that policy makers understand; journalists are a link to the people to whom policy makers should listen.
- The communication process is important; the connections made throughout this process are among the most important outcomes in Communication for Development.

See box 2.4 for a case study.

CASE STUDY

Box 2.4 Grandmothers

"We feel much stronger now because not only do we have our traditional knowledge but, in addition, we have acquired the knowledge of the doctors."

—Senegalese grandmother leader

In virtually all sociocultural settings in Africa, Asia, Latin America, and the Pacific, senior women or grandmothers are part of family and community systems in which women and children are embedded. Across cultures, in all matters related to the health and development of women and children, grandmothers are expected to teach, guide, and support the younger members of society. But policies and programs on maternal and child health and the communication strategies that support them have rarely taken grandmothers' role and influence seriously into account.

The Grandmother Project is an American NGO. The "grandmother-inclusive methodology" works through grandmother networks and leaders, using participatory methods of communication as dialogue to acknowledge the important role of grandmothers and to challenge them to combine traditional and modern knowledge in order to strengthen their contribution to promoting the well-being of women and children. Experiences in the Lao People's Democratic Republic, Mali, and Senegal using this methodology have demonstrated that the inclusion of grandmothers in maternal and child health programs increases the cultural relevance of such programs. This leads to greater community support for the initiatives and, in turn, contributes to greater program effectiveness. Qualitative results from the programs show increased self-confidence of grandmothers, better solidarity between women, the emergence of grandmother leaders, increased public recognition of their role, and increased knowledge of women's health practices.

Source: Aubel 2006.

RECOMMENDATIONS

1. Projects, policies, and programs should be culturally sensitive, beginning with recognition of what exists and building on that.
2. Training and capacity building is necessary, both to give those affected confidence to speak and to get policy makers to listen.
3. Health communication projects need initial analyses of family roles and how they influence health norms and practices.

Of Rubber and Road: Impact and Evidence

This session began by asking who the audience is for the impact evaluation. The evaluation should be for the beneficiaries but it is often more about proving the validity of data to donors and policy makers. Often funders define issues on which people are supposed to work. For example, speaking to people in Uganda, ICCD found that issues related to malaria were seen as more relevant than those related to HIV and AIDS. It is important for those planning impact evaluations to recognize that people can measure their own change and can set their own indicators. The session also discussed the usefulness of participatory evaluation and how it can strengthen ownership and long-term impact.

See box 2.5 for a case study.

KEY ISSUES

- How do you measure empowerment? A mixture of methodologies is needed to be able to measure such things as people's own sense of empowerment (for example, the impact of health care workers feeling professionally empowered).
- Communication is seldom consistent over prolonged periods of time. Change in health status takes longer than program evaluation cycles last.
- What can really be measured? For example, national AIDS prevention campaigns often cite condom use because that is relatively easy to measure, but other issues—such as women's rights and empowerment—are equally important in preventing HIV.
- The validity and presentation of data raise questions. How much scientific rigor is really needed? Is it possible to use less rigorous but still valid data? Collecting stories—that is, people telling how they perceive change—can also be an effective methodology.

Box 2.5 Scaling Up Communication for Social Change

In 1970 the Comprehensive Rural Health Project (CRHP) began as a small community-based project in Jamkhed, India, working with only a handful of villages. But every few years new villages were added, as people from villages that were not served approached the project staff. The CRHP has grown exponentially to cover some 250 villages. It has also expanded to become a training center to build the capacity of people from other community development projects, and it has started a new project in Bhandardara, a remote community of indigenous people some 150 kilometers away from Jamkhed. Twelve elements of communication for social change can be drawn from the evidence from the project:

1. Establishing open dialogue and horizontal communication between project staff and change agents and community members to build trust and confidence
2. Listening to people's needs, identifying culturally relevant ways to involve local personnel, and mobilizing local resources to meet these needs
3. Identifying ways to promote outside expert advice and information, yet ensuring that information is not merely disseminated but also allows people the means to participate in the knowledge creation process
4. Ensuring that local health workers receive continuing training and that health workers provide feedback from the communities, to be integrated in the training program
5. Designing training of health workers based on dialogue, critical thinking, peer learning, and respect for local knowledge
6. Repeating new or complex information provided during the training to ensure that health workers remember the key messages
7. Incorporating local cultural practices in designing preventive health messages and providing health workers the freedom to use their experiential knowledge in promoting and diffusing information in the villages
8. Challenging certain harmful social or cultural practices by being transparent in communication and demonstrating the ill effects of those practices
9. Using communication for personal development as a way to empower individuals
10. Organizing people in formal and informal groups and engaging in a dialogue with these groups to stimulate critical thinking
11. Building on individual-level changes to stimulate societal changes, including changing social norms and behaviors
12. Allowing community members to decide when they want the project staff to stop working with their community and move on to work in a new one

Source: Chitnis 2006.

- There is a need for an evidence base; alternative methodologies, such as Most Significant Change (MSC), are useful here. MSC is a participatory monitoring and evaluation technique that collects stories and systematically analyzes them to identify significant changes in program participants' lives. The technique does not use predetermined indicators; instead, it involves stakeholders in deciding on the type of change to search for, collecting and analyzing significant change stories, and discussing the value of those changes (Davies and Dart 2005).
- Participation of the most affected is not only about who is being heard, but also about supportive spaces where those affected can develop a sense of their own priorities—to set the agenda—and express themselves in their own ways on their own terms.
- Participatory approaches in monitoring and evaluation are important in self-learning and auto-evaluation.
- Rethinking who the impact evaluation is for is important—it should ultimately be for the beneficiaries.
- Data have limited use in policy making: data from evaluations need to be translated into language that policy makers and laymen can access and understand.

Key and Emerging Issues for the Health Strand

A number of significant issues and recommendations emerged from the health strand as a whole:

- Culture is part of people's realities and can be both an enabling factor for and a barrier to communication. Either way, it must be engaged from the beginning. People are more ready to change cultural practices or adapt them than many assume when they think of culture as static or traditional.
- Participation is not just about who is being heard but also about supportive spaces where people can develop a sense of their own priorities and set the agenda. They need to be given the capacity to express themselves in their own ways, on their own terms.
- Community monitoring is needed to hold authorities to account—an important part of building capacity that empowers communities.

- New technologies are important, but there will always be a need for face-to-face and interpersonal communication in Communication for Development.
- Power issues mean that some policy makers are not interested in Communication for Development if it opens up participation and scrutiny. "Getting people to be masters of their own reality is a threat to many," said one participant.

Papers Used in the Health Sessions

Aubel, Judi. "Using a Neglected Cultural Resource in Development Programs: Grandmother Networks and Participatory Communication."

Bamezai, Gita. "Grassroots Communication Innovations to Make Rural Health More Pragmatic and Scope for Community Ownership."

Chitnis, Ketan. "Scaling Up Communication for Social Change: Implications of the Community-Based Health and Development Model in Jamkhed, India."

Communication Initiative. "Health in a Time of Poverty: A Background Note." Background paper prepared for the WCCD—http://www.devcomm.org/devcomm/Sessions/tabid/81/Default.aspx?macroId=3&microId=302.

Goldstein, Susan, and Esca Scheepers. "Using Edutainment for Social Change—Evidence from Soul City over 6 Series."

Gray-Felder, Denise, Ailish Byrne, James Hunt, Afework Ayele, and Mirgissa Kaba. "CFSC and Youth Clubs Tackle HIV/AIDS in Ethiopia: Using and Evaluating Youth-Focused Dialogue."

Hegazi, Sahar. "Making a Difference: The Success Story of Social Communication in the Battle against Polio in Egypt."

Ogden, Ellyn, Silvio Waisbord, Lora Shimp, and Shan Thomas. "Communication for Disease Eradication: Using Social and Epidemiological Data to Increase Immunity."

Vega, Jair. "Project: Joven Habla Joven (Young People Speak)—A Communication Intervention for Social Change to Improve Sexual Responsibility."

Yahaya, Mohammed. "The Influence of Parent-Child Communication Pattern in Risky Behaviour Reduction among Vulnerable Groups in Nigeria."

Note

1. See the Treatment Action Campaign Web site: http://www.tac.org.za/.

3

Communication and Governance

The background paper on governance for the Congress notes "information and communication processes—and the media of communication—are a fundamental part of how governance systems operate in any political community. What is more, they are fundamental to the agenda of pro-poor social and political change" (DFID and World Bank 2006).

The Congress had a series of debates about the nature of governance and its application to government, the media, and civil society, and the relationships among all three. The strand on governance began with a plenary called "Communication for Good Governance, Participation, and Transparency."

The plenary started with a BBC World video, *It's All Communication,* which looked at three examples of successful communication for good governance in Bangladesh, Ghana, and Uganda. In Bangladesh, public leaders were held accountable through *Sanglap,* a TV discussion program that included government officials on the panel. It reached 5 million people. In Ghana, journalists used mobile phones to transmit election events from polling stations live on radio. This enhanced credibility of election and made it more difficult for those who lost to cry foul. Voter turnout was 85 percent. "We take our freedom very seriously," commented one interviewee on the video. In Uganda, surveys showed that only 13 percent of funds actually reached primary schools in the early 1990s. A range of reforms led to an increase to 80 percent by early 2001 (box 3.1).

A number of points emerged from this session:

1. What constitute free media? This question ran throughout the conference and was the subject of a BBC World Debate. There

Box 3.1 Uganda—Expenditure Tracking

In the mid-1990s Uganda implemented its first public expenditure tracking survey. The purpose of the survey was to collect information from primary schools to gauge the extent to which government grants actually made it to their intended destination. The survey revealed that during 1991–95, on average, only 13 percent of the grants made it to the schools. Most of the funds were used for purposes unrelated to education: to fund the local political and bureaucratic machinery or for private gain, as indicated by numerous newspaper articles about indictments of district education officers after the survey findings were made public.

As evidence of the degree to which money was leaking out of the system became public knowledge, the central government enacted a number of changes. It began publishing the monthly transfers of public funds to districts in newspapers and broadcasting them on the radio, and requiring primary schools to post information on inflows of funds. The government also replaced the central supply of construction and other materials with school-based procurement and compiled data on spending for teachers' salaries at the central government level. The objective of this information campaign was to promote transparency and increase public sector accountability.

A preliminary assessment of these reforms showed that the flow of funds improved dramatically, from an average of 13 percent reaching schools in 1991–95 to about 80 percent in early 2001. Work is under way to evaluate the impact of the information campaign.

Source: Reinikka and Svensson 2004.

was recognition that many media institutions are controlled by the "super rich." There is also the danger of control by those with political interests to pursue.

2. It was clear that governance, participation, and transparency have become a particular area of focus at multilateral, governmental, and citizen levels.
3. Good governance is not just about reducing corruption, and corruption does not occur only in developing countries. There are many examples from the industrial countries as well. As one participant put it: "Corruption is about the corruptor as well as the corruptee—and often the corruptor is from the developed world."
4. The principle of access to information as a right must cut across cultures and be universally acknowledged.

5. Good governance is helped by the free spread of information and the capacity of all levels of society to engage in debate. The rise of the Internet, satellite technology, and blogging contribute to this capacity. It becomes increasingly hard for those in power to control or limit discussion.
6. In a discussion about what happens when the good governance function of free media—holding to account, transparency, public debate—fails, it was suggested that some form of subsidies should be in place when the market fails, to uphold the public interest function.

Additional points on governance arose during the BBC World Debate on the second day of the Congress, on the subject, "Is a free media essential for development?"

7. What is a free media?
    a) The debates made clear that no common definition exists. As in the governance plenary, debate focused on whether the concept of free media is Western or universal and on skepticism about whether any media is really free from both political and commercial agendas.
    b) Free media are not always wise or just media. It was pointed out that free media could be abused in a number of ways. For example, unfettered free radio in Rwanda was used to spill out vitriolic messages that led to genocide.
    c) Free media must be held accountable by legal systems, institutions of governance and accountability, and a freedom of information act.
    d) Discussions also covered media ownership. How free can media be when they must focus on issues of interest to the people that will bring in the money?
    e) Do free media really cover the important stories?
8. Ideally, free media play at least four roles:
    a) As an important watchdog—of governments, the private sector, and public bodies
    b) As a way of giving voice to ordinary people
    c) As a way of holding politicians to account—partly through enabling people's informed participation in political processes
    d) As a "public sphere"

Although the issue was also raised in other strands and at special events, six workshop sessions focused specifically on governance:

1. Securing Political Will: The Prerequisite for Public Sector Reform
2. Strengthening Voice and Accountability: The End-Goal of Communication for Development
3. Building Media Systems: Enabling an Effective Fourth Estate
4. Fighting Corruption: Beyond Technocratic Solutions
5. Making Public Institutions Transparent: The Cornerstone of an Open Society
6. Good Governance in Practice: The Example of Infrastructure Projects

Securing Political Will: The Prerequisite for Public Sector Reform

> *"Securing political will can be achieved through recognizing that politicians have a responsibility. Although it is hard to define, it's easy to see where political will is absent—it is obvious where it is lacking."*
>
> —SESSION PARTICIPANT

"Good governance," "participation," and "pro-poor reform" are terms attached to most major development projects today. Yet whether these values are realized in the field depends in large part on the nature of the politics and the political culture of a country. How do we secure support—starting with political will—for public sector and pro-poor reform programs? What kind of advocacy is required at different levels of government and society? What role does communication play? What more/better/different should be done and by whom?

Presentations in the workshop looked at the political will of politicians and donors, and what needs to change. The session also explored how communicators can help involve citizens in change and in mobilizing their own political will both in a top-down way—being persuaded to comply with the wishes of policy makers—and in bottom-up ways—in the sense of ordinary people getting their wishes across to those in power and influencing policy. The participants also focused on political capital: politicians invest political capital in change processes and must be convinced of the return on their investment of that political capital. Communication can help them assess the political risk—the more participatory the assessment, the more responsive the politician will be to the needs of his or her constituents.

KEY ISSUES

Issues that arose during the workshop can be grouped as challenges for politicians, challenges for donors, and challenges for Communication for Development.

Challenges for politicians

1. Prefabricated ideas do not fit local contexts: a one-size-fits-all approach is not working.
2. Politicians often fail to keep their side of the bargain of being in power—to inform and to provide solutions for their people. Sometimes this is simply because they are not transparent. Fixing this problem requires political will, definite action, and capacity building within governments.
3. Sometimes politicians do not know what to do: they are given big ideas by institutions such as the World Bank and the International Monetary Fund but no details of how to realize these ideas.
4. Communication to achieve reform must engage with decision makers (box 3.2). The RAPID framework for analysis is useful here. RAPID: **R**ecommended—ideas are recommended by others; **A**gree—who needs to be included to agree to decisions?; **P**urpose—who carries out the activities?; **I**nput—input provided by experts, thinkers, advisers; **D**ecisions—who actually makes the decisions?
5. How does a politician choose which cutbacks to make, knowing that cutting back in some areas will mean other longer-term costs? Cutting back on education, for example, will lead to the extra expense of bringing back those nationals who had to leave the country to be educated elsewhere. Communication underpins the assessments and risk analyses: How do

Box 3.2 Decision Makers Want Communication—What They May Not Want Is Participation

Decision makers are interested in communication. There is no need for a hard sell here. What I see is a growing interest in the power of communication so long as it is one-way information dissemination, awareness raising, and public relations—no problem. What is sorely missing, however, is in-depth knowledge of how to build communication in such a way that the people to whom it is directed actually gain or have a say in the countless messages thrown their way. At stake is the kind of planning and research that must go into a communication effort to make it truly effective. In short, what is missing is any notion of putting in place what is commonly known as participatory communication.

In an earlier work to research decision makers' views on communication (Quarry and Ramirez 2005), the authors found that decision makers fell into three main categories. If this is the case, might it not be a good idea to first acknowledge that all decision makers are not created equal and that it would prove useful to take this into account? Second, let's acknowledge that some decision makers simply do not have participation within their mandate—whether in government for reasons of state or in banks, well, because they are banks. Next, let's consider changing our own agenda. Instead of expecting a better participatory approach from those institutions that really do not have participation within their mandate, let's work with them to help widen their understanding of what others may need to make participation effective. It is well within their mandate to foster this approach. An understanding of the importance of space for slower and longer time frames for others to enhance participation ultimately ends up being beneficial to society.

Source: Quarry 2006.

politicians know what constituents think is the most important issue in which to allocate resources? Through communication processes.

Challenges for donors

6. Donor coordination is important—there are too many donors, all working on a different strategy or agenda with different reports. Many people spend their time just writing reports.
7. The key is not to impose the solutions the donors would like but to listen to what the beneficiaries want and need.

Challenges for Communication for Development

8. Communication practitioners are transformers: they must "step down" the issues to a lower voltage so that their complexity does not electrocute policy makers and ordinary people. Sometimes recipients do not fully understand the agendas offered or solutions presented by donors or those with power. Development communicators must clarify those agendas and solutions. This is particularly important where the powerful are able to dictate terms and definitions to the powerless. Structural readjustment programs and other development paradigms are examples.
9. The saying goes that "the price of freedom is eternal vigilance." The public must work to uphold its freedoms and to hold government accountable. Too often the responsibility for such vigilance is passed on to nongovernmental organizations (NGOs) and civil society organizations (CSOs). This is not necessarily bad. It depends on the nature, legitimacy, and representativeness of the organization. The people must also take on this responsibility as part of being citizens, for example, through engagement with CSOs and vigilance over their behavior, too.
10. Communication specialists need to help people focus on the reasons why things happen. Too often they focus only on the "know what and know how." This should be complemented by the "know why" of how change happens. Communicators also need to engage the nodes of organizations in CSOs and NGOs, which can in turn galvanize public opinion, debate, and action. Communication can amplify the voices of the targets and beneficiaries of reform programs by creating spaces for people to express their voice, for example, on television and radio discussion programs.

RECOMMENDATIONS

1. Fit communication strategies to a particular context. This applies equally to politicians, donors, and Communication for Development specialists.
2. Establish a caucus of donor countries with one focal person, to reduce time and minimize conflict of donor agendas.

3. Persuade politicians to use their position to get a message across; for example, the Ugandan president ended every speech with a message on AIDS.
4. Engage all stakeholders in reform programs from the beginning. If people are included in the decision-making process, (a) it will meet their needs and (b) they will support rather than obstruct it.

Strengthening Voice and Accountability: The End-Goal of Communication for Development

The true test of development communication and information processes lies in whether they are effectively strengthening the voice of the people and their ability to hold leaders accountable for promised outcomes. How seriously are development leaders—both donors and their government partners—emphasizing this aspect? Does the current dialogue on sustainable development sufficiently recognize this aspect? Is modern development work focusing enough on the issue of voice and accountability at both the national and the local levels? What more/better/different should be done and by whom?

KEY ISSUES

1. The media can play a fundamental role in strengthening voice and accountability. But there are often limits to the media's role in ensuring government accountability. For example, in Asia and Africa many journalists are undersupported and underresourced professionally, lacking the time and resources needed to visit poor communities to research stories. Traditional reporting patterns and the enduring impact of political controls may mean that journalists fail to uncover and explore poverty and social equity issues in proper depth. Official secrecy, as well as the costs and difficulties of accessing information, can hinder research. They follow a pattern of reporting that narrates what is happening but does not go into the issues in depth.
2. Discussion covered the challenges of working with the media and how the media and other stakeholders could work more

productively together. The media are commercially oriented, so it costs money to work with them, and NGOs often cannot afford to buy airtime. Yet NGOs need to be able to access the mainstream media. The media should be sensitized to the concerns and views of communities. Skills need to be developed to use the kind of information NGOs produce. Very few journalists can understand the language of the people, and they cannot work out how to make it into a story. NGOs and CSOs need to be more aware of the professional and commercial pressures that journalists work under and what their specific needs are. Communication strategies need to fit commercial needs.

3. Media owners and editors in the increasingly commercial media environment often view poverty issues as unattractive. Stories are squeezed out by the need for advertising space. This issue needs more research. What are the limits of the target audience's interests and needs? Are we really pushing the boundaries as far as we can? How can the media play a public interest role in an increasingly commercial environment?
4. It is often exceedingly difficult for the general public—and especially poor communities—to get information from governments, which may lack focal points and coordinated structures for the interactive provision and receipt of information. Governments may not have a communication strategy in place. Sometimes it is a question of will, sometimes of lack of skills and resources. The two-way dynamic to information exchange is often missing.
5. Increasing public discussion and participation in decisions to improve the use of public resources is important for poverty reduction. There is also a need for stronger debate about addressing equity issues, which would require both governments and international institutions to be more open to considerations of a wider range of policy choices.
6. Good governance is an international issue. The debate about the international aspect of accountability needs to be broader. For example, despite often-voiced concerns about the openness of some developing country governments to transparency and participation, are governments in the industrial countries fulfilling their side of the governance bargain? Are they making progress toward Millennium Development Goal 8 (develop a global partnership for development) on debt, aid, and particularly trade? Raising public awareness of and debate on

international responsibilities for good governance—so that citizens in the industrial countries as well as the developing countries can hold their governments to account for progress in poverty reduction—is a complex challenge that communicators must address.

7. Citizens can build their own monitoring instruments to evaluate public policy without being asked by government. Doing so involves access to information and the right to access the spaces where public policy is being implemented.
8. Donors increasingly stress governance questions. But under what circumstances should donors have the right to make governance a condition of lending? Is there a danger of new forms of conditionality? If the threat of aid withdrawal is not to be used as a lever except under extreme circumstances, what other ways can be found to support civil society actors to ensure that people are empowered to get their views across and be heard by the state?
9. Content is as important as process. There is a need not only for greater voice and accountability within official policy processes but also for space for greater debate about policy content. CSOs can help poor people define their agendas and articulate them.
10. There needs to be political will to reestablish democracy, but tools are required to accomplish this. Reestablishing democracy and seeking the tools to do so is the dual role of government. Where governments are weak, government capacity needs to be strengthened and strategies created within government to increase dialogue between government and CSOs. We need champions within countries who can foster these dialogues (box 3.3).

RECOMMENDATIONS

1. More research should look into the interests of different readers, listeners, and viewers. Are we making assumptions about people's information needs?
2. Tools that can be used directly by citizens should be developed to ensure government accountability and transparency. Citizens are not generally involved in evaluating the implementation of policies, but they should be.

CASE STUDY

Box 3.3 Nicaragua—Citizen Involvement in the PRSP Process

Mignone Vega, Director of Strategic Communication for the Presidency of the Republic of Nicaragua, told participants

> *In Nicaragua we want to strengthen the connection between governments and citizens. This is a challenge that sometimes politicians don't understand. Nicaragua is portrayed as a corrupt country with low self-esteem, low private investment, and poor transparency. To change this image is a very high achievement. People do want to participate, to better their standards of living. This is participation in a deep sense. We wanted to institutionalize this dialogue between government and citizens through the PRSP process. It was important to define the role of the state, the role of people, and the nature of communication between the two. People need to know how the state spends its money. We have started a dialogue on economic issues and corruption. News on this was published in newspapers every day. The budget has been decentralized to the local government level for the first time and a finance law was discussed with them. Nicaragua today has a transparent budgetary process. The role of the media is fundamental to this.*

3. Media coverage and communication initiatives should consider new styles, formats, and genres (for example, capitalizing on youth and popular culture).
4. Communication vehicles outside the media (that is, not journalists) should be considered for the inclusion and promotion of voice. An example is community theater, which has often proved powerful.
5. Media and stakeholder groups (for example, CSOs, government bodies, research organizations) should strengthen their interaction, information exchange, and working relations so that communication on poverty reduction, including poor people's views, can be maximized.

Building Media Systems: Enabling an Effective Fourth Estate

The international development community has expressed overwhelming consensus on the important role of the media in exposing corruption and holding leaders accountable. What is needed to improve the environment—from the national to the community level—in which the media in developing countries operate? How can we better support free, pluralistic, and independent media systems? What is needed to improve media laws and policies? What more/better/different should be done and by whom?

KEY ISSUES

1. Some countries have a tremendous need for training. For example, in the Arab world at the moment less than 1 percent of the population uses the Internet but in the next 5–10 years, as young people are trained to use it, this situation will change. It is considered a freer medium than others and gets all sorts of people talking. Because this new phenomenon, as well as SMS (Short Message Service), is popular among young people, it provides an opportunity for opening up dialogue with new groups in society.
2. Communication for Development specialists need to learn from one another about media support: What are the business models that work? How can we tackle corruption and journalists being bribed?
3. Local ownership and leadership in the media are important. Direct support should be given to media outlets that contribute to a pluralistic environment—those threatened by market liberalization and political pressures (for example, repression).
4. Media donors should look at media development as a sectoral issue in itself, but at the same time, those responsible should reach out to other programmatic areas to ensure that media development is coherent. Exchanges of experience among journalists, publishers, and owners are very helpful on a global scale.
5. Media actors at the country level need to debate the role and the future direction of the media in their country: journalists, publishers, and owners should all be involved in this debate. It should not be possible to impose models of journalism from the West that do not take into account the country context. The public and civil society must demand free media, and the media must be understood to be a public good (boxes 3.4 and 3.5).

CASE STUDY

Box 3.4 Philippines—*Newsbreak*

Democracy alone cannot produce a free press. In the Philippines, the state is weak and media organizations operate in a context of corruption. There is no free and independent media culture; the media are not believed. One journalist is killed every month and the murders are not investigated. Libel is used as a weapon by the powerful: the prime minister has filed 42 libel cases.

Newsbreak is the flagship current affairs TV program. It is unique in that its business model includes advertising and donations, ensuring its independence. Media organizations must be able to compete in a commercial media marketplace in this way, to ensure sustainability. Owners of big media outfits are often part of conglomerates with other business interests. But even in the Philippines, where the media are controlled by a few, the middle class is small, and the gap between rich and poor is huge, the *Newsbreak* business model is working.

Some recommendations for reforming the media in the Filipino context:

- The media have an important role to play on the demand side of democracy and should be strengthened to help make government more accountable.
- There needs to be legislation—freedom of information acts and the like.
- People need to see that the independent media can thrive in the marketplace—extending its audience base.
- Market-based solutions are important—we need to increase audience size by working with the private sector and providing marketing training.
- Venture capital and loans and grants should be accessible for successful media in developing and developed countries.
- Donors should gather together and create something similar to the Millennium Challenge Fund, through which media groups should be able to access funds according to conditions.
- We need to learn from one another—what are the business models that work? How can we tackle corruption and journalists being bribed?
- Media organizations and CSOs need to work together. In the Philippines, a partnership between CSOs and the media addressed the practice of politicians paying off journalists, who earn low salaries and therefore are more easily tempted. The campaign resulted in a public admission by journalists of this hidden practice.

Source: Presentation at the WCCD by Marites Vitug, Editor in Chief, *Newsbreak,* the Philippines.

Box 3.5 Panos—Making Development Stories Attractive to Journalists

Many journalists in developing countries have remarked to Panos representatives that coverage of stories on issues such as poverty reduction, trade, and development often does not figure uppermost in the minds of media owners, managers, and editors operating in an increasingly competitive commercial environment. Ostensibly dry stories on trade and poverty may be deemed of little interest beyond an elite group of readers. And in the competitive battle for editorial space, with the pressure or attraction of increasing advertising revenue making its presence felt, copy on this subject may lose out to other topics.

Yet in communications with Panos, several journalists and editors have argued that innovative ways could and should be found to make such stories attractive and that there should be a greater commitment to providing editorial space for them. They claim that media houses can sometimes make narrow, short-term assumptions about their key target audiences and the limits of the public's information interests and needs. Underestimated is the public's potential appetite for well-crafted, accessible stories on poverty reduction that explain the complexities of the topic and also humanize it.

Source: Presentation at the WCCD by Jon Barnes, Panos.

RECOMMENDATIONS

1. Show success stories about the impact of responsible media organizations on democracy.
2. Improve the rule of law in general, so that media freedom laws and freedom of information acts cannot be easily overridden, for ostensible reasons of national security or the like.
3. Use entertainment formats—for example, soap operas, cultural programming—to promote dialogue on development issues.
4. Promote market-based solutions to strengthening media, such as increasing audience size and training staff in marketing.
5. Donors who support media systems should work with grassroots media organizations rather than international media institutions. These donors should also coordinate activities.
6. Donors should collaborate and coordinate more before they go into countries, especially countries in crisis. Donors should pool funding and seek strategic partnerships with other donors.

7. Donors should get together to create something similar to the Millennium Challenge Fund through which media groups can access funds, according to conditions. The media have an important role to play on the demand side of democracy and that role needs to be strengthened to help make government more accountable.
8. Media groups should lobby development donors to take media support more seriously.

Fighting Corruption: Beyond Technocratic Solutions

Anticorruption measures are almost entirely technocratic, led by specialists who concentrate on fixing institutions. While important, this kind of work is not sufficient. What can be done to wage a more comprehensive fight against corruption? How can strategic communication be used to promote disclosure, to transform attitudes, opinions, and behavior regarding corruption? What can be done to strengthen intolerance of corruption and stimulate widespread activism to combat it? What more/better/different should be done and by whom?

KEY ISSUES

1. All strategies to reduce corruption ultimately depend on citizens acting as a check against corrupt practices. Therefore, it is important that civil society be able to organize to form legal bodies; enabling and allowing this to happen requires appropriate legislation. Civil society must not be afraid of the consequences of organizing and speaking out: this requires an environment of trust, so that people will listen and respond to the issues raised.
2. Efforts to support free flows of information will only be successful if a demand for information exists.
3. Communication must be more than just access to information: it must lead to action. Legal mandates should oblige governments to explain policy decisions and to provide an enabling environment in which people can act on that information.
4. Broad-based coalitions are important for transparency efforts. For example, although the inclusion of diverse stakeholders

in drawing up Romanian and Bulgarian laws on access to information produced weak legislation on paper, the implementation of those laws is relatively high: 50 percent of requested files are provided.

5. In its ranking of media environments, Freedom House says that one-third of the world lives in environments with free media, one-third in environments with partially free media, and one-third in environments without free media (box 3.6). Although the assumption is that free media lead to a reduction in corruption, corruption can also lead to a reduction in media freedom. It is very hard, however, to measure the extent and quality of media freedom.

CASE STUDY

Box 3.6 Freedom House Findings, 2005

In 2005, of 194 countries and territories surveyed by Freedom House, 73 (38 percent) were rated free, 54 (28 percent) were rated partly free, and 67 (34 percent) were rated not free (comparable numbers for the previous survey were 75 free, 50 partly free, and 69 not free). Category shifts in 2005 suggested a trend of convergence toward the partly free category. Two countries, Timor-Leste and Botswana, moved from free to partly free, while two countries, Kenya and Mauritania, improved from not free to partly free.

In terms of population, the survey found that 17 percent of the world's inhabitants live in countries that enjoy a free press, while 40 percent have a partly free press, and 43 percent have a press that is not free. The relatively negative picture painted by examining population figures can be explained by the fact that China, with its large population, is rated not free, and the almost equally populous country of India is rated partly free, thus vastly limiting the percentage of people worldwide who have access to free media. Over the past year the percentage of people enjoying free media has declined slightly, while the percentage of people who live in countries with a media environment that is not free has decreased by two percentage points; this indicates that more countries are moving into the gray zone of partial media freedom.

The overall level of press freedom worldwide, as measured by the global average score, worsened slightly in 2005 to 46.05, continuing a four-year downward trend. Both the overall global average score and the global averages for the legal and political environment categories worsened, with the political environment category showing a particular decline.

Source: http://www.freedomhouse.org/template.cfm?page=1.

RECOMMENDATIONS

Priorities for establishing good governance and preventing corruption include the following:

1. Establish legal framework that allows for, and protects, free media and CSOs.
2. Open up the policy process to scrutiny at the national level.
3. Create transparency and publicity and incentives to promote local participation in political processes.
4. Build the role of civil society in anticorruption measures—thus promoting the demand for anticorruption efforts. This should go beyond training better administrators, imposing stronger sanctions, and the like.

Making Public Institutions Transparent: The Cornerstone of an Open Society

Government is a public trust, yet in too many countries governments are not trusted because their operations are not transparent and their citizens do not have the information to hold their leaders accountable. How can communication and information processes be used to transfer more knowledge—and thus power—from behind closed doors into the public realm? How can the balance of information-as-power be tipped in greater favor of the citizens at large? What are the success stories and what are the stubborn obstacles? What more/better/different should be done and by whom?

One of the important threads in the workshops was how information and communication can help public institutions function better. Two issues were identified as relevant here: the importance of access to information and the importance of free media and the Internet.

THE IMPORTANCE OF ACCESS TO INFORMATION

Some 70 countries have passed access to information laws, but these laws are meaningful only when they are implemented and upheld. A useful way of framing access to information is to present it as the right to access or request information: this is particularly important as information is increasingly held by private corporations.

More information leads to greater knowledge—particularly for citizen understanding about state activities, which leads to greater potential to hold the state to account. It also builds trust in two important ways: by giving out information, the state demonstrates that it trusts its citizens to know what to do with the information and also that the state has trust and confidence in the policy decisions it has made. This is particularly important at a time when trust in politicians and political institutions is very low.

But for states to implement access to information legislation, they need to believe that it is in their interest to do so and that it will not simply increase the burden on the state. Arguments for introducing access to information legislation include the following:

1. It makes government more efficient: the actions of putting documents online, keeping records, and archiving and sharing information internally create significant efficiency.
2. Politicians are always concerned about getting reelected. They often resist introducing access to information laws because they think such laws will reveal deficiencies on their part. However, such laws can also be used to show that policy failures are not their fault. They can reveal when the responsibilities for policy and social failures lie not with politicians but with external agents, or how blame should be apportioned. Blame does not always lie with politicians.
3. Where information about policy is available, civil society can help put those policies into practice—for example, by helping local authorities understand responsibilities or simply by mobilizing people.
4. Access to information also means that citizens can take part in public life—for example, through citizens' assemblies.

THE IMPORTANCE OF FREE MEDIA AND THE INTERNET

Access to information is not the most crucial condition for the functioning of free media. Although it can be useful for investigatory journalism, access usually takes too long (20 to 100 days for documents to be released) and journalists need information immediately to be able to meet daily deadlines. Paradoxically, advocates of free media sometimes resist laws on access to information, for various reasons:

1. When access to information is democratized, it can threaten the privileged position that the media hold in providing information.
2. Institutional sources that journalists depend on may no longer feel they have the same responsibility to provide information, if there is legislation to provide it through other channels.
3. Legislation on access to information can also be used to repress the media: governments can restrict the kind of information that is available, as in Paraguay and Zimbabwe.
4. Governments can also "scoop" the media: by withholding information until a decisive moment, they can choose to release the information before it is exposed by others, defusing the impact.
5. New technologies can also pose problems for access to information: governments can dump huge quantities of information onto the Internet without sorting or categorizing the information, making it very hard to identify what is important. Using new digital technologies as the key to accessing information can also exclude those who lack access to the technologies from the information, widening the digital divide.

KEY ISSUES

1. Who accesses information? In Mexico, after the passing of legislation on access to information, 150,000 requests came in—more than 50 percent from businessmen and academicians. Other requesters were journalists and other bureaucrats. Sixty percent were from urban areas. Access to information is seen as an instrument for the elite to check power. For example, a federal minister's career was compromised when information revealed his illegal dealings with casino owners.
2. The challenge is to make the legislation accessible and usable by ordinary people. A huge number are marginalized from even the potential of accessing information, and most do not know how accessing information can benefit them. So there are currently programs—external, not government funded—to explain the benefits that accessing information can bring.
3. Access to information is a human right, under Article 19 of the Universal Declaration of Human Rights. It is increasingly

recognized as important: the Inter-American Court of Human Rights recently passed access to information decrees.

4. Support to promote demand from citizens and civil society for the elements of good governance is needed. Stimulating demand for access to information legislation is as important as advocating for new laws: without the demand there is no point to such legislation (box 3.7).

RECOMMENDATION

Capacity building is needed, not only with civil society but also with the media and public institutions themselves; many second-level officials simply do not know their responsibilities.

CASE STUDY

Box 3.7 Botswana—Vision 2016

Botswana is classified as a middle-income country, on target to meet the Millennium Development Goals (MDGs). Yet it is plagued by inequality and 25–30 percent of people live below the poverty line. In the mid-1990s the government decided to establish a national agenda for the future—Vision 2016—to mark the 50th anniversary of the country. The entire population was involved in setting the agenda: politicians traveled around the country and conducted discussions with people to see what they needed and wanted for the future.

On the basis of these discussions and extensive consultations, the politicians drew up a strategy to achieve the vision expressed by the people—a strategy for achieving the MDGs, before the MDGs were initiated. It was comprehensive, covering all aspects of life from child care and health care to how the elderly would be looked after. The process of consulting the people also introduced ideas of rights holders and duty bearers.

The project raised expectations and placed huge pressure on politicians to deliver. The government sent video teams out to the villages and rural areas to ask what the impact of the plan had been so far and found that there had been no communication of the vision to the people whom it was supposed to benefit.

The president then initiated a communication plan based on the establishment of indicators, looking at the number of clinics, roads, and other benchmarks in the vision. These were consolidated into a live database that tracked the performance of the delivery of the vision on the ground. Many politicians opposed this scheme, fearing for their votes. But enlightened politicians recognized that politics is about taking risks—and they trust that greater communication between politicians and voters will lead to better development.

Source: Presentation at the WCCD by session participant.

Good Governance in Practice: The Example of Infrastructure Projects

Communication for Development has evolved beyond traditional propaganda and marketing to a greater emphasis on two-way communication flows, dialogue, and participation, which are now widely deemed essential to ensuring good governance. Beyond a shared terminology, are we also forging agreement on international standards for development communication work? Infrastructure development is one area of development that often faces charges of poor governance and corruption. In particular, large infrastructure projects have effectively demonstrated both the damage that corruption and mistrust can do and, in other cases, the value of good communication programs. They also provide many examples of learning about integrating communication into project planning and implementation. In this way, they also provide examples of good practice. What is considered international best practice, in areas such as infrastructure, for measuring the effectiveness of Communication for Development projects and programs and, in particular, the role of communication in ensuring good governance, participation and transparency? Who benefits from infrastructure projects? There is a need for national debates on needs and priorities in infrastructure development.

The workshop participants had a wide-ranging discussion on these issues. Donal O'Leary, Senior Adviser with Transparency International, and Leonardo Mazzei, Communications Officer in the Development Communication Division of the World Bank discussed their presentation on governance and infrastructure. In it, they argued

Communication is an important management tool to promote sustainable infrastructure in three primary respects:

1. *To improve the quality of infrastructure through enabling more inclusive and informed decision making at all stages of the project cycle, driving new thinking and innovation to make infrastructure more sustainable, and establishing consensus on service provision priorities.*
2. *To build consensus on governance reforms around infrastructure through raising awareness of corruption vulnerabilities at*

all stages of infrastructure development and establishing consensus on reform programs, including the partnerships and tariffs needed to make services sustainable.

3. *To take concerted action to manage corruption risks in infrastructure through maintaining pressure for implementing reforms, consensus on concrete measures to deal with corruption, and mainstreaming those actions (Mazzei and O'Leary 2006).*

KEY ISSUES

1. *The importance of building in communication from the start of a project.* Participants noted that despite consensus on the need for communication, it is still difficult to include communication systematically in infrastructure projects. Involving communication from the start is key, because upfront communication adds value to project design. It can be used for diagnostic purposes to understand the political, social, economic, and cultural context in the field and to anticipate and resolve potential conflicts. This type of assessment, when timely, can identify risks that were not previously understood and would otherwise threaten the project. Transparency is key.
2. *The role of consensus.* CSOs, media, and beneficiaries play active and direct roles in infrastructure projects. Not giving them the opportunity to play a role puts the project at risk. Infrastructure projects are large and may require involvement from the private sector, so it is important to develop consensus on plans using communication—though communication does not always lead to consensus.
3. *Corruption and transparency.* Corruption is a major threat: governments and citizens pay a price for it in terms of lower incomes and lower investment. It is a major cause of poverty. It affects the poor and vulnerable excessively; for example, they will suffer most from negative environmental impacts. Corruption starts in small ways, and communication is helpful when discussing solutions.
4. *The importance of systematizing communication.* This can be done by learning from previous projects. A few standard

methodologies, public opinion surveys, stakeholder mapping, and coalition building are needed. One way to systematize communication is to improve the way donors work with implementers, to put pressure on them to meet certain standards, ensuring a transparency and accountability process is in place. One important element is vertical integration, establishing protocol so there is a rigor to information sharing at an institutional level. Every player should know how to access information and whom to approach to get it.

Participants also identified a number of myths about communication and development in this context:

1. *The idea that increased information and communication strengthens collective action and is good for cooperation.* This is often the case, but the result of increasing information depends a great deal on the context in which the actors find themselves. Actors are not just managers of risk and uncertainties. Differences in interests and opinions are real. If people are driven by a common understanding, then information is a useful tool that can spur development. However, people are more complex and diverse than that. They act to uphold certain values, as a result of historical injustices, or to uphold their social identities. These drivers have concrete effects in large infrastructure projects.
2. *The idea that information is an effective tool in fighting corruption.* There is a high correlation between a free press and a low incidence of corruption, but a free press also has some negative effects. If increased information about corruption appears in the press but not much happens to people who are corrupt, corruption may increase because the message is that everyone else is engaging in corruption and getting away with it. In this way, a free press can legitimize corruption and make it more endemic. If the corruption is among the political leadership—if the fish rots from the head down—this is very demoralizing for a society.
3. *The idea that curbing corruption is about getting the incentives right.* Strategic financing can play a role, but it has limits. Empowering the victims is a way to increase the risk that those managing the project will get caught if they act corruptly.

> Public officials and private actors engage in corruption when the risk of getting caught is negligible. Actors are guided by incentives, but also by norms and values concerning what is right. At the workshop Dr. Patrick Stalgren of the University of Gothenberg noted, "We should continue working with incentive-oriented reform but also increasingly look at how social values influence corrupt behaviors and how these values can be changed to reduce corruption."

See box 3.8 for some case studies.

Box 3.8 Canada and Peru

Canada: The Cree Nation

The Cree have been living around hydroelectric projects since the 1950s. Historically, hydroelectric development projects in northern regions of Canada have disrupted and often destroyed First Nation communities whose lands and waters were in the path of such development. Gradually the Cree found a voice: in the 1970s they lobbied to be involved in negotiations around a river diversion project. They taught the developers in Canada about the impact on their lives. The Cree community now has its own communication strategy for negotiation with local government. This strategy also ensures that Cree community members understand the full implications of a project. They have supported local government infrastructure agencies in establishing communication strategies tailored to meet the specific communication needs of the Cree community, taking into account language issues. How the concepts are translated for the community is critical—with technical language it is often important to translate the concepts in a way that the Cree community can comprehend. As a result, the community's capacity to minimize damage from such projects has been improved.

Four key recommendations, adapted from Usubiaga, Knippel, and Jackson (2006), should form the basis for migrating this approach to development projects in other environments, whether in the public or the private sector:

1. Affected peoples should be considered equal stakeholders. Where capacity building is required to enable fully informed decision making, independent advice must be facilitated as a project or governmental cost.
2. True commitment to the principles of participatory consultation, accountability, and transparency can serve project proponents' public relations goals, preempt opposition by those who are not stakeholders, and minimize unanticipated compensation costs and legal challenges.

3. Preference should be given to project bidders who implement the best practices to meet these goals—bidders who genuinely recognize and acknowledge the challenges and the costs of putting these recommendations into practice.
4. Although pre-project costs may be higher as a result, synergies with other projects or programs can often be found or developed to reduce the costs attributable to the project. Project investors will attach value to the cost certainty that comes from effective social risk management.

Source: Usubiaga, Knippel, and Jackson 2006.

Peru: The Small Town Pilot Project—A Private-Public and Social Partnership

> *"When two persons only dialogue and there is no change, it is because they did not dialogue, they only exchanged words."*
>
> —Erich Fromm

In Peru a structural gap exists between the state and the citizens. CSOs do not have representatives in state institutions. The legitimacy of those who manage infrastructure projects is a real problem. The Peruvian Small Towns Development Project was about changing traditional municipal models on the basis of an alliance between the private and the public sector. The project was not to implement infrastructure but to develop local management capacities to provide sustainable water and sanitation service. The project's philosophy was to change attitudes and behavior, as well as perceptions of and thinking about the roles of social and sector players in the delivery of sustainable high-quality water and sanitation services. The process of change is based on an alliance between the local authority, the civil society, and a private specialized operator. There was a lot of mistrust in the private sector, so it was important to recover trust in the state. The project created a new relationship between the state, civil society, and private operators. The relationship between government, citizens, and providers improved through the building of an alliance in nine localities, based on local control of how the project would be implemented. The people and the state signed a social contract to this effect.

The experience with the Small Towns Development Project suggests the following actions:

- Document the quantitative and qualitative impact of the strategic use of communication in interventions, in order to use successful communication types as advocacy tools.
- Produce attitude and behavior change in project managers, policy makers, and decision makers at the sector and the national levels.
- Scale up tested mechanisms and tools.

Source: Schippner and Quispe Martínez 2006.

Key and Emerging Issues for the Governance Strand

1. Free flows of information and communication lie at the heart of good governance, transparency, and accountability.
2. Partnerships and coalitions across different sections of society (media, civil society, and governments) need to promote appropriate policies and ensure transparency and accountability. Should citizens be responsible for holding governments to account, or do governments need to enable citizens to hold them to account?
3. There is a crisis of political legitimacy; people do not trust politicians and political institutions. In this context even free media can contribute to increasing the sense of impunity, if they expose issues of corruption but no action is taken as a result.
4. Free media are necessary but not sufficient for addressing good governance. There is also a question of what constitute free media—and of the state's interest versus the market's interest versus the public's interest.
5. Legal mechanisms are important to complement the role of free media—but it is how they are upheld that makes the difference.
6. If Western donors are serious about the political nature of development and the importance of political systems, then the recipient government's efforts to achieve transparency, accountability, and inclusion of citizen's voices must be part of the dialogue between donor and recipient. Should aid be conditional on the trajectory to good governance?

Papers Used in the Governance Sessions

Adam, Gordon. "News Based or Needs Based? Can Journalism and Advertising Paradigms Be Replaced by Development-Driven Broadcasting Initiatives?"

Alfaro Moreno, Rosa María. "El Desarrollo en la Agenda Pública."

DFID and World Bank. "Background Note on Communication in Governance." Background paper on governance prepared for the WCCD—http://www.devcomm.org/worldbank/admin/uploads/WCCD%20Files/Governance%20BackgroundNote.doc.

Islam, K M Baharul. "National Information and Communication Infrastructure Policies and Plans towards Poverty Reduction: Emerging Trends and Issues in Africa."

Misuraca, Gianluca C. "ICTs for Local Governance in Africa."

Moreno, José Manuel, and Francisco Sierra. "The Experience of Participatory Budgets in the City of Seville: Methodology for Planning Communication Patterns and Constructing Citizenship."

Quarry, Wendy. "Decision Makers DO Want Communication—What They May Not Want Is Participation."

Salazar García, Lina María. "Policy Advocacy Effectiveness and Knowledge Assets: A Case Study about U.K. and Colombian Non-governmental Organisations."

Schippner, Beatriz, and Andrés Quispe Martínez. "Building a Private-Public and Social Partnership to Change Water and Sanitation Management Models in Small Towns."

Usubiaga, Cristina, Steffen Knippel, and Sandra Jackson. "Empowering the Tataskweyak Cree Nation—A Case Study in Effective Communication and Consultation." Paper prepared for the World Congress on Communication for Development.

Walker, Gregg, Steven Daniels, Susan Senecah, Tarla Peterson, Anthony Cheng, and Jens Emborg. "Pluralistic Public Participation: Case Studies in Collaborative Learning."

4

Communication and Sustainable Development

In the run-up to the World Congress on Communication for Development, there were a number of regional meetings on the sustainable development strand. These meetings identified the main challenges for communication for sustainable development and looked at the lessons learned from the past and the challenges for the future. A background paper, "Communication for Sustainable Development" (FAO 2006), reflected main trends, challenges, and perspectives in the field of Communication and Sustainable Development, including the recommendations of the ninth United Nations (UN) Roundtable on Communication for Sustainable Development, held in Rome, September 6–9, 2004. The WCCD included a plenary and six workshops on the subject of sustainable development, as well as a number of special events.

The Regional Meetings

FAO coordinated seven regional initiatives in preparation for the WCCD during May–September 2006, with a view to promoting learning experiences and partnerships in Communication for Development. (Based on these experiences, a publication, "Compendium on Regional Perspectives," was prepared by Wendy Quarry and Ricardo Ramirez, in October 2006.) The executive summary of the findings from these meetings outlined the main challenges and the lessons learned, as well as some issues and recommendations, along with an action plan for each region. It identified five main challenges:

1. Decision makers' lack of knowledge of and capacity in Communication for Development practice
2. The lack of trained practitioners
3. The lack of political will, as evidenced through absence of policy
4. The need for partnerships
5. Confusion about information and communication technologies (ICTs) and Internet opportunities

DECISION MAKERS' LACK OF KNOWLEDGE AND CAPACITY

Experience has shown that decision makers are comfortable with the idea of communication, particularly where it applies to public relations, information, and awareness raising. However, they have little knowledge of the breadth of communication functions ranging from public relations to participatory communication. Nor is there understanding of the need for research-based communication planning to make a communication initiative viable. This lack of knowledge can result in confusion between Communication for Development and media, and it presents a major barrier to the mainstreaming of Communication for Development initiatives.

LACK OF TRAINED PRACTITIONERS

There is a tremendous dearth of well-trained communication practitioners in all regions. There is also a certain amount of confusion across regions as to the depth and meaning of Communication for Development, making it difficult to find a common language or terminology to indicate the meaning of the process.

LACK OF POLITICAL WILL, AS EVIDENCED THROUGH ABSENCE OF POLICY

It is clear that the presence of policy supporting Communication for Development within government at the national, middle, and local levels would provide the impetus (enabling environment) to accelerate the use of communication initiatives in project and program implementation. In many regions such a policy is often implicit in countries that support participatory development (or community-based management). In others, where participatory development is not the norm, it is almost impossible to find examples of any communication initiative beyond public relations and information exchange.

THE NEED FOR PARTNERSHIPS

In several cases partnerships between government bodies, NGOs, and academia have brought communication functions together within a given program to good effect. This type of synergy is possible in countries where governments welcome the presence of NGOs and see them as complementary to the government role of service provider and regulator.

CONFUSION ABOUT ICTS AND INTERNET OPPORTUNITIES

The growth of Internet technology has given an enormous impetus to wider interest in the power of communication. It has also opened the door to more horizontal communication that cannot be controlled by government. A good example is the blogging between Israeli and Lebanese citizens during the July 2006 war. At the same time, excitement about the Internet has led many decision makers to confuse the Internet, which is a tool, with Communication for Development, which is a process that makes use of a wide array of methods and media tools.

The regional paper also pointed out that

> *While the above may appear to be a daunting task, there are numerous stories of accomplishment and innovation. It is always important to tell the stories of communication initiatives that have been able to breathe life into a wide spectrum of different projects over the years. These stories bear testament to the impact of communication in the development process and help to remind us that without communication there can be no development (Quarry and Ramirez 2006: 16–19).*

The Plenary and Workshops on Communication for Sustainable Development

> *"We hear but do not listen, listen but do not understand, see but do not see."*
>
> —Proverb

At the Congress, a plenary on sustainable development was followed by six workshops on the topic. During these events, it was noted that there are at least 89 interpretations of sustainable development. One of the central ideas is that there is no universal development model that leads to sustainability at all levels of society and the world, but many different models.

In the plenary session, participants heard presentations on the experiences of Bhutan and Burkina Faso, which looked to increase community participation in their national development plans and in environmental issues in particular. In Bhutan, community participation resulted in the development of the concept of Gross National Happiness as the measure of development, rather than the usual economic indicators.

Other issues discussed during the plenary included environmental concerns such as water and other natural resource management, climate change, migration, and globalization. There was overall agreement that sustainable development "is development that is not harmful to the future." Several points arose from the plenary:

- Policy makers need to know how communities perceive their problems before they can both develop solutions to those problems.
- Policy makers and citizens need to have bidirectional communication. Participation may trigger dialogue between citizens and decision makers. This may accompany processes of decentralization and democratization.
- Communication provides a space for people to speak; it finds a pathway for people's needs to be articulated by communities to relevant people and back to the communities.
- Panelists emphasized that information does not involve people whereas communication does, and this is a significant difference.
- Participants suggested three factors to judge whether governments and organizations are consistent with a Communication

for Development approach: (a) their policies and strategies, (b) the presence of qualified staff, and (c) the adequacy of the budget.

- There were rich discussions about the challenges of including indigenous knowledge and whether this can be scaled up when, by definition, such knowledge is local.
- The policy makers on the panel emphasized the need for policy makers to develop ways to "hear people," either by going directly to them or by gathering their input through different mechanisms.

The workshop titles were as follows:

1. Communication on Food Security, Rural Development, and Livelihood Strategies
2. Poverty Reduction and Equity Issues
3. Communication and Sustainable Natural Resource Management
4. Mainstreaming Communication in Sustainable Development Policies: Local Perspectives and Priorities
5. Communication for Development and Global Environmental Issues and Sustaining the Process: Local Appropriations of Communication for Sustainable Development

Communication for Food Security, Rural Development, and Livelihood Strategies

"When we communicate are we really communicating or are we just talking? Do we really know how to communicate fully?"

—PARTICIPANT

Food security and rural development policies have been revised in recent years, placing more emphasis on holistic approaches to rural livelihoods that focus on the sustainable use of natural resources, multisectoral collaboration, and stakeholder participation in accessing rural assets. Inherent in these approaches is the recognition of the importance of an individual's balanced portfolio of assets in which knowledge, access to information, and a means to communicate play a strategic role.

KEY ISSUES

- Food security is a term well understood by FAO and others but not by all. Has food security as an issue been communicated in a way that people see is relevant to their immediate concerns?
- There is a need to use a range of interventions as part of Communication for Development, not one single approach.
- When it comes to food security, it is crucial to give people a voice and ownership and also reinforce their ability to communicate. Apart from the obvious benefits to the community of communication, it can also increase the sense of identity among farmers. Communication is a means to recognize the cultural value of farmers and can strengthen the cultural identity of communities.
- Rural poor people need improved access to knowledge and information that enables them to take advantage of economic opportunities and improve their livelihoods.
- Opportunities need to be fostered for poor farmers to develop their capacity to generate, share, and adapt relevant local knowledge and information, as well as adapt and assimilate external information.
- All stakeholders need to engage in planning, decision making, and working toward common goals.
- Links need to be facilitated between local communities, development organizations in the field, the private sector, and different levels of policy making (from local to national).
- Links need to be improved between farmers, agricultural researchers, and extensionists.
- Public policies need to be promoted that include the financing of development communication components. These policies should give communication professionals the freedom and autonomy to design and implement rural communication programs without political or institutional interference.

See box 4.1 for a case study.

RECOMMENDATIONS

1. National policies should be developed to include participatory communication; the concept of sustainability must be built into any recommendations that the Congress produces.

Box 4.1 Tanzania—First Mile Project

The impact of the First Mile Project in Tanzania and the application of the Linking Local Learners approach in a number of contexts in East Africa are well documented and the lessons learned very concrete. Farmers used mobile phones and other communication techniques to obtain information on market prices. Before the start of the project farmers could get US$100 per ton of rice, but afterward they got US$600 through a warehouse receipts system. An additional US$350,000 per season was pulled in through the scheme. From a US$200,000 investment, there has been US$1.8 million of gross income for farmers. Farmers are willing to pay for the mobile phone calls because they can see their benefits.

The combination of structured learning with peer-to-peer sharing of ideas and lessons, and use of modern ICTs is building farmers' capacity to generate and share knowledge. It is also creating a learning environment in which farmers and other stakeholders consider the commercial viability of communication and knowledge management processes as the keys to sustainability.

Unlike many projects, which end when outside funding stops, the First Mile Project is likely to prove sustainable after funding ends in 2009. Farmers have seen the value of the information they receive from private companies that have been nurtured by but are independent of the project. Initiatives will be sustained in this way, if the activity makes sense to local people.

Source: Presentation at the WCCD by session participant.

2. A country's program approach should be developed to avoid duplication and lack of coordination between donors.
3. When dealing with rural areas, small island states are a special case and face unique challenges in Communication for Development.
4. The Mexican rural communication system should be revisited and challenges for the future identified to see what remains of the project that can be built on in the future.

Poverty Reduction and Equity Issues

Communication for Development can contribute to the effective reduction of poverty and help create better opportunities to actively involve marginalized groups and isolated populations in the decision-making process and in policy development. At the same time, it improves the relationship between urban and rural populations, facilitating economic growth and equity. Communication can also play a decisive role in promoting the empowerment of women and girls. More specifically, communication processes can give rural women a voice to advocate changes in policies, attitudes, and social behavior or customs that negatively affect them.

This session focused on the applications of Communication for Development to poverty reduction and equity programs, with specific emphasis on the role of communication in building ownership of Poverty Reduction Strategy Papers (PRSPs) through stakeholder participation in planning, implementation, and monitoring. It also considered how communication could contribute to fostering economic opportunities through remittance transfers and maximizing the dramatic growth in communication among migrant workers, their families and organizations, and the government agencies involved. In addition to this economic aspect, the session discussed the potential role of communication in enhancing the experience of migration for both migrants and host communities.

KEY ISSUES

1. Migration and the importance of remittance transfers, using new communication technology.
2. Development as more than economic growth—communication contributes to many aspects, including social and political connections.
3. The importance of using participatory, communication-driven, innovative approaches that involve people who are experiencing poverty. A Rwandan saying was quoted: "A person who has had an experience is the one who narrates the story well."
4. Development as structural change, which is required if development is to be sustainable. Communication is not the magic solution, but it is important to include it.
5. The resistance of elites to reform—assessment of resistance must form part of the analysis that is the basis for developing a communication strategy.
6. The fact that technology can be very beneficial but is not the whole answer. We must not let it distract us. As Scott Robinson of the University of Mexico pointed out, "It takes more than skills and tools to achieve social transformation."

7. The ways that communication can help make migration a positive phenomenon. It can do so through the networks that help migrants find information in their new home environment, which enables them to make a contribution to their new society. It also can help them maintain contact with those they have left at home. The new technology for communication and the processes it enables, such as funds transfer, can be structured in a way to benefit the poorest. By reducing transaction costs, more money reaches the communities from which migrants come.
8. The difficulties of and obstacles to successful Communication for Development. Top-down decision making is still taking place. The poor are often not benefiting from economic growth. To reverse this trend, communication strategies need to be based on an understanding of the obstacles that elites may place in the path of reform.

Box 4.2 provides some case studies.

RECOMMENDATIONS

1. Access to telecommunications should be broadened and costs reduced. This should include reducing the cost of transferring migrants' remittances to a maximum of 2.5 percent of the amount transferred.
2. There should be a public debate on regulation of telecommunications.
3. Community involvement should be built into all levels of design and implementation of poverty reduction programs. This is essential because the communities should set the priorities. Clear communication strategies should be part and parcel of development strategies.

Communication and Sustainable Natural Resource Management

One of the key challenges that development programs face is addressing poverty alleviation and economic growth while conserving environmental sustainability in an integrated manner. Fighting land degradation and desertification, halting deforestation, promoting

Box 4.2 Africa

Rwanda: Giving Voice to Rural Women and Youth

Communication through radio was part of the process that provoked the Rwandan genocide. But today it is used to involve women and young people in the PRSP process. The PRSP was developed in 2002 to meet the Millennium Development Goals and Vision 2020, Rwanda's 20-year development strategy. Community participation in PRSP implementation and monitoring is stressed but, in reality, is little practiced in Rwanda. For example, rural women and youth are neither aware of nor know about their health entitlements under government programs, including the PRSP.

Health Unlimited's rights-based project, Giving Voice to Rural Women and Youth, facilitates the participation of representatives from rural women and youth CSOs in monitoring the implementation of the health component of the PRSP in two of Rwanda's poorest rural provinces. The project works with existing district-level health policy makers and service providers and offers a platform for the target CSO beneficiaries to share their concerns and recommendations on health issues with the District Health Management Team members and local government officials during monthly meetings. These activities bring together people who otherwise never exchange ideas. The project is also innovative in its training of CSOs in presentation and confidence-building skills, as well as community theatre and an interactive, mainly pictorial, newsletter. By using participatory techniques, it gives a voice to those who are not usually listened to and who are most affected—in this case, the poorest rural women and youth. The project enables the target group to define and identify solutions and to share them with policy makers. In this way, poor rural women and youth directly contribute not only to their own development but also to the development of the Rwandan society at large.

Source: Uwamariya 2006.

Africa: Communication and Gender—The Dimitra Project

Communication is vital in addressing gender equality. Equality between men and women, a vital part of development, cannot be achieved without communication. Dimitra is a communication project that started by providing information to women on issues relevant to them, such as land rights. This effort built up to creating networks of women locally, which then grew to be national and Africa-wide. It developed a two-way approach—radio listening clubs—to enable women to make their own radio programs, which are played on stations and listened to by policy makers who respond to their questions.

The program focuses on rural women, who are often isolated. It includes hands-on experience and has a training aspect. It also helps highlight the contribution that rural women make to development. Radio usage is high, using local languages to reach local communities, so people can say what they need. The Dimitra project in Senegal in 2004 gave women a chance to speak to policy makers about land issues. As a result, the Rural Women National Network of Senegal succeeded in securing a seat on the Presidential Committee on Land Reform.

Source: Presentation at the WCCD by Tine N'Doye, President of the Rural Women Network of Senegal, on the Dimitra Project (www.fao.org/dimitra).

proper management of water resources, and protecting biodiversity require the active participation of rural communities through communication processes. For many years, however, communication initiatives in support of environmental and natural resources management have focused mainly on the dissemination and adoption of technical packages. These efforts have yielded only limited impacts.

Communication for Development offers an alternative. Its participatory approaches can facilitate the dialogue and exchange of knowledge and information on natural resource management, increase the community knowledge base (both indigenous and modern), promote agricultural practices compatible with the environment, and develop awareness in policy makers, authorities, and service providers. Furthermore, Communication for Development approaches can bring different stakeholders and groups into conversation with each other and allow the poorest and most marginalized to participate in the decisions about the sustainable use of natural resources. This involves establishing links among all stakeholders; developing common understanding, language, and channels for participatory communication; and responding to specific information and training needs (Ramirez 1997).

Comments and ideas from the session included the following:

- "Communities involved with the management of resources should be involved with decisions on how to manage those resources."
- "Many initiatives fail because the initiative doesn't live with the community."
- "The heart of social capital is relationships built through communication."
- "We need to enable people to understand that natural resources management can be to their benefit—make people understand that it is a better way for them . . . not only for the planet."
- "We need to note the difference between *participation* and *being participatory*—genuine versus token involvement."
- "We must not romanticize what is meant by participation—you will not be able to resolve conflict all the time through communication and participation alone."
- "Participation is not consulting but sharing governance."

KEY ISSUES

1. Communication as a right:
   - To be informed is a right of the people, not just a development strategy.
   - Many policy makers still believe in top-down approaches and need convincing to move beyond them.
   - Donors also need to be held to account.
2. Capacity building and training for Communication for Development
   - Very few experts in natural resources management have the necessary skills in Communication for Development to apply in the field.
   - There is a need for collaborative learning initiatives in development communication and natural resources management.

Box 4.3 is a case study.

CASE STUDY

Box 4.3 Uganda—Banana Farmers

Scientists from Uganda's National Banana Research Program, with support from the International Development Research Centre, agreed to research a participatory two-way communication process that promised to bridge the gap between researchers and farmers. The project was formulated and implemented in Ddwaniro subcounty, Rakai district, in South Western Uganda. It was conceived with the general objective of enabling banana farmers to acquire and use improved soil and water management technologies using a participatory development communication strategy.

By the end of the first research phase, participating farmers were realizing good banana yields because they had implemented the recommended natural resources management techniques. They were now looking for a market for their increased banana yields. They also improved their interaction within their community. From the original 60 participating farmers, more than 500 other farmers were trained within a period of a year. The farmers shared their experiences on national radio. Women members of Ddwaniro Integrated Farmers' Association overcame their original shyness and also participated. The farmers now have their own community objectives. They have acquired additional communication skills, which they can use to solve other community constraints. They say, "*Twali bubi nyo Kawanda nga tenaba kugya*" (We were badly off before researchers from Kawanda came to us).

Source: Odoi, Ngambeki, Tushemereirwe 2006.

RECOMMENDATIONS

- *Policy.* Advocate for appropriate time and resources to apply communication methodologies to natural resources management.
- *Research, evaluation, and impact assessment.* Promote research initiatives in natural resources management that have a participatory approach and involve communication and local stakeholders in design, implementation, and dissemination.
- *Evaluation.* Establish objectives and baselines at the beginning of projects. Include evaluation for social networking.
- *Training.* Support collaborative learning initiatives in development communication and natural resources management.
- *Alliance building.* Support networking activities between local and national organizations that have developed expertise in using development communication. Apply this expertise to natural resources management. Bring the private sector to the table more, because they are a key stakeholder group that is often ignored in development initiatives.

Communication for Development and Global Environmental Issues

Communication is used to address global environmental issues of general public interest. Within this framework, very often communication, education, participation, and public awareness approaches are used in an integrated manner to reach out to key groups. The emphasis of this session was on presenting experiences and evidence about the use of Communication for Development strategies and methods as applied to global environmental issues.

Participants emphasized some of the key global environmental issues of climate change, management of biodiversity, and issues raised by growing water and energy demand and also by growing socioeconomic disparity, locally and globally.

The session began with a discussion between representatives of the UN Environment Programme (UNEP) and the German NGO GTZ. They considered how successful experiences to date have been in linking global issues with local perspectives. The UNEP representative shared the positive experience of brokering the Montreal protocol relating to the protection of the ozone layer. The experience of developing the convention through a consensus process, coupled with information and awareness campaigns that targeted populations in both developing and industrial countries with relevant content, was put forward as a model.

The discussion also focused on how global environmental issues can be perceived as industrial country issues. Participants emphasized that traditionally that has been the case, but that there is a growing awareness and understanding that these are global issues and that some things can be achieved locally. Information and awareness were highlighted by the UNEP representative. He also concentrated on the need to look beyond the media in order for communication (interventions) to create processes and spaces that bring in business leaders, teachers, and others important in sustaining communication processes.

Other panelists shared experiences from South Asia, from Cameroon, and from Italian ministry programs on communication and climate change, such as the Caribbean Climate Change Center. This official center for the region acts as a clearinghouse, enabling information exchange within the region; providing expertise to facilitate community-level projects and training; and providing capacity-building and awareness-raising support with a focus on people in government and NGOs.

Comments included the following:

- "We need mechanisms in place so people can take fate in their own hands. We need to show a benefit for them and their own communities if they take steps against these large-scale, global, seemingly vague, problems."
- "Communication about the environment shouldn't be so difficult because people do care about the environment—it is important to give people a reason to care, to act."
- "Mainstreaming is very important. Communication professionals are losing and have lost the incentive and willingness to experiment. We plan years ahead. The key to success is experimentation."
- "We need to 'sell' the environment—companies sell products by linking to images of a good life; for example, energy companies, Coca-Cola. We need to learn from the private sector and sell positive images and concrete solutions. We need to infuse messages with entertainment."
- "We should worry less about our own organizations and more about the issues themselves."

KEY ISSUES

1. Development is an ongoing, multilevel process. Communication includes capacity building, networking, knowledge building, and knowledge management.
2. Communication plays a key role in environmental issues—to develop awareness and trust, to coordinate dialogue and information, to inform and empower, and to stimulate citizen action.
3. One challenge is to get the messages about global issues out there and another challenge is to sustain them. Stories can help engage people and make the link between global phenomena and issues and their own lives. The threat of skin cancer was one of these links made in relation to global warming and the industrial countries. It helped to galvanize people.
4. Too often we talk about success at the micro level and scaling up. However, it seems that the issue is really not about scaling up, but rather about working in a way that is appropriate to the scale from the beginning. Experience from the private sector here could be relevant.
5. Panelists reported the positive benefits of participatory processes. For example, children and other community members in the countries of Southeast Asia where community-based natural resource management was used had felt empowered presenting their recommendations for wetlands management to international decision makers.
6. Panelists were questioned about their organizations' commitment to participatory processes, internally as well as collaboratively. All shared positive experiences from their organizations but also acknowledged that more needs to be done for really effective partnerships.

See box 4.4 for a case study.

RECOMMENDATIONS

1. We need to move away from information toward more real communication (two-way dialogue). The global media play a necessary but not sufficient role in this move. It can help create an enabling environment, but we need to go beyond media

CASE STUDY

Box 4.4 Isang Bagsak

In Tagalog the expression "*isang bagsak*" means arriving at a consensus, an agreement. Because it refers to communication as a participatory process, it has become the working title for an initiative that began with support from the International Development Research Centre. Teams from Cambodia, Uganda, and Vietnam participated in the pilot phase for 15 months: Ratanakiri Natural Resources Management Research Action Project (Cambodia); the National Agricultural Research Organization (Uganda); and Hue University of Agriculture and Forestry (Vietnam).

The program seeks to increase the capacity of development practitioners and researchers active in the field of environmental and natural resources management to use participatory development communication to work more effectively with local communities and stakeholders. It pursues the objectives of improving practitioners' and researchers' capacities to communicate with local communities and other stakeholders and to enable them to plan communication strategies that support community development initiatives. It combines face-to-face activities with a distance-learning strategy and Web-based technology.

Through the distance component, it can answer the needs of researchers and practitioners who cannot easily leave work. It is currently implemented in Southeast Asia and Eastern and Southern Africa and is being planned for the African Sahel. In Southeast Asia, Isang Bagsak is implemented by the College of Development Communication at the University of the Philippines at Los Baños. It works in Cambodia, the Philippines, and Vietnam. In Southern and Eastern Africa, the program is implemented in Malawi, Uganda, and Zimbabwe by the Southern African Development Community's Centre of Communication for Development. Another program is being prepared for an agroforestry network in Burkina Faso, Mali, and Senegal; it will be led by the International Centre for Research in Agroforestry's Sahel Program.

Source: Presentation at the WCCD by session participant.

communication. We need to look at decision makers and build coalitions to enable change.

2. More professional communication is needed—no one Communication for Development skill or approach works on its own. A range of approaches drawing on expertise from journalism, participatory research, facilitation, public relations, technology, and more is needed. The only common strands are the need to be flexible; to adopt the approach, tools, and methods that are appropriate to a situation; and the need to be innovative.
3. We need to bridge the gap between global perspectives and tell a clear story that connects global and local experiences. This

means going beyond media communication to connect with the range of decision makers—from legislators to the private sector.

Mainstreaming Communication in Sustainable Development Policies: Local Perspectives and Priorities

This session brought together the participants and conclusions from the regional meetings held in the Sahel region, Southern and Eastern Africa, and the Middle East. The process included dialogues, meetings, e-fora, studies, and conferences, and participants emphasized their richness. The key to success in Communication for Development initiatives is to start with the participatory analysis of the needs of local institutions and stakeholders, taking into account local culture and values and promoting concerted action for development. Communication for Development can achieve relevant impacts and sustainability only if it is adequately inserted in national development policies and builds on existing experiences and capacities.

Over the years, several communication centers and systems have been established to deliver services and provide technical assistance in Communication for Development at national as well as regional levels. Economic sustainability, however, has often been the weak point of their activities.

A growing number of development initiatives have adopted the use of communication as a strategic aspect of development. New opportunities are emerging for mainstreaming Communication for Development into national policies for sustainable development, especially in agricultural and natural resource management. Nevertheless, the definition of adequate Communication for Development policies and programs should start by assessing needs, trends, and priorities at the field level and identifying lessons learned and good practices, as well as opportunities for collaboration.

Some examples of innovative and effective approaches shared in the session included the use of theatre in the development of research, in analysis, and in resolving critical issues in the community in Malawi. In another example, a group study approach that built a study circle concept was a means to develop more effective agricultural extension services.

KEY ISSUES

- Policy makers confuse communication policies and ICTs.
- There needs to be a more participatory approach to developing national communication policies. In many countries, policy makers lack understanding about what should be in them, how to develop them, and how to implement them.
- The regional workshops found that national communication policies are a strength but many countries have a corresponding weakness in that these policies were not implemented.
- There is a lack of institutional leadership on Communication for Development, for example, among UN agencies.
- The community and the field level is where impact happens: this level should be included in the communication processes about program design and implementation.

For a case study, see box 4.5.

RECOMMENDATIONS

The following recommendations were drawn from the regional process of consultation but agreed to in the workshop.

CASE STUDY

Box 4.5 Tanzania—The Involvement of Decision Makers

This example was given during the session:

> *The former president of Tanzania made a speech saying that although he was a former journalist, in all his years in tenure he had not managed to communicate policies. His message was that only then did he see that lack of communication was the missing link in development efforts. We would expect him as a journalist to be aware of this. But does any other leader really get it? They depend on non-professionals to do much of their communication—parliamentarians, etc. But they have no real formal communication training, and therefore there is no real communication of development policies across countries. How can we get this on the international agenda? How do we get the message out to policy makers?*

Source: Presentation at the WCCD by session participant.

1. *Communication and politics.* In essence, the presence or absence of free and easy communication (both vertical and horizontal) is a political act. Countries that foster dialogue, debate, and inclusion while encouraging free and open media are more likely to engage in participatory communication practices than more centrally controlled countries. The whole notion of transparency is in itself a communication function that depends on the willingness of those in power to share knowledge and information with those who are not. It is difficult to know which is the cart and which is the horse—can bottom-up participatory communication help foster a freer society, or must a society already be free for open expression to foster participatory communication?
2. *The need for policy.* The regional meetings have shown that those countries with policies to support Communication for Development are most likely to open the door to an expansion in practice. The presence of an enabling environment offers a hook for practitioners to demand the inclusion of communication at all levels of planning. While this may be self-evident, the need to fight for policy has not often been articulated clearly.
3. *The importance of fostering partnerships.* While the development of national policies to support Communication for Development is key, we recognize the differing degrees of effort and length of time each country might take to bring the issue to the table. Meanwhile, the need to foster partnerships between government agencies and other actors and among other actors is paramount.
4. *Capacity development for decision makers.* All regions report a lack of knowledge on the part of decision makers about the breadth and depth of Communication for Development. This often produces only a partial nod to communication, particularly if the communication effort involves the media or a form of public relations to enhance the government agenda. In the Near East region, for instance, participants at the regional workshop held in May 2006 felt that the lack of knowledge on the part of decision makers about the distinction between the communication functions (policy, knowledge transfer, and participation) greatly retarded the time and type of support required for implementing a participatory approach. It is clear that methods must be found to broaden decision makers' knowledge of the full communication repertoire. There may be scope to use well-

recognized approaches, such as the farmer field schools, as a familiar vehicle—though not strictly speaking a communication vehicle—to illustrate how the different communication functions contribute to the success.

5. *Capacity development for practitioners.* The corollary to the need for capacity building among decision makers is the more pressing need to develop a cadre of trained practitioners. Across all regions there is a lack of accredited training opportunities in Communication for Development. This calls for a concerted global and regional program to develop, at the very least, regional training programs. The efforts by organizations such as the Communication for Social Change Consortium to develop core reading materials and standard course templates need to be supported, and those materials should be translated, adapted, and distributed widely. Postgraduate studies in Communication for Development should also be supported.
6. *Sharing of stories and experiences.* The exchange of stories and experiences across regions and within regions provides impetus to decision makers, practitioners, and donors to get motivated in support of Communication for Development initiatives. The call for regional platforms deserves to be balanced with the need to make use of what is already available at the global level within the field and in each region, with complementary activities in related fields. For example, regional evaluation networks or farmer field school experiences could be integrated with Communication for Development platforms. The Congress sessions on sustainable development constituted one special moment for the development of regional partnerships. The findings of regional consultations and studies were further discussed during the two sessions of the Congress that reflected regional perspectives: "Mainstreaming Communication in Sustainable Development: Local Perspectives and Priorities" and "Sustaining the Process: Local Appropriations of Communication for Sustainable Development." Recommendations and conclusions from both the regional consultations prior to the WCCD and reflections during the two specific sessions were included in Quarry and Ramirez (2006).

Of particular interest for the future will be the sharing of successful mechanisms to create spaces for dialogue and change with policy makers. Reaching these circles of decision making with convincing examples of the power of Communication for Development is the challenge for the future. While the message "without communication there is no development" rings true, without expertise in reaching policy circles there is no message.

Other recommendations from the same session included the following:

- National governments, specialized agencies, international organizations, and NGOs should enhance knowledge sharing and form a Communication for Development advisory consortium at national levels.
- National governments, specialized agencies, international organizations, and NGOs should identify institutional champions within the region. They would be responsible for carrying out a Communication for Development audit, fostering collaboration and partnerships, and being a national focal point for preparing pilot projects. Facilitate documentation of good practice should be facilitated and a database should be established at the national level for a community of practice.
- We need to build a strong evidence base of Communication for Development activities and successes. To this end, we should move toward a results framework so different stakeholders can gauge progress.
- Communication for Development should be integrated into major development plans and policies; for example, PRSPs should include communication.
- If Communication for Development is to help bring about food security and natural resource management, there needs to be a legal framework for rural radio stations.

Sustaining the Process: Local Appropriations of Communication for Sustainable Development

A second set of regional perspectives focused on those countries and regions where development policies have already included Communication for Development and where there is capability in applying it to sustainable development. The focus of this session was mainly on the appropriation of Communication for Development as a process and new ways of advancing it as a cross-cutting development element.

KEY ISSUES

1. Communication for Development can relate to behavior change, social transformation, and building social capital:
   - Communication serves as a catalyst for pursuing a set of desired objectives.
   - Public interest is a useful concept but it needs to mean the interests of citizens, not government.
2. Start with the needs of the community:
   - Do we have enough evidence of the needs of the demand side rather than the supply side?
   - We need to look at integrated elements of health, education, and livelihoods, when talking to people about their needs and concerns. These may draw on different technical specialties, but the lives of ordinary people do not make such distinctions.
   - Communication for Development or communication with development—it is not a matter of experts saying what type of development people need, but of getting people (ordinary citizens) to define development.
   - We need to act as facilitators to ensure that local voices are heard.
3. There was some discussion of issues of trust. Confidence and trustworthiness is the basis of all communication. Indigenous communities, in particular, because of their experiences, may lack confidence and trust in the outside world.
4. Communication for Development as a professional discipline:
   - This label is of no relevance to the demand side (citizens)—it is useful only to define ourselves to policy makers.
   - There is a lack of knowledge about and understanding of development communication.
   - Practitioners should embrace Communication for Development as a vocation and not just a profession.
5. Capacity building and training for Communication for Development:

- There are not enough specialists in Communication for Development or knowledge of the field among those with other thematic and technical specialties. There is also a lack of understanding among the wider development community as to what Communication for Development is.
- How do we "infect" technical specialists with the Communication for Development "virus"?

6. Sustainability:
   - Partnerships are very important: coalitions and groups remain after projects and programs end.
   - We need to be able to make a business case for including Communication for Development. If the media can document in a convincing way for policy makers that its work makes a difference to the general public, then the media should be able to get funding for this work.
   - Communication for Development should be built into the budget of all initiatives.

Box 4.6 contains some case studies.

Key and Emerging Issues for the Sustainable Development Strand

Six key issues emerged from the sustainable development strand:

1. Variety is key: there are 89 definitions of sustainable development. The common theme is that today's development should not harm future generations.
2. Water, climate change, natural resource degradation, and migration were some of the major issues identified. Communication can build positive impacts for all into the migration experience. It can provide information for migrants, help migrants contribute to home and host country development, and facilitate funds transfers home with even greater benefit if costs for telecommunications and Internet fees were reduced.
3. Mind-sets matter: understanding and knowledge of Communication for Development are key but often missing. Typically experts in natural resources management are scientists who

CASE STUDIES

Box 4.6 Three Regions

Central America

The regional workshop on Communication for Development in Central America and Mexico, which was held in July 2006 in preparation for the Congress, concluded with agreements for a regional collaboration and platforms for the advancement of Communication for Development in the region. A Web site (http://www.comunicacionparaeldesarrollo.org/) has created a networking tool. The goal of this platform is to demonstrate how Communication for Development approaches contribute to improved livelihood outcomes in harmony with the environment. The specific objectives are (a) to develop and consolidate a platform as a meeting place for regional initiatives, organizations, and individuals involved with Communication for Development; (b) to develop capacities in terms of methodology, concepts, and techniques in order to enhance the effective delivery of Communication for Development projects; and (c) to influence public policy and national legal frameworks on organizations so as to integrate Communication for Development in different development sectors.

Southern and Eastern Asia

In Cambodia, where the government has embraced participatory extension on the basis of the success of the farmer field schools, additional participatory communication experiences such as Isang Bagsak will demonstrate the multiple dimensions of such approaches beyond agriculture, such as participatory evaluation.

Latin America

"*Sin comunicación no hay desarrollo*" (Without communication there is no development) is the motto at the top of the Latin America meeting report, and this phrase captures the main lesson learned. The development model that has prevailed in the region has created the conditions for a vertical, top-down way of thinking and implementing communication. The privatization thrust behind much of the development funding has left little room for the public domain of communication. The Latin America report calls for three strategic directions: (a) citizen engagement to monitor Communication for Development approaches, (b) international observations of methods and media for Communication for Development, and (c) the development of a mechanism for monitoring and exchange of participatory communication within the region beyond the Congress.

Source: Presentations at the WCCD by session participants.

often do not have a social development and participation mind-set or communication skills.

4. We need to think about being sustainable from the start and also that communication needs to be present from the start.
5. Communication for Development should not be about consultation but about genuine participation—this may mean structural or political changes. Ordinary people should have a say in governance issues, such as natural resource management of water.
6. The regional consultations on sustainable development for this Congress showed that those countries with policies that support Communication for Development are most likely to open the door to an expansion in practice. But having a national communication policy is not enough, because many countries reported challenges in implementation. All the regions recognized the need to foster partnerships among government agencies, donors, academia, international organizations, NGOs, and people.

Papers Used in the Sustainable Development Sessions

Barroso, Monica. "Waves in the Forest—Radio Communication and Livelihoods in Brazilian Amazonia."

Bessette, Guy. "Participation, Bananas, and Desertification."

Bossi, Richard, Elizabeth Booth, Tito Coleman, and Roberta Hilbruner. "GreenCOM: 12 Years of Innovation in Strategic Communication for Environmentally Sustainable Development."

FAO (Food and Agriculture Organization of the United Nations) Communication for Development Group. 2006. "Communication for Sustainable Development."

Jallov, Birgitte. "Assessing Community Change: Development of a 'Bare Foot' Impact Assessment Methodology for Community Radio."

Odoi, Nora Naiboka, Dezi Ngambeki, and Wilberforce Tushemereirwe. "Communication for Environment and Natural Resource Management."

Ogawa, Yoshiko. "Unsaid Messages: Power Relations within Agricultural Extension Training."

Papania, Patrick, Elizabeth Booth, Karabi Acharya, Tito Coleman, and Shera Bender. "Strategic Communication for System-wide Change: Experience and Results from the Medicinal and Aromatic Plant Sector in Morocco."

Quarry, Wendy, and Ricardo Ramirez. 2006. "A Compendium of Regional Perspectives in Communication for Development."

Ruiz, Jorge Martínez, Pablo C. Hernández, and José Luis M. Ruiz. "¿Hacemos de la Comunicación una Mercancía?"

Uwamariya, Josephine Irene. "Community Participation in Monitoring the Rwanda PRSP Implementation."

Vyakaranam, V. L. V. Kameswari. "Communication in Environmental Projects: Experiences from Madhya Pradesh Forestry Project."

5

Communication Labs

This section reviews the workshops from the Communication Labs strand of the Congress, which addressed the cross-cutting nature of Communication for Development, looking at methodological issues such as impact evaluation and the adoption of participatory communication approaches, as well as the use of media (including community media) and ICTs in development initiatives. This section also includes ideas and recommendations from the two special events on communication and disabilities and indigenous peoples, which were also considered important issues in which communication plays a major role.

The six workshops in this strand were as follows:

1. News Media as a Pro-Development Tool
2. Fighting Poverty—Community Media and Communication for Development in the Digital Age
3. Implementing Communication for Development Thinking in Southern Realities—Negotiating Politics, Profit, and Poverty Toward Social Inclusion
4. Impact and Assessment—Innovative Ways to Determine Communication Effectiveness
5. The Rationale, the Value, and the Challenges for Adopting Participatory Communication in Development Programs
6. Which Kind of Development Communication Does Attract Media?

News Media as a Pro-Development Tool

Panelists had no doubts about the value added of the media covering development issues. The discussion revolved instead around (a) why this is so hard to achieve, (b) what civil society needs to understand to get the news media to cover development, and (c) who needs to take what roles in order for journalists to cover development stories effectively.

KEY MEDIA TRENDS

1. The concentration of media ownership—In the United States, there has been an acceleration of ownership of all media into fewer private hands.
2. Segmentation—More and more different types of media are targeted at different audiences (for example, cooking and travel channels, the Internet, and satellite TV broadcasting).
3. The electronic media threaten the economic profitability of the traditional media. NBC recently fired several thousand employees in the United States.
4. There is ever-greater competition linked to time—always to be first. This means less and less context, especially in broadcast media.
5. In the developed world, 30–40 percent of young people are getting their news not from traditional media but from the Web and blogs.
6. We are witnessing the disappearance of the traditional Anglo-Saxon journalist. Newsgathering is more ideological than before. There used to be a clear boundary between activism and journalism, but now the line is increasingly blurred as there is less separation between news gathering and editorial roles.
7. New sources are emerging: civil society is providing a new type of expert. Civil society is more able to work with the media than are governments: they understand journalists' deadlines and their need for expertise and legitimate sources.
8. While the media sector used to lag behind when it came to adopting corporate social responsibility policies, this is now changing; good examples are the BBC and Time Warner.

RESPONSIBILITIES NECESSARY TO ENSURE GOOD JOURNALISM

Journalists must

- Be aware of the limits imposed by their personal and academic background (they are usually middle-class, are not in contact with the majority of the population, and often do not understand the social and development agenda)
- Have professional and ethical commitment
- Value and use sources of information, not uncritically, but as a link to more contextualized coverage

Media companies must

- Ensure that journalists' working conditions are decent
- Support and acknowledge journalists who cover social and development issues
- Stimulate and support investigative journalism
- Provide capacity-building opportunities
- Ensure that corporate social responsibility polices also apply to news media departments

Others play a part in ensuring good journalism:

- Journalistic bodies and universities
- Sources of information (governmental, civil society, companies, international agencies, and so on) that have a responsibility to be transparent and professional
- Media accountability systems, which can monitor editorial content, take a critical overview of coverage, and watch for media structural problems
- Citizens, who can take a critical approach to editorial content and interact with news outlets

Media monitoring is important. See box 5.1 for a case study.

RECOMMENDATION

To be effective, media monitoring and journalism training need to be part of a long-term, comprehensive strategy.

CASE STUDY

Box 5.1 Conversation Spaces

The *Fundación para un Nuevo Periodismo Iberoamericano* (Foundation for a New Iberian-American Journalism, FNPI) suggested that there are ways to train journalists and to get editors to connect better with the complexity of development issues so they can report such issues more effectively and thereby help promote development. Socially responsible companies, NGOs, and multilaterals can sponsor better journalism. The FNPI was set up in 1995 to provide a "conversation space" for journalists to reflect on their stories. It provides training and skills development in reporting and connects journalists across borders. An independent evaluation of the Foundation's work shows that, with training, journalists produce more and better stories on social issues. They need to be introduced to and helped with this work. They need to see how their stories can contribute socially. "You cannot love what you do not know," says Maria Tereza Ronderos of FNPI.

Fighting Poverty: Community Media and Communication for Development in the Digital Age

> *"We believe that communication is the fuel of everything. If we start development without fuel, it will light dimly; if we put more fuel it will light more brightly and give more power."*
>
> —Raghu Mainali, Nepal

This session was broadcast live on Bush Radio in Cape Town, South Africa. Structured like an interview, it aimed to address four questions:

- What is the added value of community media to Communication for Development methodology in fighting poverty?
- What is the human development impact of community media, specifically for poor women?
- How do community media contribute to good governance in fighting poverty?
- What are the challenges of scaling up community media centers from the government's and the stakeholders' perspectives?

The session was underpinned by two principles:

1. Access to the means that allow people to voice their views and communication is central to a people-centered approach to development, both for its intrinsic human importance and for its roles in shared culture, access to knowledge and education, civic participation in decision making, assurance of good governance through accountability, and provision of other tools that help achieve development goals. This has been acknowledged repeatedly in major international reports such as the World Development Report, the Human Development Report, the Final Report of the United Nations Millennium Project, and the Commission for Africa Report.
2. Community media has a vital role to play in providing access to voice and communication for poor and marginalized groups, which frequently are excluded from mainstream media. It has had a central impact on development and is increasingly relevant in the context of new information and communication technologies and the trend toward more liberalized communication environments. The impact and value of community media have been demonstrated repeatedly over many years, most recently in its central, critical role in Nepal in the recent peaceful transition to a new democracy.

KEY ISSUES

- Community radio takes time. It is not a short-term investment and requires commitment over a long period to make a difference.
- Opening up media legislation creates new opportunities as well as new threats. Free media can be used to create division and misinformation; however, this cannot be used as an argument against free media. Free media need to be a condition first; then we need to ensure responsible use of those media.
- Ownership is important for sustainability and participation. People empower themselves through ownership, and there is a strong relationship between participation and ownership.
- We do not know how many community radio stations continue to grow and how they sustain themselves. It is not so much about money but about social inputs. Community radio stations

are often maintained by community groups with some help from NGOs.

- Governments need to support community radio stations: their constituents are the poor and they have no money to sustain themselves.
- We need indicators to prove the impact of community media, in order to make sure that policy makers consider community radio important.
- We need to enlarge the stakeholder base to include agricultural and health scientists and academicians.
- Community radio stations are often seen as few, small, and poor, and we need to see ourselves as something different to change that perception.
- Community radio is used for reducing crime, finding missing children, and eradicating poverty. We need to convince policy makers and "sell" them on the idea of community radio stations by saying that community radios can help them save billions in health care, poverty alleviation, and crime prevention costs.
- The legal and regulatory environment must be addressed. An example of the importance of this environment: in Ethiopia an SMS service was shut down because community radio stations were using it to transmit election results.

Box 5.2 is a case study.

RECOMMENDATIONS

- National development plans should promote an enabling legal and regulatory environment for a plurality of independent media, including specific provision for the development of community media. Public funding should be provided by governments to community media through independent financing mechanisms.
- Development institutions and organizations should provide assistance to build the capacity of community media through training, strengthening of networks and sector associations, technical assistance, and investment. Support for community media should be provided on the basis of strategic long-term commitments, recognizing that impact must be measured not only in short-term results but also in community media's contribution to long-term social change.

CASE STUDY

Box 5.2 Nepal—Community Radio

In February 2005, the King of Nepal sacked the interim government and ordered the country's telephone and Internet communications to shut down. Newspapers and radio stations were shut down and a ban imposed on all news reporting. The process involved 50 radio stations, which reached 65 percent of the population.

A network of community radio stations used innovative ways to continue to report; for example, the government told them to play only music so they started to sing the news. Later the stations defied the laws and informed people of their rights and the duties of government. They started to defy government openly by hosting talk shows and made the music that they aired very message based. People from the villages were encouraged to compose songs and music to be broadcast. Civil society leaders using radio motivated the movement of peaceful protest. Community radio played an important role in ensuring that the protest was peaceful, sending messages about the dangers of violence every half hour, saying "conflict is not a way to get freedom and peace." New technology had an important role in this process because some of the community radio stations were linked in a network, which allowed for better coordination of activities.

The result: 4 million people conducted a peaceful protest in the streets calling for a resolution to the political crisis. As a consequence of the role that community radio played, the Nepali government is now very supportive of community radio. It has given licenses to 30 community radio stations over a period of two months and now encourages media diversity by ensuring that there is no financial or ideological monopoly of media companies. It took 10 years to transform Nepal into a democratic society, and community radio played a large part in this transformation.

Source: Presentation at the WCCD by Raghu Mainaly, Founding President, Community Radio Association of Nepal.

Implementing Communication for Development Thinking in Southern Realities: Negotiating Politics, Profit, and Poverty toward Social Inclusion

Development practitioners agree that there is a need for people's voices to be heard and for participation to form an integral part of development. Disadvantaged communities have opinions and demands that need to be heard; what is often lacking is an opportunity to voice these opinions and demands. The process of providing socially inclusive communication policies is very complex. Power relations need to be negotiated and success depends on numerous factors, such as the commitment of government and the private sector and the involvement of local communities. ICTs also bring a cast of new actors such as software and hardware providers, and national and international telecommunication providers. It is also crucial that CSOs be part of the negotiating process between all stakeholders. Simplistic "digital divide" analyses are no longer adequate to understand the communication gaps of a particular situation. Furthermore, implementing government commitment to "communications for all" requires support and dedication from all relevant actors, particularly from the political and business sectors (Panos 2006).

The session looked at the examples of Mission 2007 and EASSY (box 5.3) to see how each dealt with the challenges of negotiating politics, profit, and poverty to ensure access to ICTs. These projects aim to empower millions of people by providing affordable connectivity (and eventually content and increased information flows). Their successful implementation depends on numerous factors: governance, ownership access, commitment from government and the private sector, financing arrangements, different business models, and the creation of innovation technologies.

CASE STUDIES

Box 5.3 India and East Africa

India: Mission 2007

Mission 2007 was born out of the dream of an independent rural India where ICTs bring knowledge, livelihood, and prosperity. The idea was to not throw information at rural people but to make them the stakeholders in this process of generating and preserving knowledge. Mission 2007 plans to connect 637,000 villages, using both national and international support. The alliance formed to achieve this goal includes the Indian Institutes of Technology; the Ministries of Information and Broadcasting, Information and Technology, and Science and Technology; and elected village bodies. Mission 2007 aims to provide knowledge centers to all villages in India by 2007. It proposes three types of communication:

- Lab to lab (expert to expert)
- Land to lab (laymen to experts)
- Land to land (communication between farmers)

It recognizes the importance of partnerships: commitments from officials high in government are important. But it is also crucial to be able to motivate local people:

if they are ready to talk, they need to be put in touch with people who have the resources they need. A holistic approach is important. Skills building and job creation should be integrated into the process; for example, by giving people microcredit to get cell phones to start a business. The emphasis is on people, not only on the technology. Mission 2007 is an example of a successful NGO. Using external assistance from the outset, it has convinced stakeholders ranging from village councils, to government institutes, to the private sector to participate.

Mission 2007 outlines three things that are necessary for ICTs to play their role in promoting development:

1. A platform to be able to convene a multistakeholder process
2. A champion to lead a multistakeholder process
3. A broker to negotiate between parties. Brokers identify partners, their resources, and their capacities, and they identify the roles and responsibilities of each partner (Panos 2006)

The East African Submarine Cable System (EASSY)

The aim of the EASSY project is to provide fair and equitable access to communication infrastructure in Africa by providing the East Africa Submarine Cable system to serve East Africa and landlocked countries. Investment in infrastructure in Africa is low: of all the money spent on communication infrastructure in the world, only 3 percent is spent on Africa. A multitude of stakeholders are involved in the project: national and regional governments, civil society, and regulatory bodies. At first it was a private initiative, then NEPAD (New Partnership for Africa) got involved, then Telkom South Africa became interested. However, Telkom South Africa has a monopoly on existing communication infrastructure in Africa and threatened to move out when it became clear that the company's private sector interests were being jeopardized. Within NEPAD, Kenya and South Africa were also in conflict over issues. Managing expectations and communication between stakeholders was a challenge. There was no communication facilitator; therefore, powers and roles were fluid and nobody was accountable.

Issues that needed to be negotiated were ownership, branding, rules governing the selling of cable capacity, size of partnership investments, return on investment, and access to bandwidth provided for an investment. These challenges have caused delays: the project was scheduled to be completed by October 2007; now it is aiming for October 2008. The cost has risen from US$200 million to US$300 million. The problem is the lack of a framework that deals with public sector interest in projects driven by the private sector. In response to these challenges, the project has since encouraged a more inclusive process and now has a facilitator who brings together all stakeholders and manages the process.

Source: Presentation at the WCCD by session participants.

KEY ISSUES

- The key to building accessible ICT infrastructure is to be able to negotiate politics, poverty, and profit. Defined frameworks for government and private partnerships are necessary, as are rules, laws, and a policy framework that will protect the public interest.
- The role of the public sector in private sector initiatives should be clarified. Public interest projects should be recognized as such and have transparency and accountability built into them.
- Commitment from officials high in government is important.
- Access to affordable infrastructure is important because it enhances communication and makes it more effective. It also makes connectivity more affordable: in Europe 3 percent of disposable income is spent on communication; in Africa, 15 percent. This takes money away from other necessities such as education, food, and health.
- The Internet should not be considered irrelevant or a luxury: it allows access to radio and telephone, which are essential for giving people a voice. It is shortsighted to not view the Internet as essential. For example, with access to ICTs and knowledge, women can become more empowered.
- ICTs provide knowledge connectivity: knowledge deficit is a major reason for the urban-rural divide. Without knowledge there is no development. Investments in ICTs are, therefore, for knowledge connectivity and not just infrastructure.
- ICTs have the ability to overcome local diversity issues (which could potentially create a challenge) and can even bring people together through knowledge sharing.

RECOMMENDATIONS

- Government, in conjunction with the private sector, should ensure access to affordable communications infrastructure, which will enhance community participation in development initiatives.
- Multistakeholder participation is required in all development initiatives.
- Successful development initiatives require the participation of all stakeholders in their design, decision making, governance, and implementation processes.

Impact and Assessment: Innovative Ways to Determine Communication Effectiveness

The purpose of this session was to present different evaluation methodologies and to argue that the Communication for Development community should not spend time and energy disagreeing about whether one methodology is better than another. Many methodologies are valid, useful, and appropriate for different purposes and types of communication projects.

In Egypt, for example, national demographic indicators have been tracked against national multimedia family planning information campaigns for 25 years. At this level, dramatic changes in demographic indicators (population growth, attitudes, and behavior) matched systematic communication campaigns by the Information and Education Centre, campaigns that were based on research and monitoring of demographic trends.

In Nigeria, propensity score matching is used. A September 2005 household survey used multistage random sampling of 15- to 25-year-old married and single men and women to measure the rate of exposure of the population to an information campaign and the impact of the campaign on the use of modern contraceptive methods and improved ideation (beliefs about family planning). Propensity score matching is a statistical tool that can be used to refine estimation of the effects of communication interventions in situations where it is not possible to carry out the usual controls, such as pre- and post-intervention surveys, control groups, or randomized sampling. In Nigeria this involved assessing the likelihood that individuals would be exposed to a campaign. Then, when a survey was carried out to assess the incidence of the desired change (in this case, use of modern family planning and changed attitudes toward it), the results were analyzed in the light of the likelihood or "propensity" of respondents to have been exposed to the campaign. A campaign is deemed to have been effective when it has influenced the behavior of those who were not previously predisposed to the change in question.

The *Soul City* series has used evaluations. Since 1992 there have been nine independent evaluations of *Soul City*. Although they were complying with international best practice, the organizers felt that much of the impact on communities had not been told. So recently they started to record stories of change in communities brought about by *Soul City*. Part of a film was shown about an informal settlement, mainly of garbage sorters, who named their settlement "Soul City" to signal their aspirations for making the best of or bettering their lives.

Cost-effectiveness analysis is one of several different types of economic analysis that aim to compare the cost of each behavior change achieved, or the value of the health gains achieved, against the costs of a campaign. It can be useful for health communication planners to know how to invest funds best, how different interventions compare on cost-effectiveness, or how advocacy can achieve a particular type of intervention. Few such studies have been carried out in developing countries. There is a clear need for more such studies to be carried out, using known methodologies but with some standardization of approaches.

One such study was done of the 2001–03 "Smiling Sun" multimedia campaign in Bangladesh, a program to encourage the use of NGO clinics for family health. The research aimed to establish the cost-effectiveness of national full-coverage media campaigns. It found that exposure to the program produced change in a very cost-effective way—costing US$0.36 for each additional measles vaccination achieved.

KEY ISSUES

- How do we identify the impact of one intervention among several others that may have happened at the same time? One solution being tried in South Africa is for several organizations to collaborate to evaluate the impact of several interventions together.
- Should resources and effort be put into building the capacity of communities to carry out evaluation processes themselves? They probably have other priorities. However, it is useful to build the capacity of program implementers to the point where they are able to commission an evaluation and identify what questions should be asked.
- It is often said that there is insufficient evidence that Communication for Development works. Yet there is plenty of evidence that well-planned health communication interventions work. Several methodologies are available and being used to assess the impact and cost-effectiveness of communication interventions. Some methodologies meet the needs of economists,

some produce other kinds of quantitative evidence, and some produce qualitative evidence, which can be useful for assessing the achievement of objectives that are widely desired but hard to quantify, such as empowerment.

RECOMMENDATIONS

- Research and data gathering on demographic trends can be used to develop effective communication campaigns on family planning and similar issues.
- Communication campaigns influence the behavior of target populations that are not already likely to change, not merely those who are predisposed to change without the campaign, as is sometimes averred. Propensity score matching can be used to identify the impacts on those less predisposed to the desired change.
- Cost-effectiveness analysis can be used where a quantifiable outcome is achieved such as a change in specific behavior. There is a need for more cost-effectiveness studies using known methodologies but with some standardization of approaches.

The Rationale, Value, and Challenges for Adopting Participatory Communication in Development Programs

The session began with a discussion, "What Is Participatory Communication?" The following definitions emerged:

- Gives a voice to the voiceless
- Participation of the intended audience
- Starting with people for whom development is intended
- Challenging and transforming power
- Patience is required
- Not imposed
- "Users do it"
- Local, national, and global conversation
- It comes from within rather than without
- Sharing understanding.

Participants identified some of the challenges of participatory communication:

- Participation is often a lengthy and complicated process.
- It means dealing with division in the community: some parts of the community do not want to give voice to other parts of the community.
- Funding conditions are not conducive to participatory approaches. There is no room for participatory research in order to develop a project outline with the community.

Box 5.4 provides a case study.

CASE STUDIES

Box 5.4 Senegal and the Amazon

Tostan

Tostan is an international NGO based in Senegal, working on female genital cutting (FGC). Since 1997, 1,748 communities in the country have abandoned FGC. They make up 33 percent of the 5,000 communities that practiced FGC in 1997. Within the same period there have also been 20 public declarations against FGC, where the community comes together—men, women, traditional FGC practitioners, leaders, and others—and publicly denounces the practice by throwing away the tools. The Tostan approach has been so successful that the World Health Organization and UNICEF have both named it as a model program for other nations that seek to end the practice of FGC, and they have encouraged the organization to expand broadly across Africa.

Tostan's emphasis is on nondirective participatory communication that aims to empower the community. The project involves a long period of educating agents of change before they go out into the community to discuss human rights and issues affecting the community. The teaching of agents or facilitators is learner centered, using both modern and traditional communication techniques. In order to make a shift in social convention, Tostan uses a dialogue approach. FGC is tackled as a human rights issue rather than a health issue. Collective change is emphasized as opposed to individual change. This approach also helps ensure that the changes in social convention are lasting—people who want to practice FGC are denounced.

Tostan relies on the diffusion model of adopting new innovations. Villages that have made the changes and rejected FGC take it forward to other villages. It is in their interest, because they need to ensure that intermarriage can occur with neighboring villagers.

Source: Presentation at the WCCD by Molly Melching, Executive Director of Tostan.

CASE STUDIES

Projeto Saúde e Alegria (Health and Happiness Project)

Saúde e Alegria works with indigenous people in the Amazon who are socially excluded. It has a circus on a boat that brings health care and health messages to the people in an entertaining, participatory, and positive manner. The idea is to give information in a way that brings hope and happiness (hence the name of the organization). The project has set up a community press, community radio, community TV, and solar-powered telecenters. There is even a Wi-Fi zone.

The introduction of soya bean agriculture in the Amazon led farmers to destroy huge areas of forest to make space for plantations. Brazil is the fifth biggest contributor to carbon emissions in the atmosphere because of the fires used to clear agricultural land in the Amazon. New roads and a port were built into the Amazon for transporting products. No environmental impact assessments were done. The new developments brought violence and unemployment and caused the migration of indigenous rural people to urban areas where they live unemployed. Ninety-five percent of the soya beans in Europe come from the Amazon. McDonald's was one of the biggest buyers.

Together with NGOs and civil society movements, the communities started a campaign against soya production in the Amazon. They partnered with Greenpeace and mobilized the media and prominent people to help give wider coverage. The campaign involved community radio stations, the Internet, a network of 600 social movements linked through the Internet, and the creation of blogs by social movements.

Source: Presentation at the WCCD by Caetano Scannavino, Director of Projeto Saúde e Alegria.

KEY ISSUES

- Any development process must come from the bottom up, respecting local people.
- Social movements should make use of the media to help their issues gain wider support.
- Participatory communication is a practice that can and must reach beyond the local level to become national and global.
- Mass communication can model behavior to reinforce activities that are happening at the community level.
- There is a need to standardize principles for participatory communication that can be adopted in the context of each country.
- Joy and happiness should be emphasized more in participatory development. It is about bringing positive messages to people. If messages are positive, people get excited and want to become part of the process.

- Participatory development—which requires sharing and listening—should be viewed more from an ethical and spiritual point of view.

RECOMMENDATIONS

1. Project time frames must be longer than the standard one to three years. They must allow for meaningful participatory processes suitable for attaining sustainable change in relation to funding and evaluation requirements.
2. Academic institutions, donors, governments, and NGOs should form partnerships to leverage one another's strengths. Academic institutions can offer meaningful evaluation services, whereas donors and NGOs want quick assessments and results.

Which Kind of Development Communication Does Attract Media?

> *"We have a free press in India but it fails the poor. Journalism is moving toward celebrity journalism, the issues are getting lost, we have shut out the masses, and the stories of the masses are not coming through: Madonna makes news in India but not women who have no water."*
>
> —SESSION PARTICIPANT

> *"We need to go back to the question of capacity building for journalists and correspondents, and media literacy for the public, so the public knows how to hold the media to account."*
>
> —SESSION PARTICIPANT

The presentations and contributions made by the journalists at this session reflected the different types of audiences their work addresses. Several contributors involved in donor-funded work to build journalism capacity articulated dilemmas about the relationship between development agencies and media. Journalists face dilemmas over whether to exercise self-censorship in the face of development agencies—for instance, on whether to hold back from being critical when covering what editors or donors view as positive stories.

A presentation on the work of AlertNet, an international humanitarian news network set up by the Reuters Foundation, explained how the agency seeks to address the barriers and needs identified by journalists seeking to cover crisis situations. These were identified in the Fritz report produced by the Columbia School of Journalism. The most significant barriers identified by journalists were

- The cost of sending reporters to the scene and logistics
- The lack of a timely response from groups at the scene
- Inadequate supporting material on aid agency Web sites.

Four needs were identified:

- Basic primers on a crisis—crib sheets, whether on Nagorno Karabakh or Colombia
- Directories of which groups are operating in which areas
- A weekly newsletter that would inform journalists about breaking stories and give new angles
- Independently financed trips to those places.

See box 5.5 for a case study.

RECOMMENDATIONS

There were no specific recommendations from this session.

CASE STUDY

Box 5.5 Kenya—InterNews

"In Kenya NGOs weren't accessible to journalists, they would use language like 'capacity building,' they had no concept of what a news angle is—they didn't know that the opening of an office is not news. They had no personal relationships with journalists. InterNews used journalists to train NGOs, and the NGOs trained the journalists on HIV/AIDS. Now NGOs provide packaged information in a good form, and the journalists make a nice radio program on AIDS."

—Participant from InterNews

Communication for Development and ICTs: Where Do They Meet?

It is useful to take stock of both real and perceived differences between a development-centered ICT approach and the broader agenda and principles of Communication for Development, and to explore their distinct foci and potential synergies. We are now seeing a shift away from the more stand-alone variety of ICT projects toward a consideration of the broader context, in which information and communication are an integral part of all our lives, and also toward practices that incorporate the identified needs and strategies of communities. New ICTs are still part of the equation, but they are no longer the novelty they once were. Under what conditions can projects using ICT actually deliver, and what can we learn from the experience of Communication for Development?

- Experience with Communication for Development has demonstrated the importance of participation. But participation in ICT projects is sometimes complicated or inhibited by a variety of factors. For example, participation in the design, implementation, operation, and evaluation of ICT projects requires specialized knowledge that is often not locally available, and techniques developed to facilitate participation in low-tech communication processes do not necessarily work in virtual environments.
- The first decade of ICT for development was marked by pilot project after pilot project. Rapidly changing technologies cry out for pilot projects to test new capabilities, but real development requires attention to mainstreaming and sustainability.
- ICT projects have been accompanied by a wave of liberalization and privatization and an accompanying massive growth of the sector. But the inadequacies of a purely private sector model are becoming obvious. The development of ICTs by the private sector fails in bridging the gap between rich and poor. The poor, who are marginalized—and in some cases physically isolated—remain disconnected from the rest of society and what development opportunities there may be.

RECOMMENDATIONS

Recommendations fall in two categories: enabling policies, and ensuring effective use and impact at the grassroots level.

Enabling policies

- To the extent that ICT provides participatory and potentially more cost-effective tools, the policy makers and practitioners in Communication for Development need to renew their emphasis on policies to achieve universal service and universal access to ICT.
- ICT and development policies should not be technology-driven or top-down, but they should draw on principles and techniques of Communication for Development (for example, participation in all phases—including research, planning, design, and evaluation) and on multistakeholder participation to ensure responsiveness to needs.
- Policies and regulatory frameworks should facilitate and encourage innovative ways of financing and initiating ICT projects, such as community-owned or -driven networks, using a variety of possible technologies to ensure that they are accessible and usable by remote and marginalized communities.

Ensuring effective use and impact at the grassroots level

- ICT and development policies and projects must stress that the potential of ICTs is not realized through access to ICT or to ICT-enabled services alone, but through people's ability to use the technologies and services effectively to address their needs and to allow them to dialogue, to be heard, to learn, to participate in community life and democratic processes, and ultimately to improve their livelihoods.
- Policy makers and donors need to be more focused on encouraging learning rather than on reporting, moving to scale, and perpetually piloting. ICTs are now mainstream and their role in development must reflect this position.
- Intensive capacity development is vital to ensure that users can fully sustain and integrate ICTs in their daily lives. This must include a focus on addressing gender and other forms of social discrimination and may require institutional reengineering.

Communication and Disabilities

Some 650 million people, 80 percent of whom are living in developing countries, are disproportionately trapped in the poverty-disability cycle. If disabled people are not included in the development agenda, the Millennium Development Goals cannot be achieved. Articles 8, 9, and 21 of the International Convention on the Rights of Persons with Disabilities (UN General Assembly 2006) make specific reference to the use of communication as a tool for achieving results. Communication for Development has a key role to play through the inclusion of disabled people in the participatory approach to development. Disability is a cross-cutting issue in all development sectors, and disabled people should be included and portrayed in all communication efforts. For example, the participatory approach facilitated by Communication for Development in the PRSP process has achieved the inclusion of disability issues in a growing number of PRSPs.

KEY CHALLENGES

- Representation of people with disabilities. People with disabilities should be included in all media across all issues without being stereotyped. They should be spokespersons on disability but also on other social, cultural, and economic issues.
- Access to information and media. How do we design strategies and appropriate technologies to communicate with people with disabilities? What alternative formats are required to ensure digital inclusion?
- Integration of people with disabilities as decision makers and creators of media and communication (not just subjects of communication) is important. Recruitment, training, and promotion policies need to include people with disabilities. Disability issues should be integrated in academic, media, and communication courses.

RECOMMENDATION

Include and portray disabled people among beneficiaries of development in all Communication for Development programs, activities, and products.

Indigenous Peoples

In this very powerful, special session, speakers from the floor and on the panel contributed in equal parts. There was widespread recognition that communication is not just value added but intrinsic to the survival and development of indigenous peoples. It was also agreed that it is essential that indigenous communities establish and own their communication systems and determine their own way forward. Several participants stressed the right to manage their own communication systems in their own languages and cultures, and the right to participate in research, monitoring, and reporting on the media. The discussion also covered how globalization and climate change are damaging traditional, successful forms of communication used by indigenous peoples. Below are some of the contributions:

> *"We need air, we need mountains, we need communication. We are among the poorest of the poor, mainly because of lack of communication, and information. [Without communication] we don't learn about changes, we don't learn about HIV/AIDS, information doesn't get to us."*
>
> —Ignacio Profil, ONPIA, Argentina

> *"Consultation has to be ongoing, meaningful, and sustainable; too many projects are project-driven and have an end date. Communication tools have to be put in the hands of the people, and they have to have the freedom to make mistakes. It is important to look for consultants who come from indigenous communities."*
>
> —Brian Walmark, HKO Research Institute, Canada

> *"We are very strong inside but we are weak from the point of view of dialogue. This weakness is due to the fact that media is not available for indigenous people but for small groups. We want to articulate [our rights to] our territory, and this is against the interests of the groups of power, but when we use technology we can put forward our issues, struggle for our rights to our territory, and the dignity of the indigenous peoples of Bolivia, because they were not even considered by the constitution of our country."*
>
> —Eliana Rioja, CIDOB, Bolivia

> *"He who is well informed has power, that's why governments like to highjack information. We need to project our plight, assert ourselves, fight for our rights, project our culture and traditional knowledge, and have control, and [we need to] exchange information for development, for instance, about HIV/AIDS. I would like UN stakeholders to take steps to ensure that we have access to communications tools: radio, newspapers, TV, Internet, among ourselves and to others for development."*
>
> —IBRAHIM NJOBDI, CAMEROON

> *"[Communication is] absolutely essential to our self-determined development . . . because indigenous peoples have been marginalized to the point of extinction. Public spaces and networks that we have opened up, for instance through the UN, have allowed us to pursue our rights. There are huge opportunities for indigenous people if the digital divide can be overcome."*
>
> —VICTORIA TAULI-CORPUZ

> *"Communication offers huge hope for change, for solutions to problems: we don't want to [keep saying that] we are poor, that we are marginalized, we want to seek solutions for our own problems. Communication has always existed, from our ancestors, in the graffiti on our walls, we are able to communicate with our brothers, but up to now we haven't found a way to eradicate poverty, to stamp out poverty."*
>
> —MARIA SARAVIA, FEDERATION OF INDIGENOUS PEOPLES OF BOLIVIA

See also the case study in box 5.6.

RECOMMENDATION

The right of indigenous peoples to communication for self-determined development should be guaranteed. While the right to communication belongs to all human beings, this right must be guaranteed in particular to indigenous peoples in view of their invisibility in and marginalization from development processes and their significant contributions to the diversity of humankind. It is essential to promote policies, mechanisms, and initiatives that guarantee and enhance the realization of the right to communication of indigenous peoples.

CASE STUDY

Box 5.6 Voices in Nagaland

In Nagaland there is a serious lack of access to communication. Radio and TV are controlled by government agencies; there is no press freedom. There have been decades of conflict, and it is a very underdeveloped region. We have problems with HIV/AIDS, rampant corruption, restrictions on international agencies getting into the region, and constitutional barriers to change. Our strength is that we have our traditional forms of communication: oral history, traditional songs, arts, and dances that celebrate our history and tradition.

Peace is essential to development, but the development people have tended not to focus on this. The voices of the Naga mothers' association, which is the apex body of tribal women's organizations in Nagaland, have been key to creating a semblance of peace in the region. The women communicated with different factions and then with policy makers and urged them to form a base to open up Nagaland. This led to the 1997 cease-fire. They weren't directly involved in the talks, but their voices were heard. This was particularly significant given that Nagaland is a very patriarchal society, women do not have property, land, or inheritance rights, and yet despite these confines they have been very effective.

Naga young people are being supported to work as journalists within mainstream print outlets. They are the main channels for communication—they are journalists but they also link us, they pass on the news and information we want to give the communities—for instance, on health, agriculture, HIV, and AIDS. It's quite different when this information is being written in our local dialects, by our own people—it's no longer simply seen as a lecture from the government: the indigenous people themselves are doing the reporting.

Source: Presentation at the WCCD by Rosemary Dzuvichu.

The UN Declaration on the Rights of Indigenous Peoples and the Programme of the Second International Decade of the World's Indigenous Peoples (2005–15) will be part of the foundation for a proactive dialogue and action in the field of Communication for Development:

1. To promote the right to communication of indigenous peoples as an essential component of self-determined development, based on the principles of respect, equality, and nondiscrimination, especially in places such as Africa, where this right has been denied
2. To promote Communication for Development approaches and practices from indigenous peoples' perspectives, strengthen the

capacities controlling and managing communication processes, and ensure participation of indigenous women

3. To disseminate widely and implement effectively the UN Declaration on the Right of Indigenous Peoples and the Program of the Second International Decade of the World's Indigenous Peoples (2005–15) and to use them as the framework for a rights-based approach for indigenous peoples' self-determined development
4. To mainstream Communication for Development into the agenda of the Second International Decade of the World's Indigenous Peoples, as well as into national communication and development policies
5. To establish normative and regulatory frameworks and policies and provide adequate resources, to realize the right to communication of indigenous peoples for their own development

BENCHMARKS

1. By 2008 mechanisms for participation, consultation, collaboration, and sharing of experiences between indigenous peoples in Communication for Development shall be established in at least two regions.
2. By 2008 monitoring and evaluation mechanisms and related reports, managed by indigenous peoples' organizations in collaboration with the UN Permanent Forum on Indigenous Issues, shall be established in at least 10 countries.

6

Overall Recommendations

Recommendations from the Health Strand

These recommendations came from the workshops, the special events, and the health plenary.

GENERAL RECOMMENDATIONS

1. There is a need to think further about what successful change looks like, in terms of both what is seen to be a "success" and what is considered to be "good" change. Reconsidering the nature of change is an increasingly pressing need in a development context that is driven more and more by top-down global indicators of success and uniform measures of development.
2. Communication should be embedded in development planning, implementation, and monitoring of impact, not used only to consult people. It should be included in health program design, and the contribution of the communication component should be explicitly evaluated and the lessons learned applied in future programming.
3. Measurement of the achievement and impact of communication activities, through key indicators and a data collection system, needs to be integrated within health strategies. Research is needed to understand the role and impact of particular media or communication strategies for particular goals, in particular locations.
4. There is a need for consistent engagement on an issue over an extended period of time to see sustained changes in behavior.

5. There is a need for professional communication capacity, particularly for developing country practitioners, since at the moment there is too much reliance on international experts.
6. There needs to be training and capacity building, both to give those affected the confidence to speak and to get policy makers to listen to them.
7. Program results are better when they build on culturally appropriate values and communication methods. Health communication projects should do an initial analysis of gender and family roles and how these roles influence health norms and practices.
8. Effective development communication often requires first looking at our own organization—we need to get our own house in order.
9. We need to rethink what we consider evidence for Communication for Development to ensure that the process is valued as much as outputs, and that the process is seen as an output in itself.
10. Although mass media can reinforce many positive behaviors and practices, more targeted messaging provided by trusted health workers or community influencers has greater impact—especially with marginalized populations.
11. Communication jargon should be avoided. Communication professionals should talk in language that both policy makers and laypeople can understand.

SPECIFIC RECOMMENDATIONS ON HEALTH COMMUNICATION

12. Communication professionals need to work much more on harm reduction and on intravenous drug consumers. More work needs to be done on concurrent sexual partnerships, which multiply the risk of HIV transmission.
13. There needs to be more education about anal intercourse as a risky practice—and not just as an issue for gay men, because it also occurs in the context of avoiding pregnancy and "preserving" virginity, with young women often forced into it by male partners.
14. There is a need for clear communication about compensation with regard to birds destroyed to prevent avian influenza. Rates vary from minimal to about half of market rates, but communication on this issue is likely to have big effects on the willingness of many farmers and rearers, commercial and small-scale alike, to take effective measures.

15. In the case of epidemics or disease outbreaks, communication experts should be part of any outbreak investigation and response team. Advocacy, social mobilization, and interpersonal communication are all necessary for an effective disease control communication strategy.
16. Sustaining fresh messages and motivation for a program such as polio eradication is difficult; it requires a multidisciplinary approach and the active involvement of communication experts, epidemiologists, and civil society. Flexibility to react to a rapidly changing environment is paramount.
17. For donors and policy makers, it is important to factor in the communication needs of immunization and disease control programs.

Recommendations from the Governance Strand

1. There should be a legal framework to allow for and protect free media and CSOs. By improving the rule of law in general, media freedom laws and freedom of information acts cannot be overridden—ostensibly for reasons of national security and the like—so easily.
2. Communication should be incorporated into infrastructure projects from the start, ensuring a diversity of voices, not only the loudest and strongest. This is mainstreaming communication—and it must happen at the beginning and throughout the program.
3. Context is important—making sure interventions are based on needs identified by individuals in the specific context, for example, instead of imposing models of journalism from the West, and ensuring that anticorruption efforts are sensitive to local contexts. This applies equally to politicians, donors, and specialists in Communication for Development.
4. International institutions, including NGOs, need to uphold and be subject to the same principles of transparency and accountability as other organizations. There is a need to develop tools to ensure government accountability and transparency that citizens can use directly. Partnerships and coalitions across different sections of society—the media, civil society, and governments—need to ensure transparency and accountability.
5. All stakeholders must be involved in the political process—communities, government, the private sector, and donors.

Development of public policy must be based on the participation of the same stakeholders. This must include processes of information dissemination as well as dialogue and participation.

6. Systematizing communication is important. This can be done through learning from previous projects. We need a few standard methodologies: public opinion surveys, stakeholder mapping, coalition building. One important element is vertical integration, establishing a protocol so that there is a rigor to information sharing at an institutional level.
7. It is important to stimulate citizen demand for good governance and to develop the mechanisms through which citizens can advance good governance—citizens' juries, participatory budgeting, and so on. Capacity building is needed, not only with civil society but also with the media and public institutions. There is a need to broaden the debate on poverty and equity beyond the discourse of international institutions. Countries need to have the option to adopt strategies that fall outside the paradigms of international institutions.
8. The different roles within a democratic political system need to be clearly defined. People need to understand their roles and their responsibilities within those roles. To do this, journalists should create codes of conduct and citizens should create their own charters.
9. The case for communication must be made to national governments, pointing out the benefits of efficiency and legitimacy.
10. Donors should collaborate and coordinate more before they go into countries, especially countries in crisis. This might be done by establishing a caucus of rich countries, with one focal person, to speed the process and reduce the likelihood of conflicting donor agendas. Donors should look at strategic partnerships with other donors.
11. Donors should be lobbied to take media support more seriously. Those donors that support media systems should work with grassroots media organizations rather than international media institutions (such as BBC World Service Trust, for instance). One idea for the media was to create something similar to the Millennium Challenge Fund—media groups should be able to access funds according to specified conditions.

Recommendations from the Sustainable Development Strand

These recommendations came from the workshops, the special events, and the sustainable development plenary.

GENERAL RECOMMENDATIONS

1. Communication is a right, not just a development strategy.
2. Communication should be built into sustainable development initiatives and budgets from the start. The concept of sustainability is built into all recommendations that the Congress produced.
3. National policies should be developed to include participatory communication. A country's program approach should be developed to avoid duplication and lack of coordination between donors.
4. Communication for Development should be integrated into major international development plans and policies—for example, PRSPs should include communication.
5. Communication for Development should not be about consultation alone but about genuine participation—this may require structural or political changes. Communities need to be involved from the beginning of a project. Communication for Development practitioners need to act as facilitators to ensure that local voices are heard. Research initiatives in natural resources management should be promoted with a participatory approach and involvement of communication and local stakeholders in their design, implementation, and dissemination.
6. There is a need to foster partnerships between government agencies, donors, academia, international organizations, NGOs, and other actors, including the private sector and the media. Coalitions and groups remain after projects and programs have gone. These actors need to foster knowledge sharing and form a Communication for Development advisory consortium at the national level.
7. Capacity building is needed for sustainable development specialists and practitioners of Communication for Development. Natural resource management experts are often scientists whose mind-set is often not oriented to social development

and participation or who lack skills in Communication for Development. The efforts by such organizations as the Communication for Social Change Consortium to develop core reading materials and standard course templates merit support. They should be translated, adapted, and distributed widely. Postgraduate studies in Communication for Development should also be supported.

8. All regions report a lack of knowledge on the part of decision makers about the breadth and depth of Communication for Development. It is clear that methods must be found to broaden decision makers' knowledge of the full communication agenda and that this effort should include capacity building for decision makers.
9. Professional communication needs a range of tools and initiatives. There is no one Communication for Development skill or approach that works for all. A range of approaches drawing on expertise from journalism, participatory research, facilitation, public relations, technology, and other fields is needed. The only common strand is the need to be innovative and flexible enough to adopt the approach, tools, and methods that are appropriate to a situation. Technologies are just one of the tools that are needed.

SPECIFIC RECOMMENDATIONS ON SUSTAINABLE DEVELOPMENT

10. The Congress recognizes the unique challenges in Communication for Development for small island states.
11. The Mexico rural communication system should be revisited and challenges for the future identified to see what remains of the past project that can be built on in the future.
12. Access to telecommunications should be broadened and costs reduced. This includes reducing the cost of transferring migrants' remittances to a maximum of 2.5 percent of the amount transferred.
13. There should be a public debate on regulation of telecommunications.
14. Baselines should be established at the beginning of projects. Evaluation for social networking should be included. Participants suggested adding the "need to have objectives as well as having a baseline."

15. The private sector must be brought to the table more; it is a key stakeholder group often ignored in development initiatives.
16. Institutional champions within the region need to be identified. They should be responsible for carrying out a Communication for Development audit, fostering collaboration and partnerships, being a national focal point for preparing pilot projects, facilitating documentation of good practice, and establishing a database at a national level for a community of practice.
17. A strong evidence base of Communication for Development activities and successes should be assembled. To this end, we should move toward a results framework, so different stakeholders can gauge progress.
18. For Communication for Development to bring about food security and natural resources management, there needs to be a legal framework for rural radio stations.

Recommendations from the Cross-Cutting Themes

The following are the recommendations for the topics that cut across the main development themes. They are divided in general recommendations, recommendations for media, recommendations for ICTs, and impact and assessment.

GENERAL

1. Project time frames must be longer than the standard one to three years. They must allow for meaningful participatory processes that are suitable for attaining sustainable change in relation to funding and evaluation requirements.
2. Multistakeholder participation is required in all development initiatives. Successful development initiatives require the participation of all stakeholders in their design, decision making, governance, and implementation processes. Academic institutions, donors, governments, and NGOs should form partnerships to leverage one another's strengths.
3. Disabled people should be included and portrayed among beneficiaries of development in all Communication for Development programs, activities, and products.
4. The right of indigenous peoples to communication for self-determined development should be guaranteed.

MEDIA

5. To be effective, media monitoring and journalism training need to be part of a long-term, comprehensive strategy.
6. National development plans should promote an enabling legal and regulatory environment for a plurality of independent media, including specific provision for the development of community media. Public funding should be provided by governments to community media through independent funding mechanisms, and access to communications infrastructure should be affordable.
7. Development institutions and organizations should provide assistance to build the capacity of community media through training, strengthening of networks and sector associations, technical assistance, and investment. Support for community media should be provided on the basis of strategic, long-term commitments, recognizing that impact must be measured not only in short-term results but also in community media's contribution to long-term social change.

ICTS

8. ICT and development policies should not be technology-driven or top-down, but should draw on Communication for Development principles and techniques (for example, participation in all phases—including research, planning, design, and evaluation) and on multistakeholder participation to ensure responsiveness to needs.
9. Policies and regulatory frameworks should facilitate and encourage innovative ways of financing and initiating ICT projects, such as community-owned or -driven networks, using a variety of possible technologies to ensure that remote and marginalized communities can access and use them.
10. ICT and development policies and projects must stress that the potential of ICTs is not realized through access to ICT or to ICT-enabled services alone, but through people's ability to use the technologies and services effectively to address their own needs and to allow them to dialogue, to be heard, to learn, to participate in community life and democratic processes, and ultimately to improve their livelihoods.

11. Policy makers and donors need to focus more on encouraging learning rather than on reporting, moving to scale, and perpetually piloting. ICTs are now mainstream and their role in development must reflect this position.
12. Intensive capacity development is vital to ensure that users can fully sustain and integrate ICTs in their daily lives. This effort must focus on addressing gender and other forms of social discrimination and may require institutional reengineering.

IMPACT AND ASSESSMENT

13. Research and data gathering on demographic trends can be used to develop effective communication campaigns in the field of family planning and other similar health initiatives. Demographic trends, such as growth or evolution of the demographic pyramid, can inform communication campaigns.
14. Communication campaigns influence the behavior of target populations who are not already likely to change, not only those who are predisposed to change without the campaign, as is sometimes averred. Propensity score matching is a tool that can be used to identify the impacts on those less predisposed to the desired change.
15. Cost-effectiveness analysis can be used where a quantifiable outcome is achieved, such as a change in specific behaviors. There is a need for more cost-effectiveness studies using existing methodologies but with some standardization of approaches.

Key Recommendations from the Policy Makers' Forum

The participants in the Policy Makers' Forum agreed on the following recommendations regarding policy, media and dissemination, impact and assessment, and partnerships and ownership.

POLICY

1. The responsibility for ensuring that Communication for Development is embedded in development policy lies with the policy maker, not the communicator.

2. The lack of the institutionalization of Communication for Development is a problem. We need to revise ways of working and methods to incorporate Communication for Development from the planning stage through monitoring and evaluation of a project. Communication for Development should have its own budget, methodology, training guidelines, and so on. We need a road map for Communication for Development from start to finish. We need to revise its role and obligations.
3. Communication for Development should be embedded in poverty reduction. It needs to be linked into a framework for poverty beyond income poverty. It is fundamental that Communication for Development does this—that we use ICT to give voice and to enable the poor and marginalized to identify their priorities.

MEDIA AND DISSEMINATION

4. There is an international consensus that communication is a central part of development. To increasingly integrate Communication in Development initiatives, we must engage the media, not forgetting community media.
5. We need to report success. The irony is that many successful stories have happened since the turn of the 20th century, from the 1950s and 1960s, from the women's movements and others. We do not, however, document and extract the messages for the future. We need to show that Communication for Development brings results.
6. We need to demystify Communication for Development. People do not understand what it is for; if it were clearer, policy makers would feel more confident investing in the idea.

IMPACT AND ASSESSMENT

7. Benchmarking is important—there must be some goals to achieve. The benchmarks may not be perfect but they help give some focus to impact measurement.
8. Monitoring and evaluation need to be built in from the start of the process and must involve the beneficiaries.

PARTNERSHIPS AND OWNERSHIP

9. Communication for Development must be linked to the Millennium Development Goals, especially Goal 8, on partnerships. Partnerships must not only be with development organizations but also beyond them with other types of organizations not specifically working on development, such as academia, research centers, media, and community organizations.
10. There is a need to broaden the range of partnerships and perspectives and expand the network of practitioners of Communication for Development further, to make links between communicators and others.
11. Ownership of programs must be in the hands of the countries and communities responsible for the programs. Ownership is not stressed enough.

APPENDIX 1

Congress Participants

Plenary Session Speakers

Name	Last Name	Title	Organization
Opening Ceremony—Welcome			
Jacques	**Diouf**	Director General	FAO
Alfonso	**Pecoraro Scanio**	Minister of Environment and Territory	Government of Italy
Patricia	**Sentinelli**	Vice Minister of Foreign Affairs	Government of Italy
Rosa Maria	**Alfaro**	Founder	Calandria
Jorge	**Gestoso**	Moderator	GTN
Panel Discussion—Communication for More Effective Development			
José	**Ramos Horta**	Prime Minister	Government of Timor-Leste
Marta	**Maurás**	Secretary	Economic Commission for Latin America and the Caribbean
Aram	**Aharonian**	Director	Telesur, Venezuela, R. B. de
Garth	**Japhet**	Executive Director	*Soul City*
Paul	**Mitchell**	Manager, Development Communication Division	World Bank
Marcela	**Villarreal**	Director, Gender and Population Division	FAO
Piero	**Di Pasquale**	Moderator	RAI News 24
Governance Plenary			
Kevin	**Kellems**	Acting Vice President of External Affairs	World Bank
Prof. Flavio	**Del Bono**	Vice President	Regione Emilia Romagna
Joseph	**Stiglitz**	Professor Chair, Columbia University Committee on Global Thought	Columbia University
Anwar	**Ibrahim**	Visiting Distinguished Professor, former Deputy Prime Minister, and former Minister of Finance of Malaysia	Georgetown University

Fawzi	**Al Sultan**	Former President, former Secretary General	IFAD Higher Committee for Development and Reform, Office of the Prime Minister of Kuwait
Duilio	**Giammaria**	Moderator	RAI
Sustainable Development Plenary			
Lyonpo Sangay	**Ngedup**	Minister of Agriculture	Government of Bhutan
Laurent	**Sedogo**	Minister of Environment	Government of Burkina Faso
Marcela	**Villarreal**	Director, Gender and Population Division	FAO
Alfonso Gumucio	**Dagrón**	Managing Director	Communication for Social Change Consortium
Mario	**Lubetkin**	Moderator	Inter-Press Service
Health Plenary			
Hon. Nonofo	**Molefhi, MP**	Member of the National Assembly	Government of Botswana
Muthoni	**Wanyeki**	Executive Director	African Women's Development and Communication Network
Elizabeth	**Fox**	Deputy Director, Office of Health, Infectious Diseases and Nutrition	U.S. Agency for International Development
Peter	**da Costa**	Coordinator	Strengthening Africa's Media Project
Bella	**Mody**	Professor	University of Colorado, Boulder
BBC World Debate: Is a Free Media Essential for Development?			
Hilde	**Johnson**	Senior Adviser to the President, former Minister of International Development of Norway	African Development Bank
Anwar	**Ibrahim**	Visiting Distinguished Professor, former Deputy Prime Minister, and former Minister of Finance	Georgetown University, formerly Government of Malaysia

(*continued*)

Plenary Session Speakers (*Continued*)

Name	Last Name	Title	Organization
Daniel	**Kaufmann**	Director of Global Programs	World Bank Institute
Kumi	**Naidoo**	Secretary General	CIVICUS World Alliance for Citizen Participation
Dr Tonnie Osa	**Iredia**	Director General	Nigerian Television Authority
Stephen	**Sackur**	Moderator	BBC
Policy and Decision Makers Forum			
Jac	**Stienen**	Managing Director	International Institute for Communication & Development
Gerolf	**Weigel**	Head of ICT for Development Office	Swiss Agency for Development and Cooperation
Kilaparti	**Ramakrishna**	Chief Policy Adviser, Office of the Executive Director	UNEP
Matthew	**Wyatt**	Assistant President for External Affairs Department	IFAD
Mervat	**Tallawy**	Executive Secretary	UN Economic & Social Commission for Western Asia
Alfredo	**Barnechea**	External Relations Adviser	Inter-American Development Bank
Jeffrey J.	**Grieco**	Senior Deputy Assistant Administrator for Public Affairs	U.S. Agency for International Development
Sandra	**Charles**	Senior Economic Policy Adviser, Economic Development, Policy Branch	Canadian International Development Agency
Hu	**Shuli**	Editor in Chief	Caijing, China

Kumi	**Naidoo**	Secretary General	CIVICUS—World Alliance for Citizen Participation
Tesfai	**Tecle**	Assistant Director General	FAO
Marcela	**Villarreal**	Director, Gender and Population Division	FAO
Paul	**Mitchell**	Manager, Development Communication Division	World Bank
Warren	**Feek**	Executive Director	The Communication Initiative Network
Jorge	**Gestoso**	Moderator	GTN
Closing Ceremonies			
José	**Ramos Horta**	Prime Minister	Government of Timor-Leste
Alexander Julius	**Müller**	Assistant Director General—Sustainable Development Department	FAO
Bernard	**Petit**	Deputy Director General, DG Development	European Commission
Paul	**Mitchell**	Manager, Development Communication Division	World Bank
Marcela	**Villarreal**	Director, Gender and Population Division	FAO
Warren	**Feek**	Executive Director	The Communication Initiative Network
Jorge	**Gestoso**	Moderator	GTN

Full List of Participants

Name	Last Name	Title	Organization	City	Country
WCCD Secretariat Staff					
Mario	Acunzo	Communication Officer	FAO, SDR	Rome	Italy
José Manuel	Bassat	Senior Communication Officer	World Bank	Washington, DC	United States
Iride	Boffardi	Consultant	FAO, SDR	Rome	Italy
Mario	Bravo	Senior Communication Officer	World Bank	Washington, DC	United States
Michele	Bruni	Consultant	World Bank	Washington, DC	United States

(continued)

Full List of Participants (*Continued*)

Name	Last Name	Title	Organization	City	Country
WCCD Secretariat Staff, *continued*					
Maria Elena	Calabrese	Intern	FAO, SDR	Rome	Italy
Daniele	Calabrese	Communication Officer	World Bank	Washington, DC	United States
Serena	Cavicchi	Consultant	World Bank	Washington, DC	United States
Diana Ya-Wai	Chung	Communication Officer	World Bank	Washington, DC	United States
Riccardo	Del Castello	Communication Officer	FAO, SDR	Rome	Italy
Achille	Deodato	Consultant	FAO, SDR	Rome	Italy
Francis	Dobbs	Senior Film/Video Officer	World Bank	Washington, DC	United States
Eliana	Esposito	Consultant	World Bank	Washington, DC	United States
Maria Manuela	Faria	Consultant	World Bank	Washington, DC	United States
Warren	Feek	Executive Director	The Communication Initiative Network	Victoria, BC	Canada
Lucia	Grenna	Unit Head	World Bank	Washington, DC	United States
Christian	Hofer	Communication Officer	World Bank	Washington, DC	United States
Jean-Pierre	Ilboudo	Communication Officer	FAO, SDR	Rome	Italy
Zita	Lichtenberg	Consultant	World Bank	Washington, DC	United States
Andreas	Mandler	Intern	FAO, SDR	Rome	Italy
Piotr	Mazurkiewicz	Communication Officer	World Bank	Washington, DC	United States
Leonardo	Mazzei	Communication Officer	World Bank	Washington, DC	United States
Paolo	Mefalopulos	Senior Communication Officer	World Bank	Washington, DC	United States
Paul	Mitchell	Manager	World Bank	Washington, DC	United States
Kristina	Mlikota	Consultant	FAO, SDR	Rome	Italy
Ida	Mori	Public Information Officer	World Bank	Washington, DC	United States
Chris	Morry	Director of Programs	The Communication Initiative Network	Victoria, BC	Canada

Masud	Mozammel	Senior Communication Officer	World Bank	Washington, DC	United States
Marco	Nicoli	Knowledge Management Officer	World Bank	Washington, DC	United States
Anna	Norén	Consultant	FAO, SDR	Rome	Italy
Adesinaola	Odugbemi	Senior Communication Officer	World Bank	Washington, DC	United States
Clare Marie	O'Farrell	Communication Officer	FAO, SDR	Rome	Italy
Sunetra	Puri	Communications Adviser	World Bank Institute	Washington, DC	United States
German	Rojas	Communication Officer	FAO, GII	Rome	Italy
Emanuele	Santi	Communication Officer	World Bank	Washington, DC	United States
Agata	Schinina	Communication Officer	FAO, SDR	Rome	Italy
Ricardo	Torrado	Consultant	World Bank	Washington, DC	United States
Cecilia C.	Verzosa	Communication Adviser	World Bank	Washington, DC	United States
Daniele	Volpe	Consultant	FAO, SDR	Rome	Italy
Edith R.	Wilson	Communication Adviser	World Bank	Washington, DC	United States
WCCD Steering Committee					
Rosa María	Alfaro Moreno	President	Calandria	Lima	Peru
Indrajit	Banerjee	Secretary General	Asia Media Information and Communication Center		Singapore
Kwame	Boafo	Chief of the Executive Office	UNESCO	Paris	France
Claudius	Ceccon	Director	CECIP	Rio de Janeiro	Brazil
Andrew	Chetley	Programme Director	Healthlink Worldwide	London	United Kingdom
Jean	Fabre	Deputy Director	UNDP	Geneva	Switzerland
Elizabeth	Fox	Deputy Director, Office of Health, InfectiousDiseases and Nutrition	USAID	Washington, DC	United States
Rina	Gill	Senior Program Officer	UNICEF	New York, NY	United States

(continued)

Full List of Participants (*Continued*)

Name	Last Name	Title	Organization	City	Country
WCCD Steering Committee, *continued*					
Susan	Goldstein	Senior Manager	*Soul City*	Johannesburg, Gauteng	South Africa
Denise	Grayfelder	President and CEO	Communication for Social Change Consortium	South Orange, NJ	United States
Basyouni	Hamada	Professor	Cairo University & American University in Cairo	Cairo	Egypt, Arab Rep. of
Roberta	Hilbruner	Environmental Communication Officer, Development Communication & Sustainable Tourism Department	USAID	Washington, DC	United States
Patrick	Kalas	Communication for Development Officer, ICT for Development Office	Swiss Agency for Development and Cooperation	Bern	Switzerland
Christopher Fadeson	Kamlongera	Director	Southern Africa Development Community, Center of Communication for Development	Harare	Zimbabwe

Marcelo	Solervicens	General Secretary	AMARC	Montreal, Quebéc	Canada
Gerolf	Weigel	Head of ICT for Development Office	Swiss Agency for Development and Cooperation	Bern	Switzerland
WCCD Scientific Committee					
Silvia	Balit	Development Communication Consultant		Rome	Italy
Guy	Bessette	Senior Program Officer	International Development Research Centre	Ottawa, Ontario	Canada
Maria Celeste	Cadiz	Dean	University of the Philippines, Los Baños	Laguna	Philippines
Karin	Gwinn Wilkins	Graduate Adviser & Associate Professor	University of Texas at Austin	Austin, TX	United States
Nabil	H. Dajani	Professor, Department of Social and Behavioral Sciences	American University of Beirut	Beirut	Lebanon
Robert	Huesca	Professor, Department of Communication	Trinity University	San Antonio, TX	United States
Thomas Leigh	Jacobson	Senior Associate Dean for Academic Affairs, School of Communications and Theater	Temple University	Philadelphia, PA	United States
Ullamaija	Kivijuru	Professor	University of Helsinki	Helsinki	Finland

(*continued*)

Full List of Participants (*Continued*)

Name	Last Name	Title	Organization	City	Country
WCCD Scientific Committee, *continued*					
Rico	Lie	Professor, Subdepartment Communication Science	Wageningen University	Wageningen	Netherlands
Shuang	Liu	Professor, School of Journalism and Communication	University of Queensland	Brisbane, Queensland	Australia
Eric	Louw	Professor, School of Journalism and Communication	University of Queensland	Brisbane, Queensland	Australia
John	Mayo	Professor	Florida State University	Tallahassee, FL	United States
Levi	Obijiofor	Professor, School of Journalism and Communication	University of Queensland	Brisbane, Queensland	Australia
Rafael	Obregon	Professor	Ohio University	Athens, OH	United States
Charles	Okigbo	Professor	North Dakota State University	Fargo, ND	United States
Ricardo	Ramírez	Assistant Professor, School of Environmental Design and Rural Development	University of Guelph	Guelph, Ontario	Canada
Jan	Servaes	Professor and Head, School of Journalism and Communication	University of Queensland	Brisbane, Queensland	Australia
John Douglas	Storey	Associate Director for Communication Science and Research	Johns Hopkins Bloomberg School of Public Health—Center for Communication Programs	Baltimore, MD	United States

Pradip Ninan	Thomas	Professor, School of Journalism and Communication	University of Queensland	Brisbane, Queensland	Australia
Thomas	Tufte	Professor	Roskilde Universitetscenter	Roskilde	Denmark
WCCD Advisory Body					
Jaime Jose	Abello Banfi	Executive Director	Fundación para un Nuevo Periodismo Iberoamericano	Cartagena de Indias	Colombia
Jane	Bertrand	Executive Director	Johns Hopkins University CCP	Baltimore, MD	United States
Elroy	Bos	Acting Head, Global Communications Unit	IUCN—The World Conservation Union	Gland	Switzerland
Nasserie	Carew	Director of Communications	Interaction	Washington, DC	United States
Eric	Chinje	Manager, Internal and External Communication Division	African Development Bank	Tunis	Tunisia
Barbara Ann	Clay	Communication Director	Transparency International	Berlin	Germany
Charlotte	Cole	Vice President, Education and Research	Sesame Workshop	New York, NY	United States
Alberto	Contri	President	Fondazione Pubblicita Prgresso, RAI NET	Milan	Italy

(continued)

Full List of Participants (*Continued*)

Name	Last Name	Title	Organization	City	Country
WCCD Advisory Body, *continued*					
Henry	de Cazotte	Director of Communication	AFD (Agence Française de Développement)	Paris	France
Peter	Erichs	Media Program Officer	SIDA	Stockholm	Sweden
Bjoern	Foerde	Director	UNDP, Oslo Governance Centre	Oslo	Norway
Sophie	Garnham	Director, Strategy and Development	BBC WST	London	United Kingdom
Omar	Gharzeddine	Information Officer	UNFPA	New York, NY	United States
Helen	Gillman	Manager, Editorial Services	IFAD	Rome	Italy
Mario	Grieco		Association of Italian NGOs	Rome	Italy
Jeffrey	Hiday	Director General, Department of External Relations	Asian Development Bank	Manila	Philippines
Stephen	King	Director	BBC WST	London	United Kingdom
Patricia	Light-Borsellini	Communication Director	Bernard van Leer Foundation	The Hague	Netherlands
Nelsy	Lizarazo	Executive Director	ALER	Quito	Ecuador
Mario	Lubetkin	President	IPS—Inter-Press Service	Rome	Italy
Sergio	Marelli	President	Association of Italian NGOs	Rome	Italy

Sejamothopo	Motau	Chairman	Global Alliance for Public Relations and Communication Management	Rooihuiskraal	South Africa
Toni	Muzi Falconi	Senior Counsel	Methodos—Global Alliance for Public Relations and Communication Management	Rome	Italy
Donal	O'Leary	Senior Adviser	Transparency International	Berlin	Germany
Sara	Page	Deputy Director	SAfAIDS	Harare	Zimbabwe
John Lawrence	Paluszek	Senior Counsel	Ketchum—Global Alliance for Public Relations and Communication Management	New York, NY	United States
Gerry	Power	Director, Research and Learning	BBC WST	London	United Kingdom
Maria Teresa	Quiroz	President	FELAFACS	Lima	Peru

(*continued*)

Full List of Participants (*Continued*)

Name	Last Name	Title	Organization	City	Country
WCCD Advisory Body, *continued*					
Kilaparti	Ramakrishna	Deputy Director, Division of Policy Development and Law	UNEP	Nairobi	Kenya
Jose	Rimon	Senior Deputy Director	Johns Hopkins University CCP	Baltimore, MD	United States
Jac J. W.	Stienen	Managing Director	IICD—International Institute for Communication & Development	The Hague	Netherlands
Elena	Suarez	Chief, Special Programs Section	Inter-American Development Bank	Washington, DC	United States
Jakob S.	Thompson	Adviser, ICT in Development Cooperation	NORAD	Oslo	Norway
Cleofe	Torres	Professor	University of the Philippines Los Baños—College of Development Communication	Laguna	Philippines

Stijn	van der Krogt	Head of Country Programmes	IICD—International Institute for Communication & Development	The Hague	Netherlands
Veet	Vivarta	Director	ANDI—News Agency for Children's Rights	São Paulo	Brazil
Kitty	Warnock	Senior Adviser	Panos	London	United Kingdom
Mark	Wilson	Executive Director	Panos	London	United Kingdom
Sabina	Zaccaro	Journalist	IPS—Inter-Press Service	Rome	Italy
Pierre	Zemor	President	Communication Publique	Paris	France
Authors of Papers					
Tamara Mohamed Aref	Abu Sham	Project Coordinator	Bukra Network	Amman	Jordan
Gordon	Adam		Media Support Solutions	North Kessock, Ross-shire	United Kingdom
Sara	Adkins-Blanch	Senior Policy Communications Analyst	Population Reference Bureau	Washington, DC	United States
Chrys	Alakonya	Country Manager	Health Unlimited, Somalia	Nairobi	Kenya
Antonia	Antonopoulos	Assistant Project Officer	UNICEF	Dakar	Senegal

(*continued*)

Full List of Participants (*Continued*)

Name	Last Name	Title	Organization	City	Country
Authors of Papers, *continued*					
Judi	Aubel		Grandmother Project	Rome	Italy
Gita	Bamezai		National Institute of Health and Family Welfare	New Delhi, Delhi	India
Monica	Barroso		London School of Economics and Political Science	London	United Kingdom
Hannah	Beardon		ActionAid International	London	United Kingdom
Elizabeth	Booth		AED	Washington, DC	United States
Krishnendu	Bose	Director	Earthcare Films	New Delhi, Delhi	India
Richard	Bossi	Vice President	Academy for Educational Development	Washington, DC	United States
Ellen	Brazier	Director, Anglophone Africa Program	Family Care International	New York, NY	United States
Carlos	Camacho		Universidad Andina Simón Bolívar (UASB)	La Paz	Bolivia
Sarah	Cardey		University of Guelph	Waterloo	Canada

Delfina de los Angeles	Castillo Tzab	Maestra en Comunicación	Universidad Autónoma de Yucatán	Mérida, Yucatán	Mexico
Ketan	Chitnis	Program Communication Officer	Louisiana State University	Baton Rouge, LA	United States
Maria Margaretha	Claasen-Veldsman		University of Pretoria	Pretoria, Gauteng	South Africa
Alice	Colombi		University of Chicago	Chicago, IL	United States
Maritza	Concha	Director of Operations	Covian Consulting	Orlando, FL	United States
Mirtha Elizabeth	Correa Alamo	Directora Ejecutiva	Asociación de Comunicadores Sociales Calandria	Lima, Lima	Peru
Melanie	Croce-Galis	RN MPH	Alan Guttmacher Institute	New York, NY	United States
Kathrynruth	Czuczman		IFRTD	London	United Kingdom
Rochelle	Davidson		Wits University	Johannesburg, Gauteng	South Africa
Miguel	de Aguilera	Professor Doctor	Universidad de Málaga	Málaga	Spain
Dirk	de Jong	Information and Communication Officer	IRC International Water and Sanitation Centre	Delft	Netherlands
Gideon	De Wet	Professor	University of Johannesburg	Johannesburg, Gauteng	South Africa

(continued)

Full List of Participants (*Continued*)

Name	Last Name	Title	Organization	City	Country
Authors of Papers, *continued*					
Florencia	Enghel	Master in Communication for Development	Malmö University, Sweden	Buenos Aires	Argentina
Festus	Eribo	Professor	East Carolina University	Greenville, NC	United States
Sione	Fakaosi			Nukualofa, Tongatapu	Tonga
Carolyn	Fanelli	Documentation and Dissemination Manager	Catholic Relief Services/ Zimbabwe	Harare	Zimbabwe
Giuliana	Frugone			Milan	Italy
Carmen Elena	Gadala-Maria Valiente	Public Information Analyst	World Bank	Guatemala, Guatemala	Guatemala
Bishan	Garg	Professor of Community Medicine	MG Institute of Medical Sciences	Wardha, Maharashtra	India
Jude William	Genilo	Programme Director	Community-based Communi-cation and Development	Mandaluyong	Philippines
Radhey Shyam (R.S.)	Goyal	Professor	Indian Institute of Health Management Research	Jaipur, Rajasthan	India
Patrick	Griffiths		RMIT University	Melbourne,	Australia

Georg	Gruenberg	Dr. Phil.	Casa de Los 3 Mundos	Managua	Nicaragua
Qin	Guo		Macquarie University	Sydney, New South Wales	Australia
Adrian	Hadland		Human Sciences Research Council of South Africa	Cape Town, Western Cape	South Africa
Helen	Hambly Odame		University of Guelph	Guelph, Ontario	Canada
Zaeem	Haq	Senior Team Associate	Johns Hopkins University	Islamabad	Pakistan
Lisa	Hartenberger	Media Consultant	Self-employed	Austin, TX	United States
Poncelet	Ileleji	Coordinator	The Gambia YMCAs	Banjul, Banjul	The Gambia
Nick	Ishmael-Perkins	Head of Communication, Networking and Learning	Healthlink Worldwide	London	United Kingdom
K M Baharul	Islam	Chairman, SRTPC	UN Economic Commission for Africa	Addis Ababa	Ethiopia
Sandra	Jackson	Vice President, Development Services	Hobbs International	Winnipeg, Manitoba	Canada
Birgitte	Jallov	Consultant	Independent	Gudhjem	Denmark
Deependra Joshi	Joshi		IUCN Nepal	Kathmandu, Kathmandu	Nepal
Narcisse	Kalisa	Project Manager/Executive Producer	Health Unlimited, Rwanda	Kigali	Rwanda
Karen	Kaun	Executive Director	Knowledge iTrust	Darien, CT	United States

(*continued*)

Full List of Participants (*Continued*)

Name	Last Name	Title	Organization	City	Country
Authors of Papers, *continued*					
Koronel	Kema	Program Manager	AMREF	Dar es Salaam	Tanzania
Steffen	Knippel		Hobbs International	Winnipeg, Manitoba	Canada
Johannes	Kranz		Fundacion Casa de los Tres Mundos	Granada	Nicaragua
Manish	Kumar		OneWorld South Asia	New Delhi, Delhi	India
Mohammed	Kuta Yahaya		University of Ibadan	Ibadan, Oyo State	Nigeria
Pina	Lalli	Professor	University of Bologna	Bologna	Italy
Andreas	Lehnert		ASOCARS—CIM	Bergkamen	Germany
Ank	Linden	TV Journalist	MEDAC/ University of Groningen	Nijmegen	Netherlands
John Dennis	Liu	Director	Environmental Education Media Project (EEMP)	Beijing, Beijing Municipality	China
Cristiano	Lopes		Câmara dos Deputados	Brasília, Distrito Federal	Brazil
Rosmery de Urquizo	Machicado	Economist	Gabriel Rene Moreno University	Santa Cruz de la Sierra, Santa Cruz	Bolivia

Mia Martha	Malan	Senior Health Journalism Adviser	Internews Network	Washington, DC	United States
Pat	Malikhao		University of Queensland	St Lucia, Queensland	Australia
Jenevieve	Mannell		BRAC	London	United Kingdom
Adedayo	Mark-Adeyemi		Lagos Water Corporation	Lagos, Lagos State	Nigeria
Deyna	Marsh		Cook Islands National Envrionment Program	Rarotonga	Cook Islands
Jorge	Martínez Ruiz	Professor of Institutional Communication	Instituto Mexicano de Tecnología del Agua	Progreso-Jiutepec Cuernavaca, Morelos	Mexico
Doe	Mayer	Professor	University of Southern California	Los Angeles, CA	United States
Emile	McAnany	Professor	Santa Clara University	Santa Clara, CA	United States
Lisa	McArthur	Programme Manager, BCC	AMREF/Tanzania	Dar es Salaam	Tanzania
Neill	McKee	Chief of Party	Healthy Russia 2020	Moscow	Russian Federation
Steve	Menzies	Community Communications Specialist	Pacific Regional Environment Programme	Apia, Apia	Samoa
Maja	Micevska, PhD		University of Klagenfurt	Klagenfurt	Austria

(continued)

Full List of Participants (*Continued*)

Name	Last Name	Title	Organization	City	Country
Authors of Papers, *continued*					
Stefania	Milan		Inter-Press Service/ European University Institute	S. Domenico di Fiesole (FI)	Italy
Viola	Milton		University of Pretoria	Pretoria, Gauteng	South Africa
Gianluca Carlo	Misuraca		EPFL	Lausanne	Switzerland
Bella	Mody	Professor	University of Colorado	Boulder, CO	United States
Marisol	Moreno	Associated Professor	Universidad Nacional de Colombia	Bogotá, Cundi-namarca	Colombia
José Manuel	Moreno	President	Instituto Europeo de Comuni-cación y Desarrollo	Sevilla	Spain
Charles	Moumouni	Professor	Université Laval	Québec, Québec	Canada
Nancy	Muturi		Kansas State University	Manhattan, KS	United States
Marietjie	Myburg		Institute for Democracy in South Africa (Idasa)	Pretoria	South Africa

Nora Odoi	Naiboka	Development Communication Specialist	National Agriculture Research Organization (NARO)	Kampala	Uganda
Fabio	Nascimbeni		MENON Network	Bruxelles	Belgium
Leah	Nimoho		International Waterways Project		Vanuatu
Rachel	Nugent	Project Director	Population Reference Bureau	Bethesda, MD	United States
Rory	O'Connor	President and CEO	Globalvision, Inc.	New York, NY	United States
Yoshiko	Ogawa		Asian Institute of Technology	Phnom Penh	Cambodia
Ellyn	Ogden	USAID's Worldwide Polio Eradication Coordinator	USAID	Washington, DC	United States
Fiona	Otway	Project Director	Breaking the Silence	Seattle, WA	United States
Patrick	Papania	Senior Communications Strategist	Academy for Educational Development	Washington, DC	United States
Chitra	Pathak		One World South Asia	New Delhi, Delhi	India
April	Pojman		University of Guelph	Guelph, Ontario	Canada
Neeraja	Prabakar		Anna University	Chennai, Tamil Nadu	India

(*continued*)

Full List of Participants (*Continued*)

Name	Last Name	Title	Organization	City	Country
Authors of Papers, *continued*					
Maria	Protz		Independent Consultant	St. Ann's Bay, St. Ann	Jamaica
Wendy	Quarry	Senior Associate	New Economy Development Group	Ottawa, Ontario	Canada
Andres	Quispe Martinez	Consultant	World Bank	Lima	Peru
Prof. Sultan Muhammad	Razzak	Executive Director	Forum for Culture and Development	Dhaka, Dhaka	Bangladesh
Donna	Reyes	Professor	Miriam College	Quezon City	Philippines
Lina Maria	Salazar Garcia			Washington, DC	United States
Esca	Scheepers		*Soul City*	Johannesburg, Gauteng	South Africa
Beatriz	Schippner		Water and Sanitation Program	Lima	Peru
Ami	Sengupta	PhD Student	Ohio University	Baton Rouge, LA	United States
Mohammad	Shahjahan		Bangladesh Center for Communication Programs	Dhaka	Bangladesh
Arifa S.	Sharmin	Coordinator-External Relations	CARE, Bangladesh	Dhaka, Dhaka	Bangladesh
Dov	Shinar	Professor	College of Management	Tel Aviv	Israel

Terje	Skjerdal	Assistant Professor	Gimlekollen School of Journalism and Commu- nication	Kristiansand	Norway
Irela	Solórzano	Evaluation Coordinator	Fundación Puntos de Encuentro	Managua, Managua	Nicaragua
Christoph	Spurk		Institute of Applied Media Studies	Winterthur	Switzerland
Sanjay	Srivastava		Indian Forest Service	Ranchi, Jharkhand	India
Kautoa	Tonganibeia	International Waters Programme National Coordinator		Tarawa	Kiribati
Titus	Tossy	Executive Director	Kukaye, Inc.	Arusha	Tanzania
Josephine Irene	Uwamariya	Programme Manager	Health Unlimited	Butare, Butare Municipality	Rwanda
Elske J.	van de Fliert	Associate Professor	University of Queensland	Brisbane, Queensland	Australia
Nancy	Van Leuven	Ph.D. Candidate	University of Washington	Seattle, WA	United States
Manuel Jair	Vega	Assistant Professor	Universidad del Norte	Barranquilla	Colombia
Shree	Venkatram	Editor and Coordinator	Unnati Features	New Delhi	India
Vanessa	Vertiz Larrea	Communicator	Minga Peru	Lima, Lima	Peru
Prabhir	Vishnu	Business Adviser	Institute of Social Studies	The Hague	Netherlands
Ellen	Vorderbruegge	Vice President	Freedom from Hunger	Davis, CA	United States

(continued)

Full List of Participants (*Continued*)

Name	Last Name	Title	Organization	City	Country
Authors of Papers, *continued*					
V. L. V. Kameswari	Vyakaranam		G.B. Pant University of Agriculture and Technology	Pantnagar, Uttaranchal	India
Gregg	Walker	Professor	Oregon State University	Corvallis, OR	United States
Ana Maria	Zanotti	Independent Film Producer		Posadas, Misiones	Argentina
Jinqiu	Zhao	Associate Professor	Nanyang Technological University	Singapore	Singapore
Participants					
Mohamed	Abdel Aal	Professor of Agricultural Extension	University of Cairo	Cairo	Egypt, Arab Rep. of
Barbara	Affolter-Gomez	Programme Officer	Swiss Agency for Development and Cooperation	Bern	Switzerland
Sharad	Agarwal	Communications Officer, Department of Nutrition for Health and Development	WHO	Geneva	Switzerland
José Luis C.	Aguirre Alvis	Communication Specialist	SECRAD	La Paz	Bolivia
	Agyei-Amoama	Ambassador of Ghana		Rome	Italy
Cecilia	Agyeman-Anane		FAO, SDR	Rome	Italy
Johan	Akerblom	Assistant Director General, Information Department	SIDA	Stockholm	Sweden

Taysir	Al Ghanem	Information and Advocacy Manager, Resource Mobilization Division	IFAD	Rome	Italy
Fawzi	Al sultan	Consultant			Kuwait
Robyn	Alders	Director	The KYEEMA Foundation	Brisbane	Australia
Suhel	Al-Janabi	Chief Operations Officer	GeoMedia	Eschhorn	Germany
Bernadete	Almeida	Communication with Communities Coordinator	Fundação Vale do Rio Doce	Rio de Janeiro	Brazil
Michael	Als	Director	The TOCO Foundation	Toco	Trinidad & Tobago
Vanda	Altarelli	Indigenous Peoples Specialist	IFAD	Rome	Italy
Elena	Altieri	Communication Specialist	Inter-American Development Bank	Washington, DC	United States
Andrea	Ambrogetti		Municipality of Rome	Roma	Italy
Hussein Yousri	Amin	Professor and Chair, Department of Journalism and Mass Communication	American University in Cairo	Cairo	Egypt
Roberto	Amorosino	Senior Recruitment Officer	World Bank	Rome	Italy
Javier	Ampuero Albarracín		Calandria	Lima	Peru
Anne Christina	Andersson	Information Officer	Swedish International Development Cooperation Agency	Stockholm	Sweden
Margarita	Antonio	IP Communication Specialist	Radio Caribe/ URACCAN	Managua	Nicaragua

(continued)

Full List of Participants (*Continued*)

Name	Last Name	Title	Organization	City	Country
Participants, *continued*					
Subbiah	Arunachalam	Professor	M S Swaminathan Research Foundation	Chennai	India
Raimondo	Astarita		*Poste Italiane*	Rome	Italy
Domenico	Astarita		Sicurezza sul Lavoro	Rome	Italy
Ariane	Audigier		People Television	Saint Ouen	France
Beldina	Auma	Senior Communications Officer, External Affairs Group, Africa Region	World Bank	Washington, DC	United States
Francesco	Aureli			Rome	Italy
A.R.	Ayazi			Kabul	Afghanistan
Gabriela	Ayzanoa Peru	Founding Member	Milenia Radio	Lima	Peru
Stella	Babalola	Assistant Professor and Senior Evaluation Officer	Johns Hopkins Bloomberg School of Public Health—Center for Communication Programs	Baltimore, MD	United States
Marco	Baccin		Ministry of Foreign Affairs of Italy	Rome	Italy

Jorge	Ballestero	Head of Delegation	Permanent Mission of Costa Rica to the United Nations	New York, NY	United States
John	Bamba	Executive Director	Institute of Dayakologi	East Kalimantan	Indonesia
Antonio	Bancora		CESES	Milan	Italy
Amy Merrill	Bank	Executive Director	Puntos de Encuentro	Managua	Nicaragua
Carolin	Bansbach		GTZ	Eschborn	Germany
Guido	Barbera		Associazione ONG Italiane	Rome	Italy
Alfredo	Barnechea	External Relations Adviser	Inter-American Development Bank	Washington, DC	United States
Jon	Barnes	Head of Globalization	The Panos Institute	London	United Kingdom
Jeremy	Barnicle	Director of Communications	Mercy Corps	Portland, OR	United States
Alexander	Barranquero			Rome	Italy
Elisabeth	Barsk-Rundquist	Director	IFAD	Rome	Italy
Massimiliana	Baumann		Italian Association for Public Communication	Rome	Italy
Mohamed	Beavogui	Director of Western and Central Africa Division	IFAD	Rome	Italy
Sarah	Bel		CTA	Wageningen	Netherlands
Marco	Bellabarba		BNL	Rome	Italy

(continued)

Full List of Participants (*Continued*)

Name	Last Name	Title	Organization	City	Country
Participants, *continued*					
Belinda	Bergamaschi		European Commission	Brussels	Belgium
Luca	Bergamo	Director General	The Glocal Forum	Rome	Italy
Desiree	Berlangieri			Rome	Italy
Rosangela	Berman-Bieler	International Expert and Consultant		Washington, DC	United States
Gian Carlo	Bertoni			Rome	Italy
Romualdo	Bettini		Ministry of Foreign Affairs	Rome	Italy
Carlo	Bianchessi		Region Lombardia	Rome	Italy
Michael Cristian	Bieler	Assistant to Rosangela Berman-Bieler		Washington, DC	United States
Massimiliano	Bienati			Rome	Italy
Avinash	Bikha		Global Center for Information and Commu-nication Technologies in Parliament	Rome	Italy
Dennis	Bilodeau				
Honourable Rosy	Bindi	Minister of Family Planning	Government of Italy	Rome	Italy
William Robert	Bird	Director	The Media Monitoring Project		South Africa
Irma	Biseo		World Wildlife	Washington, DC	United States

Robert	Bisset	Spokesperson	UNEP Europe	Geneva	Switzerland
Kari	Blackburn		BBC World Service Trust	London	United Kingdom
Luciano	Blasi	Energy Manager		Rome	Italy
Stephanie	Blenckner	Communications Manager	Stockholm International Water Institute	Stockholm	Sweden
Claudio	Bocci		Federculture	Rome	Italy
Marie-Christine	Boeve	Communication Externe et Marketing	Coopération Technique Belge	Brussels	Belgium
Laura	Boldrini	Spokesperson	UN High Commissioner for Refugees	Geneva	Switzerland
Roxana	Bonnell	Deputy Director	Public Health Program Open Society Institute	New York, NY	United States
Teresa	Borelli			Rome	Italy
Francine	Bouchard		IDRC	Ottawa, Ontario	Canada
Dr Sarah	Bradshaw	Senior Lecturer	Middlesex University	Enfield	United Kingdom
Mathias	Braun	Supraregional Project on Knowledge Systems in Rural Development	GTZ	Eschborn	Germany
Laszlo	Breiner	Senior IT/Telecoms Specialist, Strategic Planning and Policy Division (BSP) Asia Branch	Canadian International Development Agency	Gatineau, Québec	Canada

(*continued*)

Full List of Participants (*Continued*)

Name	Last Name	Title	Organization	City	Country
Participants, *continued*					
Rosario	Brescia Franco		Telecom Italia	Rome	Italy
Paola	Brianti	Presidente Commissione Affari Comunitari e Internazionali	Consiglio Regionale del Lazio	Rome	Italy
Claudia	Brugnaletti		Associazione ONG Italiane	Rome	Italy
Gautier	Brygo	Project Manager	NGO Echos	Brussels	Belgium
Steve	Buckley	President	AMARC	Montreal, Québec	Canada
Margherita	Bufardeci		Relazioni Industriali	Rome	Italy
Eileen	Burke	Director, Special Projects	Save the Children	Westport, CT	United States
Maria I.	Busquets	Senior Adviser	DAI	Washington, DC	United States
Nestor	Busso	Vice President	ALER	La Paz	Bolivia
Christine	Butegwa		FEMNET	Nairobi	Kenya
Yves	Cabannes	Professor, Development Planning Unit	University College London	London	United Kingdom
Amparo	Cadavid Bringe	Academic Coordinator, Department of Communication	Universidad Javeriana	Bogotá	Colombia
Matteo	Calabresi			Rome	Italy
Ever Santiago	Calderon Amusquivar				
Agnes	Callamard	Executive Director	Article 19	London	United Kingdom
Alan	Campeau		IFAD	Rome	Italy

Mercedes	Campos	Consejo de Redacción	*Revista Enlace*	Managua	Nicaragua
José Edgardo	Campos	Lead Public Sector Specialist	World Bank	Washington, DC	United States
Indu Harkrishanlal	Capoor	Director	CHETNA	Gujarat	India
Mario	Cappellini		Telecom Italia	Rome	Italy
Lucio	Caracciolo		LIMES	Rome	Italy
Eleonora	Carcascio		UNICRE	Rome	Italy
Laura	Cardenas	Communication Officer	FAO Ecuador	Quito	Ecuador
Jossy	Cardenas		Movimiento Manuela Ramos	Lima	Peru
Sebastiano	Cardi		Ministry of Foreign Affairs of Italy	Rome	Italy
Monti	Carlo		RAI NET	Rome	Italy
Ulla	Carlsson	Director	Nordicom	Stockholm	Sweden
Luca	Carosella		Zone Attive	Rome	Italy
Jo	Carpenter		Panos	London	United Kingdom
Ana Filipa	Carvalho		Government of Timor-Leste	Díli	Timor-Leste
Sergio	Caserta		GVC	Rome	Italy
Marisol	Castañeda	Presidenta, Consejo Consultivo de Radio y Televisión	Ministerio de Comunicaciones	Lima	Peru
Libera	Cavaliere			Rome	Italy
Lothar	Caviezel	Head of Mission	Permanent Representation of Switzerland to FAO, IFAD, and WFP	Rome	Italy

(*continued*)

Full List of Participants (*Continued*)

Name	Last Name	Title	Organization	City	Country
Participants, *continued*					
Giulio	Cederna			Rome	Italy
Gunilla	Cederqvist	Information Department	SIDA	Stockholm	Sweden
Alessandro	Cenderello		Ernst & Young	Rome	Italy
Armando	Cerrato	Assistant FAO Representative	FAO	Managua	Nicaragua
Risha	Chande		Panos London	London	United Kingdom
Anuradha	Chandran		DFID	London	United Kingdom
Bogadi Kaseepathiah	Chandrashekar		Karnataka Legislative Council	Bangalore, Karnataka	India
Sandra	Charles	Senior Economic Policy Adviser, Economic Development, Policy Branch	Canadian International Development Agency	Gatineau, Québec	Canada
Chania	Charles	Deputy Director, Center for Civil Society and Governance	Academy for Educational Development	Washington, DC	United States
Prof. Claude-Yves	Charron	Vice President	Université du Québec à Montréal	Montreal, Québec	Canada
Naveed	Chaudhri		Oxfam Great Britain	London	United Kingdom
Raffaella	Chiodo		Movimondo	Rome	Italy
Tenzin	Chophel		Ministry of Agriculture of Bhutan	Thimphu	Bhutan

Francesca	Ciotti		Telecom Italia	Rome	Italy
Pierpaolo	Cito		*Poste Italiane*	Rome	Italy
Kirsty	Cockburn	Head of Communications	Overseas Development Institute	London	United Kingdom
Robert	Cohen	Regional Communication Officer	UNICEF TACRO	Panama City	Panama
Tom	Cohen	Media Relations Officer	Conservation International	Washington, DC	United States
Gabriella	Colella		*Poste Italiane*	Rome	Italy
Gherardo	Colombo	Judge	Supreme Court of Italy	Milan	Italy
Pierfrancesco	Consalvo		Cui Prodest LLC	Rome	Italy
Antonella	Cordono		IFAD	Rome	Italy
Franklin	Cornejo			Rome	Italy
Leonardo	Corsetti		Presidenza del Consiglio dei Ministri	Rome	Italy
Loretana	Cortis		*Poste Italiane*	Rome	Italy
Maryse	Coutsouradis		European Commission	Brussels	Belgium
Peter	Cranston	OKN, Communication Specialist			
Danilo	Crovella	Researcher in Communication for Development		Rome	Italy
Elisabeth	Crudgington		IUCN Commission on Education and Communication	Gland	Switzerland

(*continued*)

Full List of Participants (*Continued*)

Name	Last Name	Title	Organization	City	Country
Participants, *continued*					
William	Currie		Association for Progressive Communications	Melville	South Africa
Peter K. A.	da Costa	Coordinator	Strengthening Africa's Media Project	London	United Kingdom
PierLuigi	D'Agata		Assafrica	Rome	Italy
Massimo	D'aiuto		Simest	Rome	Italy
Mike	Daka	Owner and Manager	Breeze FM	Lusaka	Zambia
Pierpaola	D'Alessandro		Sviluppo Lazio	Rome	Italy
Susan	Dalgety		Scottish Government	Scotland	United Kingdom
Cecilia	Dall'Oglio		Focsiv	Rome	Italy
Martin	Dawes	UNICEF Regional Communication Adviser, South Asia	UNICEF	Thimphu	Nepal
Susana	de Funes Casellas	Communication Officer, Spanish Development Cooperation Agency	Ministry of Foreign Affairs of Spain	Madrid	Spain
Thierry	de Geyer d'Orth	Communication Officer	AFD (Agence Française de Développement)	Paris	France
Carla	De Gregorio		IFAD	Rome	Italy
Millogo	De Honore	Director	INADES	Ouagadougou	Burkina Faso

Antonio	de Martini		Incentive Spa	Rome	Italy
Cecilia	de Rosa	Training Officer, Staff Development Section	UN High Commissioner for Refugees	Geneva	Switzerland
Guillaume	de Saint Phalle	Deputy Director of Communication	AFD (Agence Française de Dévelop-pement)	Paris	France
Dr. Cobus	de Swardt	Director of Global Programmes	Transparency International	Berlin	Germany
Helga	de Vries	Administrative Assistant to Ruth Rawling	Cargill Europe	Minneapolis, MN	Germany
Ides	de Willebois	Country Programme Manager	IFAD	Rome	Italy
James	Deane	Managing Director, Strategy	Communication for Social Change Consortium	South Orange, NJ	United States
Anna Maria	Decorali		Ministry of Foreign Affairs of Italy	Rome	Italy
Prof. Flavio	Del Bono	Vice President	Regione Emilia Romagna	Bologna	Italy
Pietro	Del Sette		Movimondo	Rome	Italy
Martina	Delfino			Rome	Italy
Ulac	Demirag		IFAD	Rome	Italy
Chitra	Deshpande				
Paola	Di Gennaro			Rome	Italy
Antonietto	Di Gregorio		Government of Italy	Rome	Italy

(*continued*)

Full List of Participants (*Continued*)

Name	Last Name	Title	Organization	City	Country
Participants, *continued*					
Viviane	Di Majo		IFAD	Rome	Italy
Roberto	Di Vincenzo		Carsa Consulting	Rome	Italy
António	Dias	National Director	CORE Polio Eradication Team Angola	Luanda	Angola
Ambassador Amorim	Dias	Ambassador	Government of Timor-Leste	Brussels	Belgium
Janice	Dias	Social Programs Manager	Petrobras		Brazil
Francesco	Diasio		AMARC	Montreal, Québec	Canada
Paolo	Dieci	Director	CISP	Rome	Italy
Christopher	Dietz	Deputy Executive Director and South America	Cameco	Aachen	Germany
Jacques	Diouf	Director General	FAO	Rome	Italy
Vicente C.	Domingo	Presidente	Fundación Mundo 21	Madrid	Spain
Romeo	Dominguez Barradas			Rome	Italy
Stefania	Donaera		ActionAid International Italy	Rome	Italy
Marco	Donati			Rome	Italy
Thierry Charles	Doudet		CTA	Wageningen	Netherlands
Mohamed	Drabo		RECOM	Ouagadougou	Burkina Faso
Nicola	Drago	Expert in Project Evaluation and Management	ICS-UNIDO	Trieste	Italy

Darinka	Drapal	Managing Director	PR'P Odnosi z javnostmi	Ljubljana	Slovenia
Mojca	Drevenesk			Ljubljana	Slovenia
Aline	Duplaa		Public Health & Environment	Paris	France
Rosemary	Dzuvichu	Director	Mass Communication Centre	Nagaland	India
Alison	Eades	Geographical Coordinator and Supervisor for Asia and Central Asia	European Commission	Brussels	Belgium
Mark	Edwards	Director	Still Pictures	London	United Kingdom
Fabienne	Egal	Communication Specialist			
Madeline	Eisner	UNICEF Regional Communication Adviser, East Asia and Pacific	UNICEF	Bangkok	Thailand
Georges	Eliopoulos		European Commission DG Development	Brussels	Belgium
Tawfiq	El-Zabri		IFAD	Rome	Italy
Fatma	El-Zanaty	President	El-Zanaty & Associates	Giza	Egypt
Samuel	Eremie		IFAD	Rome	Italy
Anriette	Esterhuysen	Executive Director	Association for Progressive Communications	Melville, Gauteng	South Africa
Matilde Bernetti	Evangelista		COMPA	Rome	Italy
Alessandra	Fantini		Università La Sapienza di Roma	Rome	Italy

(*continued*)

Full List of Participants (*Continued*)

Name	Last Name	Title	Organization	City	Country
Participants, *continued*					
Patrizia	Faustini	Communication Assistant	UNICEF Innocenti Research Centre	Florence	Italy
Gabriella	Fava			Rome	Italy
Maria E.	Fernández	Research and Communication Specialist	International Support Group	Rome	Italy
Francesco	Ferrante	Senator	Parliament of Italy	Rome	Italy
Fiorella	Ferrari		Region Lombardia	Milan	Italy
Matilde	Ferraro		Associazione ONG Italiane	Rome	Italy
Mary Delcy	Figueroa Flores	Consultant		Rome	Italy
Maira Santanna	Fioravanti de Almeida			Rome	Italy
Dave	Fish	Director	DFID	London	United Kingdom
Siobhan	Fitzpatrick	Director	Children's Media Initiative	Belfast	Northern Ireland
Ross	Fitzpatrick		BBC World	London	United Kingdom
Janeth	Flores Rivas				
Elizabeth Anne	Fogarty	Information and Communication Officer	Directorate General for Development	Brussels	Belgium

			and Relations with the African, Caribbean and Pacific Countries		
Lauren	Fok		Association for Progressive Communications	Melville, Gauteng	South Africa
Cecilia	Fonseca	Project Manager	European Charter of Active Citizenship Network	Rome	Italy
Neil	Ford	Regional Adviser	UNICEF West Africa	Dakar	Senegal
Laura	Formica		*Poste Italiane*	Rome	Italy
Silvia	Francescon		Millennium Campaign, United Nations	Rome	Italy
Massimo	Franco		*Corriere della Sera*	Milan	Italy
Marco	Franza		ENEA	Rome	Italy
Colin	Fraser	Development Communication Consultant		Bogotá	Colombia
Teriana	Fratello			Rome	Italy
Musa	Freiji	President	The Wadi Group	Cairo	Egypt, Arab Rep. of

(*continued*)

Full List of Participants (*Continued*)

Name	Last Name	Title	Organization	City	Country
Participants, *continued*					
Chiara	Freschi	Researcher		Rome	Italy
Angela	Funes		Inter-American Development Bank	Washington, DC	United States
Laura	Gagliardone		IFAD	Rome	Italy
Prof. Michele	Gallina	Coordinatore Centro Dipartimentale Master, Media Management for Development e F.A.D	Università Europea di Roma	Rome	Italy
Michael	Galway	Chief, Programme Communication	UNICEF India	New Delhi	India
Domingos	Gama	Journalist	TVTL	Díli	Timor-Leste
Emilia	Gangemi		Gruppo Giovani Imprenditori di Roma, Unione Industriali	Rome	Italy
Emanuela	Gasbarroni	Journalist	TVE—MED	Florence	Italy
Piero	Gastaldo		Compagnia San Paolo	Rome	Italy
Jacob	Gayle	Vice President, HIV/AIDS	Ford Foundation	New York, NY	United States
Luca	Gentili		IULM	Rome	Italy
Nathalie	Gerbasi		CAF	Caracas	Venezuela, R. B. de
Anna	Gerrard		IICD	The Hague	Netherlands
Jorge	Gestoso		GTN	Washington, DC	United States
Gopi	Ghosh	Assistant FAO Representative	FAO	New Delhi	India
Romolo	Giacani		*Poste Italiane*	Rome	Italy

Honorable Luigi	Giacco		Ministry of Foreign Affairs of Italy	Rome	Italy
Marisa	Giannini		Poste Italiane	Rome	Italy
Dario	Giardi		Ministry of Environment of Italy	Rome	Italy
Stefano	Giovannelli	Director	UNIDO-IPO Italy	Rome	Italy
Bruce	Girard	Co-founder	World Association of Community Radio Broadcasters	Montreal, Québec	Canada
Josef	Girmai		*Fortune*	Addis Ababa	Ethiopia
Grace	Githaiga	Executive Director	EcoNews Africa	Nairobi	Kenya
Guilherme Canela de Souza	Godoi		ANDI	Brazilia	Brazil
Marcello	Goletti		MOVIMONDO	Rome	Italy
Emma	Grant		DFID	London	United Kingdom
Andrea	Grechi	Freelance journalist		Rome	Italy
Romily	Gregory	IT Project Manager	Oxfam	London	United Kingdom
Jeffrey J.	Grieco	Senior Deputy Assistant Administrator for Public Affairs	USAID	Washington, DC	United States
Luisa	Guarneri		FAO, GIIM	Rome	Italy
Juan Pablo	Guerrero	Comisionado	Instituto Federal de Acceso a la Información Pública	Mexico City	Mexico
Renato	Guimarães		Oxfam	Lima	Peru

(*continued*)

Full List of Participants (*Continued*)

Name	Last Name	Title	Organization	City	Country
Participants, *continued*					
Paul	Gully	Senior Adviser to Assistant Director General, Communicable Diseases	World Health Organization	Geneva	Switzerland
Alfonso	Gumucio Dagrón	Managing Director, Programs	Communication for Social Change Consortium	Guatemala City	Guatemala
José Luis	Guterres	Minister of Foreign Affairs	Government of Timor-Leste	Díli	Timor-Leste
Justino	Guterres		Government of Timor-Leste	Díli	Timor-Leste
May	Hani	Extension, Education and Communication Officer	FAO-RNE	Cairo	Egypt, Arab Rep. of
Teresa	Hanley	Director of Programmes	Panos	London	United Kingdom
Farhana	HaqueRahman		IFAD	Rome	Italy
Bambang	Harimurty	Chief Editor	*Tempo Magazine*	Jakarta	Indonesia
Saskia	Harmsen	Capacity Development Officer	IICD	The Hague	Netherlands
Paul	Harris	Head	Peace Initiative	San Antonio, TX	United States
Mark	Harvey	Director of Development	Internews Europe	London	United Kingdom
Jim	Harvey	Head of Sustainable Development, Environment	DFID	London	United Kingdom
Salvador	Herencia	Head of Communication and Partnership Unit	UNICEF Innocenti Research Centre	Florence	Italy

Lourdes	Hermosura-Chang	Information Associate	UN Special Unit for South-South Cooperation	New York, NY	United States
Kristina	Herngren	Organizational Development Officer, Communication for Development	Swedish Mission Council	Sundbyberg	Sweden
Gregory	Hess	Director	Peacepath Consulting Rome	Rome	Italy
Antoine	Heudre	Director	Sayara Media & Communications	Kabul	Afghanistan
Allison	Hewlitt		Bellanet International Secretariat	Ottawa, Ontario	Canada
David	Hoffman	Chairman	Global Forum for Media Development	Washington, DC	United States
Sara	Holst				
Annemarie	Hou	Director, Communication and Public Information	UNAIDS	Geneva	Switzerland
Matthew	Howick		Barkers Scotland	Glasgow, Scotland	United Kingdom
Rocio	Hurtado				
Paul	Hutchinson	Assistant Professor	Tulane University	New Orleans, LA	United States
Anwar	Ibrahim	Visiting Distinguished Professor	Georgetown University	Washington, DC	United States

(continued)

Full List of Participants (*Continued*)

Name	Last Name	Title	Organization	City	Country
Participants, *continued*					
Tonnie Osa	Iredia		Nigerian Television Authority	Abuja	Nigeria
Abiodun	Jagun		Association for Progressive Communications	Melville, Gauteng	South Africa
Dr Garth	Japhet	Executive Director	*Soul City*	Johannesburg, Gauteng	South Africa
Max	Jarrett	Officer-in-Charge, Information and Communication Service	UNECA	Addis Ababa	Ethiopia
W.	Jayaweera	Director, Division for Communication Development	UNESCO	Paris	France
Sergio	Jellinek	Communications Adviser	World Bank	Washington, DC	United States
Antonio Do Rosario	Joaquim				
Hilde	Johnson	Senior Adviser to the President	African Development Bank	Tunis	Tunisia
Susan	Jupp	Head, Communications and Information	Global Forum for Health Research	Geneva	Switzerland
Katri	Kaarniala	Director, Development Policy Information Unit	Ministry for Foreign Affairs of Finland	Helsinki	Finland
Mirgissa	Kaba	Program Officer, Youth Program Design	UNICEF Ethiopia	Addis Ababa	Ethiopia

Nickson Ochieng	Kakiri	Consultant		Nairobi	Kenya
Shalini	Kala		IFAD	Rome	Italy
Carol	Kalafatic	Community Development and International Policy Consultant			United States
Shanthi	Kalathil		USAID	Washington, DC	United States
Siapha	Kamara	CEO	SEND Foundation	Accra	Ghana
Henri	Kangete			Rome	Italy
Bevis	Kapaso	Monitoring and Evaluation Officer	Student Partnership Worldwide	Kabwe	Zambia
Sarah	Karinge	Development Consultant and Researcher	Vrije Universiteit Brussels	Brussels	Belgium
Nathaniel	Katinila	Consultant		Dar es Salaam	Tanzania
Nils	Katsberg		UNICEF TACRO	Panama City	Panama
Daniel	Kaufmann	Director of Global Programs	World Bank Institute	Washington, DC	United States
Ronald D	Kayanja		Panos Global Aids Programme	Lusaka	Zambia
Cornelis	Keijzer	Programme Assistant, Strategy and Innovation	European Centre for Development Policy and Management	Maastricht	Netherlands
Kevin	Kellems	Vice President for External Affairs	World Bank	Washington, DC	United States
Pareena	Khairdin		BBC World Service Trust	London	United Kingdom

(continued)

Full List of Participants (*Continued*)

Name	Last Name	Title	Organization	City	Country
Participants, *continued*					
John	Kidd	Communications Officer	IUCN—The World Conservation Union	Gland	Switzerland
Evelyn	Koch	Project Manager	Austrian Development Agency	Vienna	Austria
Aboubakar	Koda-Traoré	Programme Coordinator	CTA	Wageningen	Netherlands
Sebastian	Koeber		IFAD	Rome	Italy
Nicholas	Kori			Rome	Italy
Sabine	Krawitz		University of Catania	Catania	Italy
Padma	Kumar	Programme Officer	DFID India	New Delhi	India
Radhika	Lal	Policy Advisor, Bureau for Development Policy	UNDP	New York, NY	United States
Francesca	Lamanna		World Bank	Washington, DC	United States
Robert Paul	Lamb	Producer, DET TV (former)			Switzerland
Robin	Landis		World Food Program	Rome	Italy
Isabel	Lavadenz	Director, Latin America and the Caribbean Division	IFAD	Rome	Italy
Veronique	Le Vavasseur		FAO, SDR	Rome	Italy
Julien	Lecas	Chargé de mission à la sous-direction de la stratégie, des questions européennes et multilatérales	Ministère des affaires étrangères de France	Paris	France

James	Lenahan		Global Water Partnership	Stockholm	Sweden
Fabrizio	Lepri		Formazione e Comunicazione Interna	Rome	Italy
Paul	Lewis	Editor, Executive Briefing	The Economist Intelligence Unit	London	United Kingdom
Antonio	Lico			Rome	Italy
Clive	Lightfoot	Executive Director	ISG	West Sussex	United Kingdom
Paulo	Lima		Red de Informaciones para el Tercer Sector–Rits	Rio de Janeiro	Brazil
Helena	Lindborg		Panos	London	United Kingdom
Luis	Linde	Executive Director for Austria, Denmark, Finland, France, Norway, Spain and Sweden	IDB	Washington, DC	United States
Annette	Linden	PhD Student	Vrije University	Amsterdam	Netherlands
Geoffrey	Lipman	Assistant Secretary General	World Tourism Organization	Madrid	Spain
Roberto	Lippi		Ministry of Foreign Affairs of Italy	Rome	Italy
Jose Luis	Lobera		IDB	Washington, DC	United States
Fabrizio	Lonati		Ministry of Environment of Italy	Rome	Italy

(*continued*)

Full List of Participants (*Continued*)

Name	Last Name	Title	Organization	City	Country
Participants, *continued*					
Patricia	Lone	UNICEF Regional Communication Adviser, East and Southern Africa	UNICEF	Nairobi	Kenya
Philippe	Loop	Head of Information, Communication and Front Office—EuropeAid Cooperation Office	European Commission	Brussels	Belgium
Giancarlo	Loquenzi		Fondazione Magna Carta	Rome	Italy
Angelamaria	Loreto	Sociologist; Secretary General; Director	IPV; CEU Department of Information and Documentation	Rome	Italy
Maria Louisa	Loukopoulou	Expert Minister Counsellor, Hellenic Aid	Ministry of Foreign Affairs of Greece	Athens	Greece
Mark	Lowcock	Director General	DFID	London	United Kingdom
Bruno	Lucarelli			Rome	Italy
Vitullo	Luciana		*Poste Italiane*	Rome	Italy
Typhaine	Mace		Barkers Scotland	Scotland	United Kingdom
Dr Wade	Magatte	Principal Communications Officer	African Development Bank	Tunis	Tunisia
Charles	Magloire Le Combat		Public Health & Environment	Paris	France

Amar Jyoti	Mahapatra	Project Manager and Communications Adviser	Orissa Public Enterprise Reform Project	Bhubaneswar	India
Dr Cheick Omar	Maïga	Conseiller Technique Principal	FAO Cameroun	Yaoundé	Cameroon
Raghu	Mainaly	Founding President	Community Radio Association of Nepal	Kathmandu	Nepal
Bunmi	Makinwa	Head	UNAIDS Ethiopia	Addis Ababa	Ethiopia
Phil	Malone	Director	Countrywise Communication	Northants	United Kingdom
Wahba Mint	Maloum		FAO, SDR	Rome	Italy
Cynthia	Malvicini	Head, Public Information and Disclosure Unit, Department of External Relations	Asian Development Bank	Manila	Philippines
Olivier	Malvoisin	Film Director		Brussels	Belgium
Paolo	Mancini	Director, School of Journalism	University of Perugia	Perugia	Italy
Gianni	Manisco			Rome	Italy
Francesca	Manno		Ministry of Finance of Italy	Rome	Italy
Manuel	Manrique	UNICEF County Representative	UNICEF	Guatemala City	Guatemala
Fabio	Manzione	Agronomist; Secretary General	Action Committe for the Three Global Conventions	Roeme	Italy

(continued)

Full List of Participants (*Continued*)

Name	Last Name	Title	Organization	City	Country
Participants, *continued*					
Honourable Norbert	Mao	Governor	Gulu District	Gulu Municipality	Uganda
Sarah	Marciant				
Silvio	Marino		Regione Lazio	Rome	Italy
Jonathan	Marks			Amsterdam	Netherlands
Gabriella	Martini			Rome	Italy
Barbara	Marziali		Movimondo	Rome	Italy
Mustapha	Masmoudi	President	Association Tunisienne de la Communication	Tunis	Tunisia
Stephen	Masty	Consultant		London	United Kingdom
Federica	Matteoli		Ministry of Environment of Italy	Rome	Italy
Nelida Erendida	Matzar	Leader, Youth Peer Educator Group	Asociación Payasos Atz'anem k'oj	Iximulew	Guatemala
Blessing	Maumbe	Researcher	Cape Peninsula University of Technology	Cape Town	South Africa
Marta	Maurás	Secretary	Economic Commission for Latin America and the Caribbean	Santiago	Chile

Parkie Shakantu	Mbozi	Director	Panos Southern Africa	Lusaka	Zambia
Ida	McDonnell	Coordinator, Informal Network of DAC Heads of Information	OECD Development Cooperation Directorate	Paris	France
Brian	McCotter	Principal Consultant	PAConsulting	Arlington, VA	United States
Louise	McDonald		IFAD	Rome	Italy
Sandra	McGuire	Director of Communications	IFAD	Rome	Italy
James E.	McHale	Senior Vice President of Programs	Kellogg Foundation	Battle Creek, MI	United States
Mary Ann Joan	McKenna	Journalist		Minneapolis, MN	United States
Adriana	Medina	Communication Specialist			
Marie Anne	Medori		Ministry of Foreign Affairs of Italy	Rome	Italy
Molly	Melching	Executive Director	Tostan	Dakar	Senegal
Robert	Menard	Secretary General	Reporters sans Frontières	Paris	France
Pierluigi	Mennitti			Rome	Italy
Enrico	Mentana		Mediaset	Rome	Italy
Alessia	Mephalopulos			Rome	Italy
Lucina	Mercadante		INAIL	Rome	Italy
Gilles	Mersadier	Coordinateur FIDAFRIQUE	IFAD	Dakar	Senegal
Christian	Mersmann	Managing Director	IFAD	Rome	Italy
Cecilia	Mezzano			Rome	Italy
Irene	Mia		World Economic Forum	Geneva	Switzerland

(continued)

Full List of Participants (*Continued*)

Name	Last Name	Title	Organization	City	Country
Participants, *continued*					
François	Milis	Secretary General	NGO Echos	Brussels	Belgium
Doug	Miller		GlobeScan Incorporated	London	United Kingdom
Carol Lynn	Miller	International Communication Lead	American Red Cross	Washington, DC	United States
Cristian	Minelli		Fondazione Magna Carta	Rome	Italy
Massimo	Mirabella		Ministry of Environment	Rome	Italy
Cristina	Miranda Beas	Head of Communication	Consejo Nacional del Ambiente—CONAM	Lima	Peru
Linda	Mitchell	MSc Student	University of London	London	United Kingdom
Stefania	Mittica		Leonardo Business Consulting	Rome	Italy
Bruce	Moats	Senior Manager, Head of Corporate Relations	IFC	Washington, DC	United States
Martha	Mogus	Communication Officer	UNECA	Addis Ababa	Ethiopia
Lavinia	Mohr	Director of Programmes	World Association for Christian Communication	Toronto	Canada

John	Molefe	Senior Manager, Marketing and Public Affairs	Soul City	Johannesburg, Gauteng	South Africa
Honourable Nonofo Ezekiel	Molefhi	Member of National Assembly	Government of Botswana	Gaborone	Botswana
Gerardo	Mombelli			Rome	Italy
Eleonora	Mongelli		ERA ONLUS	Rome	Italy
Adriano	Montagni				Italy
Marco	Montrone		Ministry of Foreign Affairs of Italy	Rome	Italy
Antonio	Morabito	Counselor	Ministry of Foreign Affairs	Rome	Italy
Claudia	Mordini		Ministry of Finance of Italy	Rome	Italy
Sarah	Morgan		IFAD	Rome	Italy
Riccardo	Moro			Rome	Italy
Daniela	Morreale			Rome	Italy
Charlotte	Moser	Manager, Global Online Communities	Development Gateway Foundation	Washington, DC	United States
Guy-Loup	Motte	Director	TOTAL	Paris	France
Ziad	Moussa	Professor, Environmental and Sustainable Development Unit	American University of Beirut	Beirut	Lebanon
Geraldine	Mpoumalgmo		IFAD	Rome	Italy
Mary Margaret	Muchada	Ambassador and Permanent Representative of Zimbabwe	FAO	Rome	Italy

(continued)

Full List of Participants (*Continued*)

Name	Last Name	Title	Organization	City	Country
Participants, *continued*					
Lucy	Mulenkei	Chairperson	African Indigenous Women's Organi-zation—Indigenous Information Network of Africa	Nairobi	Kenya
Cristina	Müller	Communication Officer	UNECA	Addis Ababa	Ethiopia
Alexander Julius	Müller	Assistant Director General for Sustainable Development	FAO	Rome	Italy
Katiana	Murillo	Global Communications Officer	COM+ Alliance	San Jose	Costa Rica
Daniel	Murillo-Licea	President	IFSA		Mexico
Kumaran Shunmugam (Kumi)	Naidoo		CIVICUS World Alliance for Citizen Participation	Johannesburg	South Africa
Eliane	Najros	Project Coordinator	DIMITRA	Brussels	Belgium
Vikas	Nath	Special Adviser to the Executive Director	South Centre	Geneva	Switzerland
Maurizio	Navarra			Rome	Italy
Ibrahim	Ndjobdi Amadou		Mbororo Social and Cultural Development Association of Cameroon	Yaoundé	Cameroon

Tine	N'Doye	President	Rural Women Network of Senegal	Dakar	Senegal
Honorable Papa Kwesi	Nduom	Minister of Public Sector Reform	Government of Ghana	Accra	Ghana
Eskedar	Nega		Economic Commission for Africa	Addis Ababa	Ethiopia
Laura	Neuman	Assistant Director, Americas Program	The Carter Center	Atlanta, GA	United States
Hansjörg	Neun	Director	CTA	Wageningen	Netherlands
Honourable Lyonpo Sangay	Ngedup	Minister of Agriculture	Ministry of Agriculture	Thimphu	Bhutan
Salvatore	Nigro	Director Glocal Advocacy Department	The Glocal Forum	Rome	Italy
Ilaria	Nizzo		Focsiv	Rome	Italy
Sonia	Nobile		Associazione ONG Italiane	Rome	Italy
Hugo	Noe Pino	Executive Director for Central America and Belize	IDB	Washington, DC	United States
Alfredo	Noto		Comune di Roma	Rome	Italy
Nadia	Nsabimbona	PhD Student	Université de Genève	Geneva	Switzerland
Enrico	Nunziata		Ministry of Environment of Italy	Rome	Italy
Elizabeth	Nyawira			Rome	Italy

(*continued*)

Full List of Participants (*Continued*)

Name	Last Name	Title	Organization	City	Country
Participants, *continued*					
Esther	Obdam	Project Coordinator	Radio Netherlands Training Centre (RNTC)	Hilversum	Netherlands
Manfred	Oepen	Consultant		Jakarta	Indonesia
Dorothy	Okello	Coordinator	Women of Uganda Network	Kampala	Uganda
Joris	Oldenziel		SOMO—Centre for Research on Multinational Corporations	Amsterdam	Netherlands
Celeste	Oliphant				
Adebisi Samuel	Olowoyo	Corporate HSE Manager	Brass LNG Limited	Lagos	Nigeria
Rasha	Omar		IFAD	Rome	Italy
Dominic	Omolo	Information and Reporting Officer, Emergency Coordination Unit	FAO	Khartoum	Sudan
Lapo	Orlandi		Era Onlus	Rome	Italy
Collins Kwabena	Osei		Crops Research Institute	Kumasi	Ghana
Marie	Ouvrard	Researcher, Communication Anthropology	Nomadic Dream Machines	Paris	France

Vesper	Owei	Researcher	Cape Peninsula University of Technology	Cape Town	South Africa
Sue	Owen	Director General	DFID	London	United Kingdom
Jack Otieno	Owiti	Sign Language Interpreter		Nairobi	Kenya
Alessandro	Pacifici			Rome	Italy
Maria Grazia	Padoan			Rome	Italy
Josephine	Pagani	Communications Manager	OECD Development Co-operation Directorate	Paris	France
Giorgio	Pagano		Transnational Radical Party	Rome	Italy
Sara	Page	Deputy Director	SAfAIDS	Harare	Zimbabwe
Inga	Paichadze	Communications Officer	World Bank	Tbilisi	Georgia
Camilo	Palacios	Regional Communication and Public Relations Adviser for Latin America and the Caribbean	Plan International		Panama
Claudia	Palazzi			Rome	Italy
Sabine	Pallas			Rome	Italy
Klas	Palm		Amazonas Relationship Management Ltd	Stockholm	Sweden
Stephen	Palmer	CEO, Europe, United Kingdom, Middle East and Africa Operations	Lonely Planet	London	United Kingdom
Chase	Palmeri		IFAD	Rome	Italy
Alessandro	Palmieri	Lead Dam Specialist	World Bank	Washington, DC	United States

(continued)

Full List of Participants (*Continued*)

Name	Last Name	Title	Organization	City	Country
Participants, *continued*					
A. S.	Pannerselvan		Panos South Asia	Chennai	India
Maria Luisa	Panzica La Manna		Ministry of Economy and Finance	Rome	Italy
David	Paqui		IFAD	Rome	Italy
Ruggero	Parrotto		Relazioni Industriali	Rome	Italy
Anita	Pasha	Content Director	Rruga Sesam/ Ulitsa Sezam Sesame Kosovo Project	Pristina, Kosovo	Serbia
Mauro	Pasqualucci		Sace	Rome	Italy
Anna Maria	Pastore		Northwestern University	Chicago, IL	United States
Alessia	Pastorutti		Ministry of Foreign Affairs of Italy		Italy
Sala	Patterson		Peacepath Consulting Rome	Rome	Italy
B.K.	Pattnaik	Principal Secretary, Department of Public Enterprises and Chief Minister's Office	Government of Orissa	Orissa	India
Brenda Lee	Pearson		Cui Prodest LLC	Rome	Italy
Honourable Alfonso	Pecoraro Scanio		Ministry of Environment	Rome	Italy

Ludovico	Peirce		Arthur D. Little	MA	United States
Maria Carolina	Pellati	Head of Administration	Green Cross Italia Onlus	Rome	Italy
Giulio	Pelonzi		Municipality of Rome	Rome	Italy
Enrico	Pennarola		Leonardo Business Consulting	Rome	Italy
Francesca	Peraldo Bertinet		Ethics Governance	Rome	Italy
João Gomes	Pessoa Lima	Associate Director	MARAPA	São Tomé	São Tomé and Principe
Bernard	Petit	Deputy Director, DG Development	European Union	Brussels	Belgium
Amalia	Petriconi	Assistant to Paola Brianti	Consiglio Regionale di Lazio	Rome	Italy
Marco	Petrini			Rome	Italy
Stefania	Petrosillo			Rome	Italy
Norma	Pevell			Rome	Italy
Israel	Phiri	Chief Engineer	Ministry of Energy and Water Development of Zambia	Lusaka	Zambia
Danilo	Piaggesi	Chief, ICT for Development	Inter-American Development Bank	Washington, DC	United States
Paola Anna	Piccione			Rome	Italy

(continued)

Full List of Participants (*Continued*)

Name	Last Name	Title	Organization	City	Country
Participants, *continued*					
Anna	Pietikainen		IFAD	Rome	Italy
Anna Cristina	Pizzorno		Danae Communications Consulting	Rome	Italy
Beata	Plonka	Consultant	World Bank	Washington, DC	United States
Marialaura	Pollice		Regione Abruzzo	Rome	Italy
Deborah	Porter				
Giovanni	Posani		Arpes	Rome	Italy
Ignacio	Prafil	Indigenous Peoples Communication Specialist	ONPIA	Buenos Aires	Argentina
Hara	Prasad Padhy	Programme Specialist-Communication and Information, Communication and Information Sector, Communication Development Division	UNESCO	Paris	France
Simona	Primavera		Movimondo	Rome	Italy
Vanni	Puccioni	Regional Representative	TVE—MED	Florence	Italy
Marcovalerio	Pugini			Rome	Italy
Pierluigi	Puglia			Rome	Italy
Stefano	Puglia			Rome	Italy
Simone	Quatrini	Analyst	IFAD	Rome	Italy
Vicky	Quinlan		IFAD	Rome	Italy
Gabriele	Quinti		ALFABETA	Rome	Italy

Caroline	Rahal	Assistant Director, Communications Branch	Canadian International Development Agency	Gatineau (Québec)	Canada
Rinalia Abdul	Rahim	Executive Director	Global Knowledge Partnership Secretariat	Kuala Lumpur	Malaysia
Alessandra	Rainaldi		Italian Institute of Foreign Trade	Rome	Italy
Jeffrey	Raleigh		U.S. Department of State	Rome	Italy
Concepcion	Ramilo		Association for Progressive Communications	Melville, Gauteng	South Africa
José	Ramos-Horta	Prime Minister	Government of Timor-Leste	Díli	Timor-Leste
Hugo Guy	Raybaudo	Coordinator	Nomadic Dream Machines	Paris	France
Lara	Rayess Calvo		FAO, SDR	Rome	Italy
Roberto Maria	Razeto		IULM	Rome	Italy
Matteo	Rebesani		Municipality of Rome	Rome	Italy
Beatriz	Recio Aguado	Professor	Universidad Politecnica de Madrid	Madrid	Spain

(continued)

Full List of Participants (*Continued*)

Name	Last Name	Title	Organization	City	Country
Participants, *continued*					
Anke	Redl		Media Monitor	Beijing	China
Dennis	Redmont		The Council for the United States and Italy	Rome	Italy
Marja	Reina			Tegucigalpa	Honduras
Maria Grazia	Reitano		Telecom Italia	Rome	Italy
Sonia	Restrepo	Development Communication Consultant		Bogotá	Colombia
Julie	Reynes	Vice President for International Services	American Red Cross	Washington, DC	United States
Gerry	Reynolds	Head of Communications	Concern	Dublin	Ireland
Deborah	Rezzoagli	Area Manager for Europe	CISP	Rome	Italy
João Paulo	Ribeiro Capobianco	Secretary of Biodiversity and Forests	Ministry of Environment and Natural Resources	Brazilia	Brazil
Jenny	Richards		TVE—Television Trust for Environment and Development	London	United Kingdom
Chiara	Rinadlini		Ministry of Foreign Affairs of Italy	Rome	Italy

Eliana	Rioja	Communication Specialist	CIDOB	Santa Cruz	Bolivia
Carlos	Rivadeneyra	Comunicador	AMARC-ALC	Lima	Peru
Luz Marina	Rizo	Facilitadora	Iniciativa de Comunicadores para el Desarrollo	Managua	Nicaragua
Kina	Robberts	Senior Consultant in Communication			Sweden
Scott	Robinson	Professor of Anthropology	Universidad Metropolitana de Mexico	Mexico City, DF	Mexico
Elizabeth	Robinson	Deputy Director, Research Dissemination	Family Health International	New York, NY	United States
Josephine	Rodgers		Countrywise Communication	Wilby	United Kingdom
Adam	Rogers	Head of Communications and Public Information	United Nations Capital Development Fund	New York, NY	United States
Annette	Roman	Author	Viz Media	San Francisco, CA	United States
Isaia	Romanello			Rome	Italy
Susan	Rose-Ackerman	Co-director, School Center for Law, Economics and Public Policy and Head of Club de Madrid	Yale University	New Haven, CT	United States
Manuel	Rosini		World Bank	Rome	Italy
Gil	Rossellini	Producer			Switzerland
Silvia	Rossi		Federculture	Rome	Italy
Raul	Rupailaf Maichin	Director	Proyecto Origines	Santiago	Chile

(continued)

Full List of Participants (*Continued*)

Name	Last Name	Title	Organization	City	Country
Participants, *continued*					
Salvatore	Russillo		Government of Italy	Rome	Italy
Kambarami Lorraine	Rutendo		African Capacity Building Foundation	Harare	Zimbabwe
William N.	Ryerson	President	Population Media Center	Shelburne, VT	United States
Marianne	Sagen	Research Associate, Access to Information Programme	UNDP Oslo Governance Center	Oslo	Norway
Tebeka Aberra	Sahle	Media Pluralism Officer	Panos Eastern Africa	Kampala	Uganda
Chantal	Salako	Communication Specialist			
Silvan	Salako	Communication Specialist			
Seidy	Salas Viquez				
Sandra	Salazar	Director	Voces Nuestras	San José	Costa Rica
Charles T.	Salmon	Dean	Michigan State University	East Lansing, MI	United States
Roxanna	Samii		IFAD	Rome	Italy
Waheeda	Samji	Managing Director	Carpe Diem Ink	Dar Es Salaam	Tanzania
Simone	Santi		Leonardo Business Consulting	Rome	Italy
Nelson	Santos		Government of Timor-Leste	Díli	Timor-Leste

Fabio Maria	Santucci	Professor	University of Perugia	Perugia	Italy
Ashish	Sanyal	Director-eGovernance, Department of Information Technology	Government of India	New Delhi	India
Abba	Sanyang	Planning Officer, Directorate of Planning	Department of State for Education	Banjul	The Gambia
Maria	Saravia Paredes	Communication and Research	CIDOB	Santa Cruz	Bolivia
Anthony	Savadie	Project Manager, Proyecto Payaso	Asociación Payasos Atz'anem k'oj	Guatemala City	Guatemala
Filippo	Scammacca	Head of International Financial Institutions, Directorate General for Development Cooperation	Ministry of Foreign Affairs of Italy	Rome	Italy
Caetano	Scannavino	Director	Saúde e Alegria	Santarém, Pará	Brazil
Lucie	Scheepers	Project Assistant	CTA	Wageningen	Netherlands
GianMarco	Schiesaro	Communication Specialist		Rome	Italy
Emrys	Schoemaker		Panos	London	United Kingdom
Chantal J.	Schryer	Director, Communications and Government Relations	IDRC	Davos	Switzerland
Emanuela	Sciattella				Italy
Riccardo	Sciolti		TRASPORTI	Rome	Italy
Massimiliano	Scogna		ENEA	Rome	Italy
Costanza	Sebastiani		LUISS	Rome	Italy
Pietro	Sebastiani		Ministry of Foreign Affairs of Italy	Rome	Italy
Rahmatou	Seck	Director	Green Sénégal	Dakar	Senegal

(continued)

Full List of Participants (*Continued*)

Name	Last Name	Title	Organization	City	Country
Participants, *continued*					
Honorable Laurent	Sedogo	Minister of Environment	Government of Burkina Faso	Ouagadougou	Burkina Faso
Diane Annick Helene Elise	Senghor		Panos West Africa	Dakar	Senegal
Patrizia	Sentinelli	Vice Minister of Foreign Affairs	Government of Italy	Rome	Italy
Hani Mohamed Mousa	Serag	Director, Health Policies and Systems Programmes	AHED (Association for Health and Environmental Development)	Cairo	Egypt, Arab Rep. of
Antonio	Sergi		INTERSOS	Rome	Italy
Basheerhamad	Shadrach	Programme Manager	Telecentre.org South Asia Division	New Delhi	India
Minouche	Shafiq	Director General	DFID	London	United Kingdom
Murali	Shanmugavelan	Programme Officer	Panos Institute	London	United Kingdom
Pamela	Shao		World Food Program	Rome	Italy
Salil	Shetti	Director	The Millennium Campaign—UNDP	New York, NY	United States
Lora	Shimp	Senior Technical Officer, Immunization Basics	John Snow Institute	Washington, DC	United States
Thaninga	Shope-Linney	Head of Communications and Outreach	NEPAD	Johannesburg, Gauteng	South Africa

Ambasciatore Francisco	Sigarro			Rome	Italy
Julien	Signolet	Expert in Communication Systems	Nomadic Dream Machines	Paris	France
Jacopo	Signorile			Rome	Italy
Joanne Marcia	Silberner	Health Journalist	National Public Radio	Washington, DC	United States
Guillermo	Siles Paz	Comunicador Social	ALER	La Paz	Bolivia
Paolo	Silveri		IFAD	Rome	Italy
Massimo	Simone		*Poste Italiane*	Rome	Italy
Mikias	Sissay	Coordinator of Communication and Information Management Unit	FAO	Addis Ababa	Ethiopia
Toni	Sittoni	Communications Specialist, Water and Sanitation Program-Africa Region	World Bank	Nairobi	Kenya
Birir	Sittoni			Rome	Italy
Dr. Faouzi	Skali	Director General	The Fès Festival of Sacred World Music	Milan	Italy
Leticia	Soberon Mainero	Coordinator, Red Informatica de la Iglesia en America Latina	Pontifical Council for Social Communications	Vatican City	Vatican
Henry-Bernard	Solignac-Lecomte	Head of Unit, Policy Dialogue and External Cooperation	OECD Development Co-operation Directorate	Paris	France
Jean Baptiste	Sourou, phd		Università Gregoriana a Roma	Rome	Italy

(*continued*)

Full List of Participants (*Continued*)

Name	Last Name	Title	Organization	City	Country
Participants, *continued*					
Sioasi	Sovaleni	Adviser, Information, Communication and Technology, Pacific Gender and Energy Network	South Pacific Applied Geoscience Commission	Suva	Fiji
Fatoumata	Sow	Coordinator, Project CMC	UNESCO	Dakar	Senegal
Theodosia	Sowa	Policy Adviser and Consultant		London	United Kingdom
Franco	Spicciariello		Microsoft	Rome	Italy
Martina	Spisiakova		IFAD	Rome	Italy
Fr. Jacob	Srampickal	Director of CICS	Pontificia Università Gregoriana	Roma	Italy
Patrik	Stalgren	Expert in Infrastucture and Governance	University of Gothenberg	Gothenberg	Sweden
Urbano	Stenta	Counselor	Ministry of Foreign Affairs of Italy	Rome	Italy
Mark	Sterling	Regional Director East and Southern Africa	UNAIDS	Johannesburg, Gauteng	South Africa
Joseph	Stiglitz	Professor	Columbia University	New York, NY	United States
Marie	Struthers	Programme Manager	Open Society Foundation	London	United Kingdom
Teresa H.	Stuart	Regional Adviser	UNICEF	Kathmandu	Nepal

Denise	Stuckenbruck	Coordinator of Program and Communication of the Save the Children Sweden for Latin America and the Caribbean	Save the Children Suécia		Peru
Fr. Bernardo	Suate		Signis Services Rome	Rome	Italy
Aruna	Sundararajan	CEO, Common Services Centre Initiatives	Government of India	New Delhi	India
Vittoria	Taborelli		Ministero dell'Ambiente e della Tutela del Territorio	Rome	Italy
Mervat	Tallawy	Executive Secretary	UN Economic & Social Commission for Western Asia	Beirut	Lebanon
Stefania	Tamborini		Region Lombardia	Rome	Italy
Prof. Yash	Tandon	Executive Director	South Centre	Geneva	Switzerland
Carlo	Tassara	Director	CISP	Rome	Italy
Victoria	Tauli-Corpuz	Chairperson	UN Permanent Forum on Indigenous Issues		Philippines
Eamoinn	Taylor	Head of Development Section	DFID	London	United Kingdom
Tesfai	Tecle	Assistant Director General	FAO	Rome	Italy
Giorgio	Tellini		Sace	Rome	Italy
Lucinda	Terrazas Herbas			Rome	Italy

(continued)

Full List of Participants (*Continued*)

Name	Last Name	Title	Organization	City	Country
Participants, *continued*					
Maria Letizia	Tesorini			Rome	Italy
Gopakumar	Thampi	Executive Director	Public Affairs Foundation	Bangalore	India
Jeanette	Thomas	CGAP Communications Manager	World Bank	Washington, DC	United States
Yvonne	Thomas		Panos	London	United Kingdom
Dick	Thompson	Team Leader, Pandemic and Outbreak Communication Communicable Diseases Section	WHO	Geneva	Switzerland
Mauricio	Tolosa	Director Ejecutivo	Proyecto Origenes	Santiago	Chile
Victoria	Tomás	Evaluator	Asociación Payasos Atz'anem k'oj	Iximulew	Guatemala
Arno	Tomowski	Head, Environment and Infrastucture Division	GTZ	Eschborn	Germany
Gianpaolo	Toriello		Finmeccanica	Rome	Italy
Oscar	Toro Peña	Head of Communication	Doñana 21	Almonte, Huelva	Spain
Elauli	Torres	Rural Sustainable Development Specialist			Germany
Paola	Tovar	Head of Communication	Municipality of Bogotá	Bogotá	Colombia
Lena	Tranberg	Information Officer	Ministry of Foreign Affairs of Sweden	Stockholm	Sweden

Valeria	Trapanese		Italian Ministry of Environment	Rome	Italy
Jean-Philippe	Tre	Agricultural Economist, Middle East and North Africa Region	World Bank	Washington, DC	United States
Marina	Troiani		*Poste Italiane*	Rome	Italy
Bernard	Trude	Executive Director	Healthlink Worldwide	London	United Kingdom
Adelaida	Trujillo	Director	Citurna and Fundación Imaginario	Bogotá	Colombia
Tiziana	Turcio	Webmaster	Green Cross Italia Onlus	Rome	Italy
Wilberforce	Tushemereirwe	Head	National Banana Program	Kampala	Uganda
Jashim	Uddin		Ajker Khabar		Bangladesh
Cristina	Usubiaga		Hobbs International	Winnipeg, Manitoba	Canada
Matthew	Uzzell	Senior Consultant, Communications and Aid Effectiveness	Adam Smith International	London	United Kingdom
Nikki	Van der Gaag	Lead Rapporteur	Panos	London	United Kingdom
Sara	Vari		Budapest University	Budapest	Hungary
Mitu	Varma	India Director	Panos South Asia	Chennai	India
Jorge Iran	Vasquez Zeledon	Forestry Engineer		Managua	Nicaragua
Dr Luis Felipe	Vega	Consultant		Bogotá	Colombia

(continued)

Full List of Participants (*Continued*)

Name	Last Name	Title	Organization	City	Country
Participants, *continued*					
Mignone Sanchez	Vega	Secretary	Presidency of Nicaragua	Managua	Nicaragua
Judith	Veldhuizen	Programme Officer, Knowledge Sharing	IICD	The Hague	Netherlands
Anja	Venth	Editorial Director	The Communication Initiative	Johannesburg	South Africa
Ambassador Sergio	Vento	Senior Adviser	McDermott Will & Emery	Rome	Italy
Gabor	Vereczi	Programme Officer	World Tourism Organization	Madrid	Spain
Vittorio	Viccardi			Rome	Italy
Marco	Vicenzino	Consultant	World Bank	Washington, DC	United States
Tim	Vickery II	Development Communications and Aid Effectiveness Specialist		Stockholm	Sweden
Rosa Maria	Vidal	Deputy Director	Pro-Natura Chiapas	San Cristóbal de las Casas, Chiapas	Mexico
Geraldo	Vieira	Communication Director	AVINA Foundation	Rio de Janeiro	Brazil
Paolo	Viero		Ministry of Foreign Affairs of Italy—DGCS	Rome	Italy
Maura	Viezzoli	Head of Innovation and Resources	CISP	Rome	Italy

Marco	Vignudelli	Press Officer	Directorate General for Development and Relations with the African, Caribbean, and Pacific Countries, EU	Brussels	Belgium
Juan Jose	Vilacha Velasco			Rome	Italy
Silvia	Villani		Com-PA	Rome	Italy
Maria Elena	Villar			Rome	Italy
Robin	Vincent		Panos	London	United Kingdom
Gloria	Visconti	Director General	Ministry of Environment of Italy	Rome	Italy
Ma. Theresa Danguilan	Vitug	Editor in Chief	*Newsbreak*	Pasig City	Philippines
Carlo	Viviani		Presidenza del Consiglio dei Ministri	Rome	Italy
Juergen	Voegele	Sector Manager, Environmentally and Socially Sustainable Development, Europe and Central Asia Region	World Bank	Washington, DC	United States
Marco Claudio	Vozzi		Ministry of Foreign Affairs of Italy	Rome	Italy
Loredana	Vullo		The Roman Forum	Rome	Italy

(*continued*)

Full List of Participants (*Continued*)

Name	Last Name	Title	Organization	City	Country
Participants, *continued*					
Silvio	Waisbord	Senior Program Officer, Advocacy	Academy for Educational Development	Washington, DC	United States
Peter	Walker		Pielle Consulting Group	London	United Kingdom
Chris	Wallace	Managing Director	Barkers Scotland	Glasgow, Scotland	United Kingdom
Ian	Walmark	Research Director	HKO Research Institute	Ontario	Canada
Jonathon	Walter		International Federation of the Red Cross and Red Crescent Societies	Geneva	Switzerland
Muthoni	Wanyeki	Executive Director	FEMNET	Nairobi	Kenya
Denise Patricia	Waples				
Armorer	Wason		Panos	London	United Kingdom
Corentin	Wauters	Journalist	The Roman Forum	Rome	Italy
Kosima	Weber		Internews Europe	Paris	France
Jo Lin	Weir		Reuters Foundation	London	United Kingdom
John	West	Executive Director	Internews Europe	Paris	France

Keith	Wheeler	Chairman	IUCN Commission on Education and Communication	Gland	Switzerland
Jon	White			London	United Kingdom
Anette	Widholm Bolme	Regional Adviser Culture and Media Southern Africa and Sida HIV/AIDS team	SIDA	Lusaka	Zambia
Jeannette	Wijnants	Country Manager	Health Unlimited	Kigali	Rwanda
Susanne	Willner	Program Manager, Pilot Project Rioplus	GTZ	Eschborn	Germany
Kevin Robert	Wilson	Head of Communications	BBC World Service Trust	London	United Kingdom
Ellen	Winters	Presidential Management Fellow	U.S. Mission to the UN Agencies in Rome	Rome	Italy
Jacek J.	Wojciechowicz	Senior Communications Officer	World Bank	Warsaw	Poland
Paul	Wu		IFAD	Rome	Italy
Matthew	Wyatt	Assistant President	IFAD	Rome	Italy
Peter	Young	International Director	Adam Smith International	London	United Kingdom
Ellen	Yount	Senior Adviser, Development Outreach and Communications	USAID/MSI	Washington, DC	United States
Faria	Zaman		World Food Program	Rome	Italy

(*continued*)

Full List of Participants (*Continued*)

Name	Last Name	Title	Organization	City	Country
Participants, *continued*					
Elena	Zambelli		Ministry of Foreign Affairs of Italy—DGCS	Rome	Italy
Arturo	Zamora	Sociologist		Managua	Nicaragua
Nicola	Zamperini		Regione Lazio	Rome	Italy
Tommaso	Zanaica	Project Organizer	NGO Echos	Brussels	Belgium
Jo	Zaremba		Oxfam	London	United Kingdom
Silvana	Zeppieri		*Poste Italiane*	Rome	Italy
Veruschka	Zilvetti			Rome	Italy
Susan	Zimicki	Senior Technical Adviser	Academy for Educational Development	Washington, DC	United States
Melanie	Zipperer	Senior Communication Officer, Independent Evaluation Group	World Bank	Washington, DC	United States
Alessandro	Zurzolo		Bilancio	Rome	Italy

APPENDIX 2

Media Attendees

Name	Title	Media Organization
A		
Atiya Achakulwisu	Assistant Editor	*Bangkok Post*
Aram Aharonian	Director General	Telesur
Washington Akumu	Journalist	National Media Group
Aboubakr Al Jamai	Editor in Chief	*Le Journal*
Mansoor Al Jamri	Editor in Chief	Al Wasat
Cristián Alarcón	Journalist	Freelance
Susan Alexander	Journalist	IPS
Massimo Angelilli	Journalist	Freelance
Lucia Araujo	General Manager and Journalist	FUTURA/TV Globo's educational channel
Datuk Azman Ujiang	Editor in Chief	*Biznes-vestinik Vostoka*
B		
Vincenzo Baldelli	Cameraman	Telegiornale 3/Tg 3 RAI
Daniela Bandelli	Journalist	MAE
Constanza Barone	Journalist	CBS NEWS
Ikiebe Barth	Journalist	Voice of Nigeria
Massimiliano Belli	Journalist	Ufficio Stampa Anti Corruzione
Claudio Brufola	Freelance	Freelance
Patrick Butler	Vice President, Programs	International Center of Journalists
C		
Leopoldo Calabria	Journalist	AMARC
Alan Camargo	Journalist	Radio Vaticano
Agneta Carleson	Journalist	Global Reporting
Tiziana Caroselli	Journalist	ANSA
Giuseppe Carrisi	Journalist	RAI International
Valentina Cavicchiolo	Journalist	RAI News 24

(*continued*)

Name	Title	Media Organization
Giulio Cederna	Delegate	AMREF
Jemaiyo Chabeda	Journalist	Africa Network for Environmental Journalists-ANEJ
Mohuya Chaudhuri	Producer	New Delhi Television
Sukhdev Chhartbar	Correspondent	Daily News AP
Stefania Coccato	Journalist	APCOM
Jenine Coezer	Reporter	Channel Africa
Anna Agnese Costa	Journalist	AISM
Mónica Cuevas	Journalist	Freelance
D		
Pietro Del Salda	Journalist	AMREF
Luigina D'Emilio	Journalist	*L'Unità*
Raimondo Deriu	Journalist	*il Velino*
Antonio Devito	Journalist	*Corriere di Roma*
Pierluca Di Pasquale	Filmmaker	EarthLive Channel
Piero Di Pasquale	Journalist	RAI News 24
Monica Di Sisto	Journalist	ASCA
Claudia Diez De Medina	Journalist	IPS
Georges Drouet	Journalist	*Prospective Internationale*
Frederic Dubois	Journalist	ACP News
Lucas Duran	Journalist	Radio Vaticana
E		
Imad El Atrache	Brussels Bureau Chief	Al Jazeera
Eman Embaby	Editor	Al Ahram
F		
Lucia Ferrari	Journalist	Telegiornale 3/Tg 3 RAI
Lenise Figuredo	Journalist	TV Globo
Ross Fitzpatrick	Journalist	BBC
Roberto Formicola	Journalist	Freelance
Marina Forti	Journalist	*il Manifesto*
Elena Frova	Journalist	Fox
Matthias Funk	Journalist, Head of the School of Journalism in Edinburgh	ARD
G		
Aldo Garzia	Journalist	ASCA
Duilio Giammaria	Journalist	RAI

Name	Title	Media Organization
Carmine Giannattasio	Journalist	RAI News 24
Maria Gabriella Giannice	Journalist	ANSA
Anna Maria Giordano	Journalist	RAI—Radio 3 Mondo
Roberto Gisotti	Journalist	Radio Vaticana
Celestin Gnonzion	Journalist	Freelance
Gustavo Gonzales	Journalist	School of Journalism, Chile
Gustavo Gorriti	Investigative Journalist	*La Prensa,* Panama and *Caretas* Peru
Riccardo Grassi	Journalist	IPS
Marta Guglielmetti	Journalist	Millennium Campain
Gabriella Guido	Delegate	AMREF
H		
Aziz Hakimi	Executive Director	The Killid Media Group
Bambang Harimurty	Editor	*Tempo*
Deon M. Higgins	Journalist	*Carib News*
Philippa Hitchen	Journalist	Radio Vaticana
Monika Hoegen	Freelance Journalist/ Reporter	*Deutsche Welle*
Shuli Hu	Editor	*Jianging*
I		
Mojahidul Islam	Technical Editor	eBiz/Ittefaq Group of Publications
Saiful Islam	Senior Reporter	BSS Center for Social Communities
K		
Tanya Kahrzstan	Journalist	Freelance
Henri Kangete	Delegate	AMREF
Herman Keppy	Journalist	Focus (ND)
Louis Keumayou	President	Panafrican Press Association
Nicholas Kori	Delegate	AMREF
Prashant Kumar Aryal	Assistant Editor	*Nepal National Weekly*
Rahul Kumar	Web Editor	Oneworld South Africa
L		
Dinesh Lakhanpal	Journalist	Lakhanpal Productions
Maria Amparo Lasso	Journalist	Tierramerica

(*continued*)

Name	Title	Media Organization
Olayinka Lere	Journalist	*The Class News*
Carl Gustav Linden	TV Journalist	Finnish Broadcast Corporation TV
Alessandra Lombardi	Journalist	ANSA
Angelo Loy	Journalist	AMREF Italia
Mario Lubetkin	Director	IPS
Clare Lyons	Producer	BBC
M		
Massimiliano Maggi	Cameraman	RAI International
Giuseppe Mancini	Journalist	RAI News 24
El Nemr Mandi	Journalist	Kuwait News Agency
Gianno Andrea Manisco	Journalist	Liberazione
Galdiero Marino	Journalist	Radio Inblù
Davison Maruziva	Editor	*The Zimbabwe Standard*
Alex May	Journalist	Radio Vaticana
Claudia Mazzaferro	Journalist	EarthLive Channel
Joseph Mballa Zang	Journalist	Radio Reine
Antonio Mendoza	Journalist	Associazione della Stampa Estera/ Freelance
Karen Molgaard	Managing Editor	World Development
Stefano Monciotti	Journalist	Globecast
Carlo Monti	Journalist	RAI
Roberto Montoya	Journalist	Metropolis (Gruppo Espresso)
Goffredo Morgia	Journalist	Inform
Antonia Moro	Journalist	RAI Economics
John Muiruri	Delegate	AMREF
Alessandro Mulieri	Journalist	Dire
N		
Renata Negri	Journalist	Reporter Gestione Editoriali/Freelance
Anadou Ibrahim Njobdi	Journalist	Radio Campus
Marco Nuzzo	Journalist	RAI Net
Elizabeth Nyawira	Delegate	AMREF
O		
Rory O'Connor	Journalist	CBS
Jimmy Okello	Journalist	Radio Apac
Francesca Oliverio	Journalist	Ecoradio
Pietro Orsetti	Journalist	Arcoiris TV

Name	Title	Media Organization
Mario Osorio	Journalist	Notimex—Mexico
Souleymane Ouattara	Coordinator	interf@ce
P		
Micol Pancaldi	Journalist	Freelance
Alberto Passalacqua	Journalist	Telegiornale 3/Tg 3 RAI
Marta Petrosino	Journalist	SIR
Dario Pettinelli	Journalist	ITALIA TV
Giuliana Pigliucci	Journalist	VIS
Ferruccio Piluddu	Journalist	Orizzonti
Lawrence Pintak	Director	Adham Center for Electronic Journalism, The American University in Cairo
Stefano Polidori	Technician	Globecast
Arial Prashant Kumar	Journalist	*Nepal National Weekly*
David Prosser	Executive Producer	BBC
Q		
Emilio Quinto	Journalist	Wawe Europe
R		
Xosé Ramil	Journalist	Canal Solidario One World
Sandra Ramirez	Journalist	Radio Vaticano
Waldir Ramos Ary	Journalist	Freelance
Khalifa Reem	Journalist	Al Wasat
Maurizio Regosa	Journalist	VITA
Gerry Reynolds	Head of Communications	Concern Worldwide
Kristina Robberts	Journalist	Global Reporting
Maurizio Roberto	Journalist	Freelance
Roberto Romagnoli	Journalist	*Il Messagero*
Isaia Romanello	Delegate	AMREF
Maria Teresa Ronderos	Journalist	*Semana*
Umberto Rondi	Journalist	Freelance
Giampaolo Rossi	Journalist	PRESS RAI NET
S		
Stephen Sackur	Presenter	BBC
Salah Al Bazzaz	Journalist	Ufficio Stampa Araba Della FAO
Giancarlo Santoni	Managing Director	EarthLive channel
Flavio Santoro	Journalist	Fox

(*continued*)

Name	Title	Media Organization
Giovanni Scafuro	Journalist	Ufficio Stampa Anti Corruzione
Alessandro Scattone	Cameraman	RAI International
Joanne Silburner	Health Reporter	NPR
Marco Silenzi	Journalist	RAI News 24
Tommy Simmons	Delegate	AMREF
Roberto Simon	Journalist	*Lecturas*
Victor Soholwicz	Journalist	Freelance
Ramata Sore	Journalist	L'Evènement
Ibrahima Soumare	Director	Africa Television News
Gianbattista Sourou	Journalist	Radio Vaticana
Giavanni Spinelli	Journalist	IPS
Lidia Spoto	Journalist	RAISAT
Stefano Carofei	Journalist	Agenzia AGF
Claudia Stila	Journalist	ZIVA
T		
Paolo Tata Nardini	Journalist	Freelance
Luca Tenti	Journalist	Freelance
Derek Thorne	Freelance Journalist	BBC
Henri Thuo	Delegate	AMREF
Aldo Torchiara	Journalist	Sky
Maria Triglia	Journalist	Figlie di Maria Ausiliatrice
Nello Trocchia	Journalist	Ecoradio
U		
Jashim Uddin	Executive Editor	Ajker Khabar
V		
Euridice Vásquez Oviedo	Editor	Latin American Network
Giuseppe Vazzano	Journalist	RAI News 24
Svletlana Vdovina	Deputy Editor in Chief	*Biznes Vestnik Vostoka*
Gaia Vendettuoli	Journalist	AGI Cooperazione
Rodrigo Vergara	Journalist	Arcoiris TV
W		
Emma Wallis	Radio Producer	BBC
Charmaine Wilkerson	Journalist	FAO, CBS NEWS
Wandji Wandji Willy	Producer	UICN Radio Environnement
Kevin Wilson	Head of Communications	BBC
Josef Woldekidan Girmai	Editor in Chief	*Fortune*

Name	Title	Media Organization
Alex Wood	Production Assistant	BBC
David Wood	Regional Projects Manager, SE Asia	BBC
Y		
Aiguo Yang	Journalist	Agenzia Stampa Nuova Cina
Z		
Maria Zampaglione	Communication Officer	OIE
Luciana Zanuccoli	Journalist	TV Danese NRV
Elena Zervopoulou	Delegate	AMREF
Rosina Zimbaro	Journalist	RAI America
Irene Zissimos	Executive Producer	EarthLive Channel

APPENDIX 3

Communication for Development: Making a Difference

A WCCD Background Study

Jan Servaes (Editor)
Nicholas Carah
Martin Hadlow
Eric Louw
Pradip Thomas
University of Queensland

Silvia Balit
Independent Consultant

Maria Celeste H. Cadiz
University of the Philippines Los Baños

Nabil H. Dajani
American University of Beirut

Cees J. Hamelink
University of Amsterdam

Thomas Jacobson
Temple University

Ullamaija Kivikuru
University of Helsinki

John Mayo
Florida State University

Rafael Obregón
Ohio University

Douglas Storey
Johns Hopkins University

Thomas Tufte
Roskilde University

Karin Gwinn Wilkins
University of Texas at Austin

January 1, 2007

The current conception of Communication for Development can be summarized in the Rome Consensus document prepared and endorsed by the participants of the first World Congress on Communication for Development: "a social process based on dialogue using a broad range of tools and methods. It is also about seeking change at different levels including listening, building trust, sharing knowledge and skills, building policies, debating and learning for sustained and meaningful change. It is not public relations or corporate communication."

Development communication creates mechanisms to broaden public access to information, empowers grassroots communities to be involved in participatory communication processes, and enables communication activities that are grounded in research (World Bank 2006a). This document highlights three key themes that formed the main framework of the World Congress on Communication for Development: Sustainable Development, Health, and Governance. The fourth area of interest forming the basic structure of the Congress was labeled Communication Labs. It included sessions dealing with cross-cutting issues relevant to communication methods, media, and ICTs (information and communication technologies). Since methodological issues are addressed throughout the various sections and given their growing relevance, the authors of this paper decided to focus on ICTs as a fourth area of interest.

The cross-cutting and flexible nature of Communication for Development allows its application regardless of the sector in which it is being used. The themes being dealt with in the Congress and in this publication are by no means the only ones where Communication for Development can make a difference. They have been chosen for practical reasons, based on a number of criteria (mainly their priority in the current development agenda of policy makers) deemed appropriate by the organizing bodies of the Congress. This was consistent with the main goal of the Congress, mainstreaming Communication for Development.

Communication is a needed ingredient to guarantee sustainable development, and that is why it has been instrumental in contributing to the success of many sustainable development programs throughout the developing world. For instance, the innovative Rural Communication System established within PRODERITH (*Programa de Desarrollo Rural Integrado del Trópico Húmedo*) in Mexico in the 1980s is still today an example of the successful use of communication for participatory planning, social change, and sharing of knowledge and skills. Communication for Development approaches have been successfully used in a number of local development projects, such as in Cambodia, where indigenous knowledge has been a valuable input to achieve successful and sustainable results.

Health and development communication has become crucial, as wider development strategies have begun to focus on social and public health. Critical development issues and goals such as population and family planning, primary health care, maternal and child health and, most recently, HIV/AIDS have focused attention on the role of communication in public health programs. Effective health communication programs integrate their strategy in targeting individuals, policy makers, and practitioners. For example, Egypt's Health and Population Program (1980–2006) has reduced the average number of children born in a woman's lifetime. This was made possible by long-term multisectoral commitment at the highest levels of the Egyptian government to support national, regional, and local communication programs. In Uganda, a current youth reproductive health program uses a radio serial to engage with cultural attitudes toward sex: the program promotes open public discussion to break through taboos and shift social gender norms that put Ugandan youth at risk.

Governance and development communication reinforces the importance of an engaged and active civil society, especially in developing countries. For example, in India, growing literacy rates have increased the demand for newspapers. This, coupled with media liberalization and a need to locate new markets, has led to local newspapers becoming important sources of information and dialogue in rural areas. The vibrancy of these local newspapers demonstrates the possibilities for the liberalization of other media channels, especially radio, which could enable the development of dialogue and debate leading to people-oriented social change.

Being part of the wider discipline of Communication for Development, ICTs can be used in any sector or development. They are important tools in efforts to achieve the Millennium Development Goals (MDGs) in health, education, and community development. They can deliver a range of services, help capacity building, empower communities, and bridge social divides. For example, rural artisans in Thailand are now able to use the Internet to market their crafts to a global audience. Urban women in Senegal use the power of networked technologies to advocate for gender policies on employment and for environments conducive to entrepreneurial activities by women. The Virtual Souk project for artisans in the Middle East and North Africa provides people the opportunity to maintain their traditional livelihood as craftspeople through a system of locally controlled Web e-commerce. The use of ICTs, however, needs to be carefully weighed, planned, and integrated into a wider communication approach, in order to avoid the pitfalls first encountered when the blind faith in mass media led to great expectations about their capacity to foster national development, expectations that were hardly met.

Even if limited by the themes treated for the purpose of this paper, several policy recommendations are made in key areas in order to advance the theory of the discipline and practice in the field. Recommendations cover legal and supportive frameworks required, donor coordination, and policy trajectories to establish a supportive environment in which Communication for Development can continue to flourish. Within these frameworks, specific institutional structures, training, and capacity-building initiatives are recommended to support best-practice programs that are given long-term funding support and integrated across themes. The recommendations also include support for ICTs and the needed "technological and cultural capital" that enable the poor, marginalized and indigenous to harness Communication for Development and social change. Finally, recommendations are made to continue a theoretical practice of Communication for Development to support applied efforts in the field.

Communication for Development is brought about by people who are involved in participatory communication processes that facilitate a sharing of knowledge in order to effect positive development change. There is no universal formula capable of addressing all situations and, therefore, Communication for Development and social change initiatives should be based on, respond to, and adapt to the cultural, social, political, and economic context. Communication that underpins and leads to successful and sustainable development places the people who are most affected at the center of the discussions, debates, choices, and decisions needed to guide their own development.

Introduction

When Nelson Mandela called on the world to "make poverty history," his words rang loud and clear across the globe, reverberating in the hearts of millions. "Poverty is not natural," he reminded us all. “It is man-made and it can be overcome and eradicated by the actions of human beings.”

But how far has humankind come in the last 50, 20, or even 10 years in achieving the goal of freeing people from what Mandela called “the prison of poverty”? In the year 2006, it is estimated that 1.3 billion people worldwide still live in absolute poverty. Most are in developing countries, but poverty also reaches into industrial regions, such as North America and Europe.

The MDGs set by the member states of the United Nations strive to address critical poverty issues and solve some of the most pressing problems within the next decade. But will they be successful? Are citizens in donor countries fatigued by endless calls to arms? Is there really light at the end of the long, dark tunnel of inequality? Why have we not yet resolved the key problems? Is there enough political will and commitment? And have any poverty alleviation solutions of the past really worked?

In the 21st century, humanity holds within its grasp some of the most powerful technologies ever invented. In particular, modern communication tools have enabled us to make the world a smaller place, as well as providing us with gateways to knowledge and pathways to information. However, these very structures, without which the global economy would not function and humankind would not be able to instantly communicate across continents, have been relatively marginalized as partners in the development process. Now is the time to recognize the potential and power of these instruments and to utilize them in unshackling people from their “prison of poverty.”

But Communication for Development and social change is more than satellite television, community radio, mobile phones, ICTs, and the Internet. Certainly, it can call on all these resources. However, at its heart, it is about individuals and about employing the most appropriate methods and tools to facilitate positive change, empowering those individuals to set their own agendas and achieve their own defined goals. Often, development projects and programs have stalled, reversed, or even failed for want of simple communication discourse with the recipients. Thus, just as it is unthinkable that an engineer would build a road in Europe or construct a bridge in North America without discussion and interaction with the end users, so it should be mandatory that the clientele of any donor-funded development project be fully involved in the design, planning, and outcome-setting process from the outset of that project's genesis. To do otherwise flies in the face of reason. The logic seems obvious. However, every day, donors defy logic by planning grand visions without once consulting with those who will live with the decisions. Therefore, development projects necessarily have to engage with power relationships among the various stakeholders.

For more than 60 years, Communication for Development professionals have been working with grassroots communities to break the cycle of habit and further enable end users to interact with donors, not just as partners in development, but as leaders in their own advancement. Countless examples exist of measurable outcomes where the "value added" of communication has aided the successful implementation of worthwhile and life-changing programs and where locally designed best practices are working to "make poverty history."

Communication that underpins and leads to successful and sustainable development action puts the people who are most affected at the center of the discussions, debates, choices, and decisions needed to guide their own development. It is a sociocultural process of dialogue, information sharing, building mutual understanding, agreeing to collective action, and amplifying the voice of people to influence policies that affect their lives. It makes use of a variety of communication vehicles from mass to community media and new technologies to traditional and folk media and interpersonal communication. Its central goal is to empower people to take action to positively effect their own development according to their own cultural and social needs and requirements.

Communication for Development, therefore, utilizes the society's entire communication system including interpersonal, social, community, organizational networks as well as conventional and electronic media, in a communication environment that underpins knowledge and media accessibility, content diversity, and good governance.

To work most effectively, Communication for Development requires an enabling environment that includes

- Free, independent, and pluralistic media systems, accountable to their audiences, through which open dialogue and debate can occur
- Open, transparent, and accountable government that encourages public debate, discussion, and input

- Broad public access to a variety of communication media and channels, as well as a regulatory environment that promotes pro-poor licensing for local radio and low-cost universal access to Internet and telephone services
- An open society in which all groups and sectors are able to participate fully in development discussions, debates, and decision-making processes

Nelson Mandela's 2005 call to the world to "make poverty history" recognized this environment. He said that we live in "times in which the world boasts breathtaking advances in science, technology, industry, and wealth accumulation." However, given that islands of plenty exist within a sea of injustice, he ranked the scourges of poverty and inequality "alongside slavery and apartheid as social evils."

For fatigued citizens in donor countries, is it a battle lost or a battle that can be won? The World Bank has estimated that it would require the contribution of only 1 percent of developing countries' consumption to abolish extreme poverty. The Food and Agriculture Organization of the United Nations (FAO) goes a step further in simplifying the challenge and presenting it in more personal terms. It says that a contribution by the citizens of developed countries of just US$13 per person per year would solve the problem of poverty—a small price to pay to "make poverty history."

The Basics of Communication for Development

Historians have eloquently explained how each historical epoch has had to solve a particular problem. While feeding the people was the major challenge during the agricultural age, the industrial age provided material well-being. Now we are said to be living in the information age, with its demands on ever more and faster (universal) services. In each epoch initial problems of scarcity (hunger, poverty, and information poverty) have been taken over by more sophisticated structural problems: overabundance (pollution and waste, extreme wealth, and information overload), inequality (ecological, economic, educational, and cultural) and (digital and other) divides. In this overview, we wish to concentrate on the issue of "Communication for Development," sometimes also called "development communication" or "communication for social change." How to deal with these issues in real-world environments will be the key challenge for citizens, and how to regulate this in a democratic way will be the challenge for public authorities.

Academics can assist citizens and public authorities in structuring the debate and identifying the real issues. However, government officials, practitioners, and others working in the development field may have different perceptions of what the defining characteristics of development communication are. Early in its history, some spoke of it as "development support communication," suggesting that the communication function was a subcomponent of various development sectors. Today some argue that development communication should itself be a sector.

The suggestion has also been made that development communication is interpersonal communication and that mass communication is something else. Others would argue that a "development communication" approach dominated by face-to-face communication has inherent limitations if one measure of success is widespread change of behavior in short periods of time, a goal that might be highly appropriate in some circumstances. Framing the discussion as mediated communication versus face-to-face communication is probably not the best approach.

This topic can be addressed according to the different perspectives on communication and the relative functions they are expected to perform. They are usually divided in two broad camps (which will be discussed in more detail in the following pages). One camp envisions communication as a way of organizing and delivering information in order to fill knowledge gaps or persuade audiences to change their intended behavior. The other perspective considers communication more broadly, going beyond the delivery of information and envisioning it as a process needed to build trust, seek consensus, and assess the situation involving all stakeholders. It is a process contextual to the situation where it is occurring, hence based on the specific sociocultural environment.

Within these two perspectives, there are a number of other intermediate ones, even if each of them would tend to be closer to one of the two perspectives mentioned above. The approaches related to the first perspective are often linked to diffusion models and tend to rely more heavily on mediated communication, either alone or in conjunction with interpersonal communication. The opposite is true in the case of the second perspective.

Clearly the role of media and new ICTs is affecting both perspectives and though there are different ideas about how they could best be used for development purposes, their role is considered important. Usually media and ICTs are seen in isolation neither from the overall communication effort, nor from other channels being used.

One could, for instance, examine the role and benefits of radio versus the Internet in terms of their impact on development and the emergence of democratic institutions. Both the Internet and the radio enhance certain kinds of interactivity. However, if, as many believe, better access to information, education, and knowledge would be the best stimulant for development, the Internet's primary development potential is as a point of access to the global knowledge infrastructure. The danger, now widely recognized, is that access to knowledge increasingly requires a telecommunication infrastructure that is inaccessible to the poor. There also is a danger that the ICT thrill may weaken the potential embedded in radio: governments tend to be very careful about the local empowerment capacity of local radio and hence control the license procedures very strictly, while the ICT does not often meet such an indirect resistance. Therefore, the digital divide is not about technology per se, but rather about the widening gaps between the developed and developing worlds and the information-rich and the information-poor.

While the benefits offered by the Internet are many, its dependence on a telecommunications infrastructure means that they are only available to a few. Radio, on the other hand, is a much more pervasive, accessible, and affordable medium for most people. Blending the two could be an ideal way of ensuring that the benefits accruing from the Internet have wider reach.

Since the Second World War, Communication for Development is no longer predominantly, or even exclusively, focused on information dissemination and the diffusion of innovations. The scope of Communication for Development has broadened to include the interpersonal dimension, that is, dialogue, which is needed to achieve mutual understanding, build trust, and seek consensus, thus facilitating the achievement of sustainable changes. This means that communication should not be included only halfway through the project, but it should be a key ingredient from the beginning of any development initiative. However, the responsibilities of donors and development agencies should also be looked at in a more structural and historical way. They have both supported certain modes of communication (like community radio in the 1980s and early 1990s and the ICTs nowadays) and muffled down certain modes (such as public service broadcasting in the past 15–20 years in the name of media independence and pluralism) via their financing decisions.

THEORIES AND MODELS

After the Second World War, the founding of the United Nations Organization (UNO) stimulated relations among and between sovereign states, not only the North Atlantic nations and developing countries, but also the new states emerging out of a colonial past. During the cold war period the superpowers—the United States and the former Soviet Union—tried to expand their interests in the developing countries.

In fact, the United States was defining development and social change as the replica of its own political-economic system and opening the way for the transnational corporations. At the same time, the developing countries saw the "welfare state" of the North Atlantic nations as an appropriate one for their own development. These nations were attracted by new technologies and the advantages of state planning in agriculture, education, and health, as well as communication. They also viewed development as a unilinear, evolutionary process. Underdevelopment was seen in the quantifiable differences between so-called poor and rich countries on the one hand, and traditional and modern societies on the other hand (for more details on these paradigms, see Servaes [1999, 2003]).

As a result of the general intellectual "revolution" that took place in the mid-1960s, this Western or ethnocentric perspective on development was challenged by Latin American social scientists, and a theory dealing with dependency and underdevelopment was born. The dependency approach formed part of a general structuralist reorientation in the social sciences. The *dependistas* were primarily concerned with the effects of dependency in "peripheral" countries, but implicit in their analysis was the idea that development and underdevelopment must be understood in the context of the world system.

This dependency paradigm played an important role in the movement for a new world information and communication order from the late 1960s to the early 1980s. During this period, the new states in Africa and Asia and the success of socialist and popular movements in Cuba, China, Chile, and other countries were striving for political, economic, and cultural self-determination within the international community of nations. These new nations shared the goal of independence from the superpowers and moved to form the nonaligned nations. Contrary to the North Atlantic nations, which viewed development and modernization primarily in terms of economic growth, the nonaligned movement defined development as political struggle.

Since the demarcation of the First, Second, and Third Worlds has broken down and the cross-over between center and periphery can be found in every region, there emerged a concept of development that emphasized cultural identity and multidimensionality. The present-day "global" world, in general, as well as in its distinct regional and national entities, is confronted with multifaceted crises. Apart from the obvious and ongoing economic and financial crisis, social, ideological, moral, political, ethnic, ecological, and security crises also have appeared. By the same token, the previously held dependency perspective has become more difficult to support because of the growing interdependency of regions, nations, and communities. From the criticism of the two paradigms above, particularly that of the dependency approach, a new viewpoint on development and social change has come to the forefront. The common starting point here is the perspective of "bottom-up" self-development at the community level. At the same time, it is assumed that there are no countries or communities that function completely autonomously or that are completely self-sufficient, nor are there any nations whose development is exclusively determined by external factors. Every society is dependent in one way or another, both in form and in degree. Thus, a framework was sought within which both the center and the periphery could be studied separately and in their mutual relationship.

More attention is also being paid to the content of development, which implies a more normative approach. "Another development," a term first coined by the Dag Hammerskjöld Foundation in the late 1970s, questions whether or not "developed" countries are in fact advanced and whether or not their achievements are sustainable or even desirable. It favors a multiplicity of approaches based on the context and the basic, felt needs, and the empowerment of the most oppressed sectors of various societies at divergent levels.

A main thesis is that change must be structural and occur at multiple levels in order to achieve desirable ends.

DIFFUSION AND PARTICIPATORY COMMUNICATION

The above more general typology of development paradigms (for more details, see Servaes [1999, 2003]) can also be found at the communications and culture level. The communication media are, in the context of development, generally used to support development initiatives by the dissemination of messages that encourage the public to support development-oriented projects. Although development strategies diverge widely, the usual pattern for broadcasting and the press has been predominantly the same: informing the population about projects, illustrating the advantages of these projects, and recommending that they be supported. A typical example of such a strategy is situated in the area of family planning, where communication media such as posters, pamphlets, radio, and television attempt to persuade the public to accept birth control methods. Similar strategies are used in health and nutrition campaigns, agricultural and education projects, and the like.

This model portrays the communication process as one of messages going from senders to receivers. This hierarchic view on communication can be summarized in Laswell's classic formula, "Who says What through Which channel to Whom with What effect?" and dates back to (mainly American) research on campaigns and diffusions in the late 1940s and 1950s. The American scholar Everett Rogers (1962) was the first to apply diffusion theory within a developmental context. Building primarily on sociological research in agrarian societies, Rogers stressed the adoption and diffusion processes of cultural innovation. The mass media were especially important to him in spreading awareness of new possibilities and practices. At the same time, he noted that interpersonal communication was instrumental in persuading people to adopt innovations.

Subsequent development communication theorists claimed that Rogers' approach to development communication was severely limited. They argued that the diffusion model is a vertical or one-way perspective on communication, and that sustainable change occurs through people's active involvement in the process. Research has shown that while people can obtain information from impersonal sources like radio and television, such information has relatively little effect on behavioral changes.

The participatory model, on the other hand, views change within a framework of multiplicity. It stresses the importance of cultural identity of local communities and of democratization and participation at all levels—international, national, local, and individual. It points to a strategy, not merely inclusive of, but largely emanating from, the traditional "receivers." Paulo Freire (1983: 76) refers to this as the right of all people to individually and collectively speak their word: "This is not the privilege of some few men, but the right of every (wo)man. Consequently, no one can say a true word alone—nor can he say it for another, in a prescriptive act which robs others of their words." In order to share information, knowledge, trust, commitment, and participation are required. Reflecting on this view, the International Commission for the Study of Communication Problems, chaired by the late Sean MacBride, argued that "this calls for a new attitude for overcoming stereotyped thinking and to promote more understanding of diversity and plurality, with full respect for the dignity and equality of peoples living in different conditions and acting in different ways" (MacBride 1980: 254).

Naturally, embracing one or the other of these two conceptual perspectives carries a number of implications in the application of daily practices. Approaches close to the diffusion model are aimed at filling information gaps or persuading people to change behaviors through ad hoc messages. Despite the refined level of feedback included in these models, the flow remains basically linear, and the outcome is usually predetermined (for example, use condoms). Approaches in participation, on the other hand, have a heuristic connotation, using dialogue to build bridges between different groups of stakeholders in order to explore options and identify the best course of action for change. The communication flow is circular, as the sender and the receiver operate as a single entity, and the outcome is usually largely shaped by whatever the result of the interaction is. This is perhaps why they are most useful in exploring and assessing the situation at the initial phases of the intervention.

The adoption of a participatory model in communication does not lead to a model opposing its predecessor, but, rather, it broadens the scope of communication. In some ways, it breaks out of the traditional boundaries of communication, since it aims not only to inform or transmit specific messages, but it also uses its communicative and cross-sectoral nature to build trust, exchange knowledge and perceptions, investigate problems and opportunities, and finally reach a consensus on the intended change among all stakeholders (Mefalopulos 2005). Thus, the scope of Communication for Development broadens beyond the transmission and sharing of information and includes the empirical research and joint definition of problems and solutions with the participation of relevant stakeholders.

UNDERLYING PREMISES

The coherence of "Communication for Development and social change" is expressed in its different common underlying premises that incorporate:

- *The use of a culturalist viewpoint*
  By means of such a viewpoint specific attention is given to communication in social change processes. By highlighting the importance of other social science disciplines can significantly contribute to the field of "Communication for Development and social change."
- *The use of an interpretative perspective*
  Participation, dialogue, and an active vision of human beings as the interpreters of their environments are of the utmost importance. Respect and appreciation must be shown for the uniqueness of specific situations and identities in social change environments.
- *The use of integrated methods and theories*
  In the field of "Communication for Development and social change," it is important that research methods are connected to one's theoretical perspective. Development communication requires openness, diversity, and flexibility in its methods and techniques. In practice it generally means triangulation and a preference for qualitative methods. This does not mean, however, that quantitative methods are excluded, and indeed an emphasis is placed on evidence-based scientific methodologies.
- *To show mutual understanding and attach importance to formal and informal intercultural teaching, training and research*
  Tolerance, consciousness-raising, acceptance, and respect can only be arrived at when members of different cultures not only hear but also understand each other. This mutual understanding

is a condition for development and social change. In order to prevent all forms of miscommunication, intercultural awareness, capacity building, and dialogue are deemed to be very important.

FROM THEORY TO PRAXIS

As noted throughout this section, a variety of theoretical models can be used to devise communication strategies for development. In contrast with the more economically and politically oriented approach in traditional perspectives on modernization and development, the central idea in alternative, more culturally oriented versions of multiplicity and sustainable development is that there is no universal development model that leads to sustainability at all levels of society and the world, that development is an integral, multidimensional, and dialectic process that can differ from society to society, community to community, context to context. As each case and context is different, none has proven to be completely satisfactory. In other words, each society and community must attempt to delineate its own strategy to sustainable development. This implies that the development problem is a relative problem and that no one society can contend that it is "developed" in every respect. Therefore, we believe that the scope and degree of interdependency must be addressed in relationship with the concept of development.

Many practitioners find that they can achieve the greatest understanding by combining more than one theory or developing their own conceptual framework. Where previous perspectives did not succeed in reconciling economic growth with social justice, an attempt should be made to approach problems of freedom and justice from the relationship of tension between the individual and the society, and limits of growth and sustainability are seen as inherent to the interaction between society and its physical and cultural ecology.

The so-called Copenhagen Consensus Project is worth mentioning in this context. Though still dominated by economic perspectives and researchers (some of them Nobel Prize winners), the panel of experts evaluated a large number of development recommendations, drawn from assessments by UN agencies, and identified 10 core challenges for the future:

- Civil Conflicts
- Climate Change

- Communicable Diseases
- Education
- Financial Stability
- Governance
- Hunger and Malnutrition
- Migration
- Trade Reform
- Water and Sanitation

The major challenge identified by this panel was the fight against HIV/AIDS. (For more details, see a number of reports in *The Economist,* April–June 2004; or visit http://www.copenhagen-consensus.com.)

Distinct development communication approaches and communication means used can be identified within organizations working at distinct societal and geographic levels. Some of these approaches can be grouped together under the heading of the above diffusion model, others under the participatory model. The major ones could be identified as follows (for more details, see Servaes and Malikhao [2004]):

- Extension/Diffusion of Innovations as a Development Communication Approach
- Network Development and Documentation
- ICTs for Development
- Social Marketing
- Edutainment (EE)
- Health Communication
- Social Mobilization
- Information, Education, and Communication (IEC)
- Institution Building
- Knowledge, Attitudes, and Practices (KAP)
- Development Support Communication (DSC)
- HIV/AIDS Community Approach
- Community Participation

This report presents a summary of four themes that have been selected as the backbone of the first World Congress on Communication for Development since they are key for current Communication for Development initiatives, incorporating some of the above-mentioned approaches. The four themes are: (a) Communication in Sustainable Development, (b) Communication for Development in Health, (c) Communication for Development in Governance, and (d) ICTs for Development.[1]

Though it is realized that there are many more themes that could be explored under the broad theme of "Communication for Development," there are a number of reasons why the overview is limited to these four. Time pressures, intellectual limitations to cover such a varied and complex field, relevance in the development agenda, and academic considerations are the obvious ones. From a research perspective, different kinds of evidence exist for different types of outcomes. The evidence for social structural change (for example, empowerment, equity, policy change) is largely of the anecdotal or qualitative type, and evidence for individual change (for example, behaviors including participation, efficacy/self-confidence, gender attitudes, and the like) is predominantly quantitative. There is nothing wrong with anecdotal and qualitative evidence, but they invite different inferences. On the other hand, quantitative evidence may provide short-term advice, which is not reliable for long-term or contextualized recommendations. It is possible to quantify higher-order changes, but to do so requires methodological approaches that few projects have the time, resources, or donor support to undertake.

Current Communication for Development Initiatives

COMMUNICATION IN SUSTAINABLE DEVELOPMENT

> *"Communication for Development is a social process, designed to seek a common understanding among all the participants of a development initiative, creating a basis for concerted action."*
>
> —FAO (1984)

Perspectives and challenges

Communication for sustainable development theory and practice have been changing over time in line with the evolution of development approaches and trends and the need for effective applications of communication methods and tools to new issues and priorities.

Communication in sustainable development has addressed the specific concerns and issues of food security, rural development and livelihood, natural resource management and environment, poverty reduction and equity, and gender and ICTs.

In the last 20 years, sustainable development has emerged as one of the most prominent development paradigms. In 1987, the World Commission on Environment and Development (WCED) concluded "sustainable development is development that meets the needs of the present without compromising the ability of future generations to meet their own needs" (Elliott 1994). Three dimensions are generally recognized as the "pillars" of sustainable development: economic, environmental, and social.

Different perspectives have, over the years, influenced the holistic and integrated vision of sustainable development. Nevertheless, a unifying theme is that there is no universal development model. Development, as indicated earlier, is an integral, multidimensional, and dialectic process that differs from society to society, community to community, context to context. In other words, each society and community must attempt to delineate its own strategy to sustainable development starting with the resources and "capitals" available (not only physical, financial, and environmental but also human, social, institutional, and so on) and considering needs and views of the people concerned. Sustainable development implies a participatory, multistakeholder approach to policy making and implementation, mobilizing public and private resources for development and making use of the knowledge, skills, and energy of all social groups concerned with the future of the planet and its people. Within this framework, communication plays a strategic and fundamental role by (a) contributing to the interplay of different development factors, (b) improving the sharing of knowledge and information, and (c) encouraging the participation of all concerned.

Approaches and guiding principles

In line with this vision, at the end of the 1980s the participatory approach became a key feature in the applications of Communication for Development to sustainable development. Development communication is about dialogue, participation, and the sharing of knowledge and information. It takes into account the needs and capacities of all concerned through the integrated and participatory use of communication processes, media and channels. It works by

- Facilitating participation by giving a voice to different stakeholders to engage in the decision-making process
- Making information understandable and meaningful. It includes explaining and conveying information for the purpose of training, exchange of experience, and sharing of know-how and technology
- Fostering policy acceptance by enacting and promoting policies that increase rural people's access to services and resources

Within this framework, communication is viewed as a social process that is not just confined to the media or to messages. Development communication methods are appropriate in dealing with the complex issues of sustainable development in order to

- Improve access to knowledge and information to all sectors of the society and especially to vulnerable and marginalized groups
- Foster effective management and coordination of development initiatives through bottom-up planning
- Address equity issues through networking and social platforms influencing policy making
- Encourage changes in behavior and lifestyles, promoting sustainable consumption patterns through sensitization and education of large audiences
- Promote the sustainable use of natural resources considering multiple interests and perspectives, and supporting collaborative management through consultation and negotiation
- Increase awareness and community mobilization related to social and environmental issues
- Ensure economic and employment opportunities through timely and adequate information
- Solve multiple conflicts ensuring dialogue among different components in a society

Guiding principles

Approaches differ according to what development issues are involved. What they have in common is a set of guiding principles and steps to follow. The emphasis now is on the process of communication and on the significance of this process at the local level. Furthermore, according to the approach of different agencies, communication for sustainable development coincides with the enhancement of local capacities and the appropriation of communication processes and media by local stakeholders, and especially by vulnerable and marginalized groups. Capacity building in communication, including "bridging" of the digital divide, is now seen as an essential condition for sustainable development and the fulfillment of the UN Millennium Development Goals.

Communication initiatives for sustainable development start with a participatory analysis of the needs of local institutions and stakeholders, taking into account local culture and values and promoting a concerted action for development. Development communication can achieve relevant impact and sustainability only if adequately inserted in national development policies and building on existing experiences and capacities.

Nowadays, an increasing number of development initiatives emphasize the use of communication as a strategic tool, and new opportunities are emerging for mainstreaming development communication into national policies for sustainable development, especially in agriculture and natural resource management.

Challenges for the future

Communication for sustainable development has been facing new challenges in the last decade, as a consequence of globalization, media liberalization, rapid economic and social change, and the emergence of new ICTs. Liberalization has led not only to greater media freedom, but also to the emergence of an increasingly consumer-led and urban-centered communication infrastructure, which is less and less interested in the concerns of the poor and rural people. Women and other vulnerable groups continue to experience marginalization and lack of access to communication resources of all kinds. The issue of ensuring access to information and the right to communication as a precondition for empowering marginalized groups has been addressed by several meetings and international conferences (World Summit on the Information Society, 2005 World Summit, and World Social Forum).

Conserving environmental sustainability

One of the challenges faced by rural development programs is how to alleviate poverty and stimulate economic growth while, at the same time, preserving the environment. Fighting land degradation and desertification, halting deforestation, promoting proper management of water resources, and protecting biodiversity require the active participation of rural communities through communication processes.

Communication for Development focusing on participatory approaches can facilitate dialogue, increase the community knowledge base (both indigenous and modern), promote agricultural practices that are compatible with the environment, and develop awareness among policy makers, authorities, and service providers. Furthermore, participatory communication approaches can bring together different stakeholders and enable the poorest and most marginalized to have a voice in the use of natural resources (Ramírez 1997).

Today, development communications programs address global environmental issues, such as biosafety and risk management in disaster prevention and mitigation. Within this framework, communication, education, participation, and public awareness approaches are used in an integrated manner to reach out effectively to the key groups who are needed to protect the environment.

Promoting food security, rural development, and sustainable livelihood

Food security and rural development policies have been revised in recent years, placing more emphasis on holistic approaches to rural livelihoods and the sustainable use of natural resources. Furthermore, the spread of digital communication technology has made information and communication services increasingly cost-effective options for providing basic information to dispersed rural producers, in particular to those settled in remote and poorly accessible areas. The focus remains on the needs of rural people, rather than on communication media per se. The critical aim is to enhance the capacity of local stakeholders to manage communication processes, to develop local contents, and to use appropriate media tools. Communication development strategies must be context specific and reflect the values, perceptions, and characteristics of the people and institutions involved.

Empowerment of women, girls . . . , and senior citizens

Communication can also play a decisive role in promoting the empowerment of women and girls with a more equitable framework of gender dynamics. Communication processes allow rural women a voice to advocate changes in policies, attitudes, and social behavior or customs. Through Communication for Development, women can take control of their lives and participate as equals with men in promoting food security and rural development. In a similar way, the power and expertise of senior citizens, who in many societies enjoy great authority and respect but are often left outside development efforts, should be recognized. Many societies may have to reconsider their contributions and potential anyway, given other social and demographic developments.

Narrowing the digital divide

The issue of equal access to knowledge and information is becoming one of the key aspects of sustainable development. Vulnerable groups in the rural areas of developing countries are on the wrong side of the digital divide and risk further marginalization. In the rush to "wire" developing countries, little attention has been paid to the design of ICT programs for the poor. The trend ignores many lessons learned over the years by Communication for Development approaches, which emphasize communication processes and outcomes over the application of media and technologies. There needs to be a focus on the needs of communities and the benefits of the new technologies rather than the quantity of technologies available. Local content and languages are critical to enable the poor to have access to the benefits of the information revolution. The creation of local content requires building on existing and trusted traditional communication systems and methods for collecting and sharing information.

Poverty reduction

Communication can contribute to the effective reduction of poverty and offer better opportunities for the inclusion of marginalized groups and isolated population in the policy development and decision-making process. Although poverty cannot be divorced from uneven power structures, and communication cannot substitute for structural change (Balit 2004), the appropriation of Communication for Development processes and technologies by marginalized and vulnerable groups, including indigenous people (Yasarekomo 2004), can ensure that they have a voice in decisions that affect their lives.

EVIDENCE AND VALUE ADDED BY COMMUNICATION FOR SUSTAINABLE DEVELOPMENT

Indigenous forest management: ICTs and political engagement

An example of a local level development communication project involved indigenous people living in the highland jungles of Cambodia's Ratanakiri Province (Waldick 2001). The purpose of the project was to secure a livelihood from the forests they inhabited. The project orginated in a tense interface emerging between the rising economic value of the highland jungles for timber and the threat of this economic resource to the indigenous culture and ecological importance of the highland jungles. Logging of the highland jungles was having dire consequences for the indigenous inhabitants of the jungle, who relied on it for their livelihood.

The project strategically used communication in two ways, through advocacy and participatory communication (ethnographic action research). Indigenous highlanders were removed from Cambodia's social and political processes. The importance of the jungle to their culture and livelihood was not understood in Cambodian society. Advocacy at the political level was hindered further by an absence of documented research to explain the ecological, economic, cultural, and social importance of the jungle to the indigenous people.

Cambodian researchers worked with community members to train them to map local resources and to document local knowledge. The community members were also taught participatory action research techniques to train other indigenous highlanders. The researchers then used ICTs such as global positioning systems to verify the indigenous land use maps. The documentation of this knowledge and resources proved to be useful in lobbying provincial and national governments for protection of the jungle for a host of reasons. The project documented the strategic and purposive use of the forest resources by the indigenous highlanders and influenced sustainable forest management at governmental levels. Indigenous confidence in their management of the forest was improved by the project as information communication technologies, Western research techniques, and indigenous knowledge intersected to create a sustainable and viable forest management plan, one which balanced economic, ecological, cultural, and social concerns across many stakeholders. In sum, the project created an integrated forest management policy and a transferable model for aligning indigenous with Western "scientific" knowledge in sustainable development.

Video for participatory planning

One of the most successful rural communication programs ever developed was created in Mexico within PRODERITH (*Programa de Desarrollo Rural Integrado en el Trópico Húmedo*), a large, integrated, rural development program sponsored by the government of Mexico, with support from the World Bank and FAO. The communication methodology developed in the 1980s is still valid today.

In the 1960s the Plan Chontalpa had been a major initiative to develop the tropical wetlands in the Gulf of Mexico through drainage systems, roads, bridges, and other infrastructures, including new settlement villages. However, the plan was launched without first engaging farmers in the process. Not surprisingly, the farmers never identified with the project and failed to maintain the infrastructure. The result was an enormous investment in infrastructure that was never properly utilized or maintained.

When the first phase of PRODERITH was contemplated at the end of 1978, to avoid another Chontalpa, government planners decided that future development in the tropical wetlands would have to be planned and executed with the informed and active participation of the local people. When the project was launched the objectives included an innovation: besides increasing agricultural production, improving the living standards of poor farmers, and conserving natural resources, there would have to be community participation. A communication process was needed. Thus, the Rural Communication System was planned and budgeted for from the outset. It worked principally with video and supporting printed materials to cover the program's three types of communication needed: (a) situation analysis and participatory planning with peasants, (b) education and training for peasants and for PRODERITH's own staff, and (c) institutional information for better coordination and management.

Much research was done with peasants before designing any development action. Video proved to be an excellent tool to bring the local communities into the planning process and to reach their consensus on the development actions to be taken. At planning meetings, local people's attitudes and needs were elicited using video and audio recordings that were then played back as a basis for discussion. A true dialogue between the rural communities and planners stimulated a debate on the past history of the community, its present situation, the problems facing it, and possible options for development initiatives that could be supported by PRODERITH. The outcome was a local development plan about which a video was also made and which was passed on to management.

Peasants felt that they were listened to and they actively participated in PRODERITH's development strategy (see box A.3.1). This strengthened their sense of community and gave them a better understanding of who they were and how they could work together to attain improved livelihoods.

PRODERITH had two phases, the first from 1978 to 1984, and the second from 1986 to 1994, under the newly created Mexican Institute for Water Technology. At the end of the first phase the methodology for rural development and communication was applied in a 1.2 million hectare area, affecting 650,000 people. In the second phase the project was expanded beyond the humid and subhumid tropics and helped meet one of the greatest challenges ever faced by the Mexican agricultural sector: in 1989 the government began to transfer the responsibility for administration and maintenance of large and medium-sized irrigation schemes to the producers' organizations that were using them. In 1994, after five years of intense institutional changes, around 300,000 farmers had received the technical and economic responsibility for the schemes, across an area of about two million hectares, thanks also to the rural communication system.

Executing the local development plans invariably called for orientation and training. During both phases more than 700 videos were

CASE STUDY

Box A.3.1 Participation by Peasants

The old Mayan, Clotilde Cob, 82 years of age, spoke of his culture, his history, the history of his people, their traditions. All this was caught on tape by PRODERITH. Other peasants from other villages viewed the tape, again and again. It was the first time they saw themselves on video, speaking their own language, speaking about themselves. A door was thus opened. The peasants welcomed PRODERITH, as the cultural richness of the past spread through the communication technologies of the present.

produced and used with some 800,000 people, covering a wide range of agricultural and rural development topics. Videos became communication facilitators: farmers could analyze and identify problems and options for development; peasants and staff could be trained and receive education on several issues; and institutional information was also improved, resulting in better coordination and management of the program. The training videos were accompanied by printed materials for course participants and technicians.

Local people were trained and formed communication committees in many farming communities, and in some, Local Communication Units were established. These consisted of a loudspeaker system to reach the whole community and a covered meeting area where videos could be shown and discussions could take place. These were instrumental in many cases of social mobilization, which led to concrete development actions in the communities, especially concerning issues such as water supply, women's activities, and health. No community with a Local Communication Unit had a single case of cholera during the epidemic, which produced many cases in the nearby areas, and there were significant reductions in infant deaths caused by diarrhea.

The cost of the rural communication system remained below 2 percent of the global investment and, according to the former director general of the National Water Commission, enhanced project implementation and rapid transfer of technology contributed to an internal rate of return 7 percent higher than initially planned by the project. The World Bank considered PRODERITH to be among the most successful projects it supported, and it was on record as having stated that the rural communication system had been instrumental to that success (box A.3.2).

Communication for Development in Health

> *"Everyone has the right to a standard of living adequate for the health and well-being of himself and his family, including food, clothing, housing, and medical care and necessary social services, and the right to security in the event of unemployment, sickness, disability, widowhood, old age, or other lack of livelihood in circumstances beyond his control."*
>
> —ARTICLE 25, UNIVERSAL DECLARATION OF HUMAN RIGHTS

CASE STUDY

Box A.3.2 Secret of a Good Communication System

In 1989, a senior FAO staff member visited the areas covered by the PRODERITH rural communication system and met many of the participating communities, organizations, and individuals. At the end of the trip he discovered what, to his mind, was one of the most important methodological "secrets" of the Mexican experience. He said: "The main challenge faced by a good communication system in the field is not, as one might generally think, filling a social space with words. It consists in the establishment of an initial silence, where the actors present recognize each other as equals, with the same rights and possibilities for generating the new knowledge required to improve the quality of life and working conditions."

Source: Santiago Funes, Former CTA UTF/MEX/027.

HEALTH COMMUNICATION IN BRIEF

The field of development communication has evolved in parallel with changes in the broader concept of development. It is widely acknowledged that until the 1960s and 1970s most of the world's experience in the area of development communication was driven by the agriculture sector. During the last quarter of the century, however, the learning and knowledge curve shifted from agriculture to public health, where developments in the biomedical sciences (for example, population and family planning, primary health care, maternal and child health, and most recently HIV/AIDS and infectious diseases) have increasingly focused attention on the role of communication in public health programs. Evidence-based public health practice assumes that interventions must be grounded in empirical research that supports decisions about health promotion and policy, taking into account the complexity of human behavior and social contexts (Kemm 2005). In part because of its origins in medical and health science, health communication has been one of the most successful subfields of communication in terms of producing a body of empirical evidence that communication works.

Health communication interventions have been part of development efforts since the 1960s, especially in the area of family planning programs. The importance of health communication rose on the international public health agenda in the 1990s, mainly as a result of important conceptual changes in the 1970s and 1980s. The Declaration of Alma Ata (1978) and the Ottawa Charter (1986) represented a fundamental point of departure from supply-driven approaches centered on technology and hospital-based care to increased demand-driven participatory and empowerment-based approaches. Recognition grew that individuals and communities could play an important role in determining their health. Following the Cairo and Beijing conferences in the 1990s, the public health field moved toward a rights-based approach. In the last decade, new momentum has built around these and other initiatives including the Millennium Development Goals, the "3 by 5" initiative, the UNAIDS HIV/AIDS Communication Framework, the Rockefeller Foundation Communication for Social Change Programme now being carried out by the Communication for Social Change Consortium, the FAO, and others. These approaches establish principles that cut across health issues such as emphasis on rights-based approach, leadership, participation, and empowerment as fundamental features of sustainable public health.

FROM BEHAVIORAL TO ECOLOGICAL APPROACHES IN HEALTH COMMUNICATION

For many years health communication focused on delivering messages about healthy practices to a variety of audiences: health workers, patients, community members, opinion leaders, and policy makers. In earlier eras, healthier behavior was the most commonly sought objective and often it was assumed that information and education delivered effectively would cause behavior change and raise standards of public health. Health behavior change strategies have become increasingly sophisticated and much more responsive to the needs and cultural sensitivities of stakeholders. The success of these strategies is indisputable, and the overwhelming preponderance of evidence of the effects of communication on health comes from research at the individual level. But the assumption that individual behavior change alone can solve public health problems is fundamentally flawed, particularly considering the structural and policy challenges of contemporary issues such as HIV/AIDS and environmental health and the cultural and political complexity of health inequities that disproportionately affect women and the poor.

Behavior change communication continues to play an important role in public health programs, but as early as the late 1950s the World Health Organization was pushing efforts to define health and well-being away from a narrow disease prevention perspective to "a state of complete mental, physical, and social well-being and not merely the absence of the disease" (WHO 1958). Along these lines, Evans and Stoddart (1990) proposed their 21st-century field model, an ecological framework that includes interactions among multiple factors that determine health: physical, family, and social environments, primary and secondary prevention systems, as well as individual characteristics and behaviors.

The World Bank, the World Health Organization, USAID, and other organizations increasingly have focused on social determinants of health to help them prioritize investments (WHO 2004). The ideal intervention strategies, therefore, do not just implore people to change, but help them live healthier lives from birth and make appropriate health decisions throughout life by building and strengthening healthy, participatory communities and effective health care delivery systems, supported by enlightened health policy.

One of the newer ecological approaches to health communication focuses on the concept of health competence as a way to link environmental influences, health systems, and human behavior in an ecological model of health improvement (USAID 2001). Communication is central to achieving and maintaining health competence. According to this perspective, health-competent service delivery systems provide access to quality services and products; have adequate capacity in their workforce (leadership, management, training, professionalism); and have governance structures through which stakeholders can access and be involved in the operation of health systems. Health-competent environments allow decision making through debate and dialogue among the media, community, and civil society, and provide access to health information. Communities are involved in setting health agendas, and policies create opportunities for the individual to flourish. At the individual level, people make health-enhancing lifestyle choices across a range of health issues (reproductive health, diet, substance use, child care, and so on), express appropriate demand for care-seeking and care-providing behaviors and adhere to treatment protocols, because they understand the determinants of disease and health.

Other sources of conceptual guidance for the health competence framework include health literacy, variously defined as knowledge and comprehension resulting from health education (for example, Simonds 1974) and as a broad set of factors that empower and facilitate achievement of health (for example, Nutbeam 2000; IOM 2004). Social capital refers to characteristics of social organizations that "combine to facilitate cooperation among people for their mutual benefit" (Kawachi, Kennedy, and Lochner 1997). In terms of health, social capital facilitates social mobilization for health improvement; enhances access to and the flow of information; and increases the likelihood of social and emotional support for behavioral decision-making. The Integrated Model of Communication for Social Change (Figueroa et al. 2002) describes the relationships among many of these individual and social level processes. Built around the process of community dialogue leading to collective action, this model draws from a broad literature on development communication, particularly the work of Latin American theorists (Beltrán 1974; Díaz Bordenave 1994). It also incorporates theories of group dynamics, conflict resolution, and network/convergence, as well as less often considered perspectives on such topics as leadership (for example, Senge 1994; Stogill 1948; Lord and Brown 2004; Tirmizi 2002; Chemers 2000) and equity (Gumucio-Dagrón 2001; White 1994; Moser 1993).

Similarly, the UNAIDS framework calls for greater attention to five contextual domains: (a) government and policy, with a focus on the role of policies and laws in supporting or hindering intervention efforts; (b) socioeconomic status, with a focus on issues such as income and its impact on communications interventions; (c) culture, with emphasis on positive, neutral, or negative aspects of culture that may help or prevent the adoption of healthy practices; (d) gender relations, focused on the status of women in society and how it impacts their vulnerability to HIV/AIDS; and (e) spirituality, focused on the role of religion/spiritual practices in the adoption/rejection of certain healthy practices (UNAIDS 1999; Airhihenbuwa, Makinwa, and Obregón 2000). Communication plays a specific role in helping produce change in one or more of these five contextual domains, which in turn affects behavior. Gender issues illustrate this point very well. While many HIV/AIDS prevention programs emphasize the use of condoms, a lack of focus on gender imbalances and the power men have in determining sexual practices would reduce program impact. Shifting gender norms associated with sexual practices can empower women and changes the dynamics of sexual negotiation.

In sum, more than 30 years of research and experience lead health communication away from a narrow focus on communication channels and technologies of information delivery for individual behavior change and toward the socially and culturally embedded processes of dialogue and discussion that are fundamental to everyday life. As a result, more attention is being paid to the social and political environments (Deane and Scalway 2003; Vincent 2003; Airhihenbuwa and Obregón 2000; UNAIDS 1999; Rockefeller Foundation 1999) in which people live and earn a livelihood and the influence of communication within those environments on lifestyle and behavioral choices. "The individual is no longer a target, but a critical participant in analyzing and adopting those messages most suited to her or his own circumstances" (Jacobson 1997).

It has become clear that no single approach is likely to achieve the goals of all health communication projects, programs, and activities. Effective health communication must focus on identifying and utilizing the most appropriate approaches, methods, and communication tools to stimulate and support a sustainable communication process that leads to social change at required levels—social, community, family, individual. Determining which will work in a given situation requires skill, patience, and sufficient time to understand the economic, social, and political situation and the health and communication needs of the people involved.

EVIDENCE AND VALUE ADDED OF EFFECTIVE COMMUNICATION FOR HEALTH AND DEVELOPMENT

Through each of the eras of health communication and development outlined above, applied research and the evaluation of health communication programs across multiple cultural and geographic settings and under varied economic and access conditions have sought to improve the effectiveness of health communication practice. Fortunately, those efforts have produced a compelling body of evidence that the right kind of communication used in the right way will produce results.

For example, communication has been shown to have effects on the political and social environment through policy and media advocacy and through social activism and social movements, which create pressures on political leaders to respond to expressed needs. Coalition building and institutional coordination, both of which require responsive and transparent communication systems, and the development and implementation of national communication strategies facilitate efforts to address health and other development topics. Supportive environments are in turn more likely to provide broader access to health information and allow and encourage informed decision making through debate and dialogue among the media, community, and civil society (box A.3.3).

At the health service systems level, studies have shown that improving the communication skills of health care providers and the quality of job aides makes health systems more responsive to clients and increases the effectiveness of client-provider interactions, both in terms of clients' informed choice and satisfaction with services and in terms of uptake of and adherence to services and treatments. Increasing the communication skills of clients, such as question-asking skills and self-confidence, through client education and modeling of active client behavior in the media, lead to clients being more demanding

CASE STUDY

Box A.3.3 Changing Social Norms Related to Female Genital Cutting in Nigeria

While more than half the women in Nigeria's Enugu State have undergone female genital cutting (FGC), a cultural practice that involves removing some or all of the female genitalia, a successful multimedia strategic communication program called *Ndukaku* increased support for discontinuing the practice after just one year. A partnership between two Nigeria-based organizations—the National Association of Women Journalists and Women Action Research Organization—used a non-confrontational approach to begin discussing this highly sensitive topic with Enugu families. Based on the Community Action Cycle (CAC), the program consisted of community mobilization activities, advocacy, and mass media interventions. Community activities included viewing of the film *Uncut—Playing with Life* at group gatherings, while advocacy consisted of activist visits to traditional leaders, regular newspaper columns, radio call-in shows, and public forums on FGC.

Research found that support for FGC declined significantly after exposure to the program. In addition to a drop in support for FGC, the proportion of women who believe that FGC is beneficial declined from 42.1 percent to 24.6 percent after exposure to *Ndukaku.* Women participating in *Ndukaku* became empowered agents for change through the community mobilization activities, leading to increased support from cultural leaders, including a public pronouncement against FGC from the traditional leader of Eha Amufu, who also banned the practice in his domain. His action led to a health bill before the Enugu State House of Assembly that included language on the elimination of FGC.

Source: Babalola 2005.

and proactive in seeking and choosing health services and treatments. Communication programs have also been shown to influence the motivation of providers and health service facilities to deliver on promises to clients and to be more client-oriented (box A.3.4).

At the health service management level, the communication of consistent and up-to-date technical standards has been shown to improve service performance and professionalism. Communication among service providers and managers has been shown to increase peer pressure to perform and to adhere to standards. And communication systems linking health facilities and institutions have been shown to improve referral systems that increase client access to appropriate services as needed.

At the community level, communication within social networks has been shown to extend the reach and local adaptation of health information, resulting in changes in health behavior comparable to those achieved through direct exposure to mass media campaigns (Boulay, Storey, and Sood 2002). Communities that have the opportunity to participate in community dialogue leading to collective action (Figueroa et al. 2002; Kincaid and Figueroa forthcoming) are more likely to get the kind of health services they need because they can express their needs clearly and with a collective voice (box A.3.5).

Box A.3.4 Improving Reproductive Health Service Utilization in Nepal

From 1998 to 2003, the Nepal Adolescent Project (Malhotra et al. 2005) provided a community-based reproductive health intervention in two communities (one rural and one urban) that attempted to actively engage disempowered youth, such as those living in poverty, young women, and ethnic minorities, in activities to address social norms and inequities. Activities included peer education and counseling linked with adult education programs and improved access to economic livelihood opportunities. Changes in the study communities were compared with changes in two control sites that had not received an intervention. At baseline, both the study and control sites showed substantial differences between wealthy and poor young women's access to health facilities for pregnancy delivery. For example, before the intervention, an urban young woman in the study site was 16 times more likely to receive prenatal care than her rural counterpart. By the end of the project urban women were only 1.2 times more likely to receive prenatal care. The control sites did not show a similar improvement.

CASE STUDY

Box A.3.5 Community Mobilization and Life Skills Education in Tanzania

SiMchezo!, a bimonthly Swahili language magazine for semiliterate, rural, out-of-school youth, is an integral part of the multimedia and community-based HIP effort to involve stakeholders in HIV/AIDS prevention, bridge generational communication gaps, foster dialogue about culturally sensitive issues, build life skills, and provide social support to vulnerable adolescents and their parents. Road shows, school-based activities, and clubs, together with media campaigns and the FEMINA family of magazine, broadcast media, and learning tools, provide entertaining life skills education. *SiMchezo!* is edited and produced partly in the field with community and NGO involvement in order to address issues of importance to its readers and in ways that they find appealing and useful. Since 2002, the magazine has become a popular discussion tool for peer educators and parents. Testimonials from youth and parents alike attest to the impact *SiMchezo!* has had: "The magazine increases communication among people here in Njombe. According to African culture, men cannot talk to their daughters on issues relating to sexuality and sexually transmitted infections. Some of the parents have the courage to talk to their daughters and sons: it is good, but for those who cannot talk, then they should use the magazine to communicate." (A father from Njombe)

Source: Fuglesang 2005.

They are also more likely to experience an equitable distribution of benefits from those services, because they help set the agenda and determine how and what kind of services will be delivered. They are also better able to mobilize local resources, such as emergency transportation systems, that can reduce maternal mortality due to obstetric complications by conveying women to an appropriate service center in a timely fashion.

The greatest body of evidence of communication effectiveness comes from research on communication at the individual level. That research is extremely diverse, ranging from work on microlevel psychological processes to relatively macrolevel sociological processes. It is beyond the scope of this paper to review the evidence in detail. Suffice it to say that research over the past 40 years in both Western and Southern contexts has shown that communication programs can help people make health-enhancing lifestyle choices across a range of health issues (reproductive health, diet, substance abuse, and so on), express appropriate demand for care-seeking and care-providing behaviors, and adhere to treatment regimens, because they understand the determinants of disease and health and have participated in decisions about how to deal with them (box A.3.6).

At the individual and interpersonal level, research has shown that health behavior choices are made on the basis of perceived benefits, perceived social support and perceived barriers to action (Ajzen and Fishbein 1997); on the basis of social observation and learning from others in one's nearby social environment (Bandura 1986); on the basis of information about the benefits and consequences of action (Rogers 2003); and on the basis of rational and emotional reactions to disease threats (Witte, Meyer, and Martell 2001). It has been shown in a wide variety of social and cultural

CASE STUDY

Box A.3.6 Adolescent Reproductive Health in Bangladesh

The Adolescent Reproductive Health (ARH) Communication Program in Bangladesh (Center for Communication Programs 2006a) addresses the gap between knowledge and practice through a multipronged communication strategy focusing on issues identified by adolescents themselves. The comprehensive program works to create an enabling environment that supports adolescent knowledge and service-seeking behaviors. All ARH materials and media are identified by the logo and slogan, *NijekeJano* (Know Yourself), which provides a rallying point for youth and youth supporters. Adolescents were involved in all stages of program development: formative research, character development and story writing for scripts and comic books, retesting, acting, and evaluation. Four life skills facilitators' guides with videos are used in workshops, where adolescents practice decision making, problem solving, critical and creative thinking, and interpersonal skills. In addition, a 39-episode TV series and 52-episode radio series follow a variety-show format, with adolescent anchors and field reporters who conduct interviews with adolescents, parents, teachers, service providers, and community leaders on issues. The entertainment education program also features songs, poems, quizzes, and mini-dramas using the same characters as the comic book. About the program, Tanzila Khatun, an adolescent girl, says, "I was depressed and afraid of a deadly disease when I saw first blood dropping out of my body without any reason. Everything happened around me so dramatically that I was feeling distressed. At that time I heard about BCCP's video show at Chowdhury Bari, which I attended. Through watching the video show and reading the booklet (*My Puberty*), I knew about the changes that occur in the human body during adolescence and also I knew what I should do to take care of myself."

settings, that communication influences the social, psychological, and emotional factors that increase the probability of healthy behavior, even under unfavorable and resource-poor conditions (box A.3.7). The uses of and response to communication varies depending on where an individual lies on a spectrum ranging from relative apathy and isolation to engagement and social connection. An individual's position on this continuum determines the specific factors that are most strongly related to performance or nonperformance of behavior. (For an overview, see McKee et al. [2000].)

CASE STUDY

Box A.3.7 Creating Space for Women's Health and Gender Equity in Nicaragua and Peru

Every two months María Castillo and Esperancita Núñez travel long distances from their homes to the national capital, Managua. There, they make their way to Puntos de Encuentro (fig., Common Ground), a feminist NGO that has specialized in the use of entertainment-education for social change since 1991. The women are typical links in a network of roughly 500 NGOs that Puntos has forged since its founding. Their goal is to pick up and help distribute 26,000 copies of the periodical *La Boletina,* which is designed to support and strengthen Nicaragua's women's movement and change norms around gender relationships and violence against women. Puntos de Encuentro builds this kind of commitment and mobilization for social change through publications like *La Boletina,* as well as telenovelas (for example, *Sexto Sentido*), interactive radio programs, youth camps, newsletters, and many other forms of communication, most of them produced for and by stakeholders. After one national campaign on violence against women in 1999, 85 percent of men surveyed said that they had changed as a result of exposure to the campaign (Rodríguez 2005).

In Peru, the reproductive health radio program *Bienvenida Salud!* attempts to move sexual and women's health out of the private arena and into the public sphere. Programs are written for and by rural indigenous women in the Department of Loreto in the Peruvian Amazon. Through interviews, news, testimonials, listeners' letters, and radio novellas, the infrequently heard voices of these women reach a wide audience. Listening groups, facilitated by locally recruited community promoters, listen to the programs together and have produced plays, community histories, and other materials that are subsequently aired. A 2003 journal article on *Bienvenida Salud!* reports that the station has received hundreds of letters from both men and women and that the proportion from women is increasing with comments like: "In our community, everyone listens to *Bienvenida Salud!* . . . Thanks to your show, I participate in community activities so I can progress, together with our community, to build a better future for our children . . ."

Evidence from specific subareas of health

Population and reproductive health

Although significant gaps in reproductive health still exist between low- and high-income countries, there has been progress worldwide in the past 50 years in such areas as pregnancy care, family planning, unsafe abortion, sexually transmitted infections, adolescent risk behaviors, and access to health services (Population Reference Bureau 2006) (box A.3.8). Piotrow et al. (1997) documented nearly 20 years of USAID-funded population communication efforts in more than 50 countries that have had measurable success in increasing contraceptive use and birth spacing, raising the age of marriage and age of sexual debut, shifting norms about childbearing and gender preference, and increasing interpersonal communication—both between spouses and in the community at large—about fertility and reproductive health.

Child survival and immunization

Enormous gaps in child survival still exist—under-five mortality is 7 per 1,000 in high-income countries compared with 120 per 1,000 in low-income countries—yet worldwide progress has been made in such areas as the use of diarrheal rehydration therapy and, particularly, immunization. Since the launch of the Expanded Program on Immunization (EPI) in 1974, vaccination programs have been one of the world's most cost-effective public health strategies. As a result of universal immunization campaigns in the 1980s, over 70 percent of children globally received the basic six vaccines. Yet coverage has stagnated since then, due in part to a decline in funding for immunization communication, and differences in coverage between lower and higher income countries continue to be severe (for example, 17 countries in Sub-Saharan Africa have complete immunization coverage levels under 50 percent).

Even when services are available, a substantial number of caregivers still fail to complete the immunization schedule, in part due to a lack of communication about differences in types of immunizations, the introduction of new vaccine types, and adherence to immunization schedules. In addition, health authorities in some countries have faced public skepticism about vaccine safety. All of this points to the need for continued advocacy for immunization

CASE STUDY

Box A.3.8 Political Commitment to Population and Health Communication in Egypt, 1980–2006

The Information, Education, and Communication Center of the State Information Services (SIS) is Egypt's lead agency in behavior change communication for family planning and family health, with a mission to contribute to national development by using strategic communication to help all Egyptians plan their families and achieve better health. Founded in 1979 by the government, the SIS-IEC Centre has for nearly 30 years coordinated the talents of Egypt's leading celebrities, artists, planners, media personnel, medical experts, religious leaders, and NGOs in creating programs that have captured the imaginations of two generations of Egyptians.

Programs in the 1980s and 1990s built awareness of the link between population growth and family well-being. President Hosni Mubarak's 1986 policy statement, "Over-population swallows all development. . . . Family planning is the solution," created political commitment at the highest level. Endorsements of this policy came from religious and political leaders at all levels, and popular celebrity involvement helped put family planning on the public agenda. Entertainment education (for example, the popular "Doctor's Diary" featuring actress Karima Mochtar) focused attention on social norms and attitudes, most notably around husband-wife communication and increased male responsibility for reproductive health. Service quality improvement efforts, such as the Gold Star program, backed up rising demand for contraception, and in 1994 interministerial collaboration was formalized with a partnership between SIS and the Ministry of Health and Population to provide quality improvement communication. Since the year 2000, the focus has been on supporting a new generation committed to households and communities as producers of health. The national *Mabrouk* (Congratulations!) initiative treats marriage as the entry point to a lifetime of good family health with media-based and community-based programs on nutrition, second-hand smoke, hygiene, handwashing, avian flu prevention, hepatitis C prevention, and HIV/AIDS awareness. Community outreach by NGO volunteers—both male and female—links traditional male *dawar* councils and *Arab Women Speak Out* empowerment workshops with village health committee structures. Private sector pharmacies are linked through a national "Ask-Consult" network, as a first source of contact for basic health information, home health products, and service referral.

The result is an increase in contraceptive use by married women of reproductive age from 24 percent in 1980 to 59 percent in 2005. The average number of children borne in a woman's lifetime dropped from 5.3 in 1980 to 3.1 in 2005 (El-Zanaty and Way 2006). Maternal and infant mortality rates have declined along with the fertility rate. There are 39 million fewer people today than were projected in 1979 and Egypt is on track to achieve replacement-level fertility by 2017.

Source: Robinson and El-Zanaty 2006.

CASE STUDY

Box A.3.9 Growing Popular Support for Children's Immunization in Colombia

The *Puye* campaign in Colombia was developed by the Ministry of Social Protection, the United Nations Children's Fund (UNICEF), the Pan American Health Organization (PAHO), and the National Health Institute in 2003, with the purpose of supporting the regular program of vaccination and stimulating sustainable mechanisms of supply and demand for vaccination services. The name of the campaign is a play on words in which the term *puyar* refers both to the action of injecting vaccines and a popular expression meaning "to demand, to hurry up, or to press for."

On top of routine information campaigns about immunization, *Puye* tried to motivate parents to be on the alert about the vaccines their children need; to motivate neighbors and friends, to remind parents about vaccination; and most importantly, to motivate authorities, to act in favor of vaccination of children of their municipality or department.

An evaluation of the program in 931 municipalities (526 that received traditional campaigns and 405 that received *Puye*) over a five-month period found that immunization coverage improved monthly in 77 percent of the *Puye* areas compared with only 48 percent of the non-*Puye* areas.

Source: Salamanca 2004.

and other child survival initiatives, particularly those that take into account local sociocultural and political influences (box A.3.9).

HIV/AIDS

One of the brightest spots in global health communication has been in the area of HIV/AIDS prevention and care. Huge new communication initiatives have been launched to advocate for increased access to and use of AIDS drugs, accompanied by massive efforts to reduce risk factors (individual, social, and structural) associated with heterosexual, homosexual, mother-to-child, and other forms of transmission. Linkages between AIDS, tuberculosis, malaria, malnutrition, and other diseases are being publicized and addressed through the Global Fund, leading to coordinated country-level plans, changes in national health policies and increased funding.

Much AIDS research during the 1980s and early 1990s focused on counting such things as the number of sexual partners and the frequency of sexual practices. But more recent research experience with sexually transmitted diseases has shown that the relationship between positive attitudes and healthy behavior is neither simple nor linear (see Terry, Gallois, and McCamish 1993; Maticka-Tyndale et al. 2004; Sandfort 1998; Sukda 2000). Behavior change models based largely on rational, volitional thinking overlook the importance of emotional and contextual factors related to sexual practices (Servaes and Malikhao 2004; Malikhao 2005).

Information about HIV/AIDS is more effective if exchanged through dialogue and debate, rather than merely transmitted, and healthy behaviors are more likely if decided through negotiation. Consequently, since the 1990s, research has shifted toward a perspective in which people are seen as the agents of their own change, but in relation to social norms, policies, culture, and supportive environments. AIDS communication programs are more likely to take these factors into account—and in locally appropriate ways—when they are developed and implemented through partnerships with stakeholders and local infrastructure (Deane and Scalway 2003) (box A.3.10).

Mass media campaigns, using appropriate communication strategies and local idioms, are an essential element of strategy, but they need to foster—sometimes in conjunction with other communication approaches—inclusive public discourse about the complexity of and differing views around HIV/AIDS and the fundamental normative and structural changes necessary to reduce AIDS and care for people living with HIV/AIDS (PLWHA). Coordinated behavior change and other communication efforts, supported by a positive policy environment, must be integrated into national HIV/AIDS programs that engage government, local and national media, and civil society (DFID 2004).

Stigma continues to be a major impediment to progress in preventing and treating HIV infection, a problem that is readily addressed by communication programs (box A.3.11). Approaches such as the ongoing Treatment Action Campaign (http://www.tac.org.za) have moved from merely disseminating messages to fostering an environment where the voices of people living with HIV/AIDS can be heard and their needs moved to the center stage of dialogue and action. Increased representation of PLWHA and of their perspective on living with HIV in the mass media can help bring previously taboo subjects into the light of day and raise the importance of HIV/AIDS prevention, treatment, and care efforts on public and policy agendas. And modeling community dialogue and discussion among partners through mass media has been shown to increase public discussion

CASE STUDY

Box A.3.10 Young, Empowered, and Healthy in Uganda

In Uganda, a current youth reproductive health program, Young, Empowered, and Healthy (YEAH), uses a radio serial called *Rockpoint 256* to raise questions about culturally based attitudes toward transactional sex, the quest for multiple partners, sexual coercion, and alcohol abuse (Center for Communication Programs 2006b). The serial models not just individual behavior but also community response to and adult support for changes that will protect the reproductive health of vulnerable women and youth. A second phase of the program focuses on creating public dialogue about what it means to *Be A Man,* thereby shifting gender norms away from male control and toward male responsibility and gender equity. At the launch of the *YEAH* radio serial in December 2005, youth writers and producers successfully defended the serial's frank treatment of youth sexuality against threats by the First Lady of Uganda to cancel the program. They argued successfully with the First Lady that open public discussion was necessary to break through taboos and shift social and gender norms that put Uganda youth at risk of unplanned pregnancy and HIV/AIDS.

Using their own resources, local and regional youth groups that collaborate under the YEAH program organize and implement community activities with schools, clubs, and church groups. Through these activities, young men and women explore traditional male and female gender norms and their impact on sexual relationships, health, and social well-being and encourage adult community leaders to confront tradition and support youth in their quest for respect and better reproductive health. After only three months of program activity, survey research shows that gender norms are already beginning to shift. Young men ages 15–24 years old who have been exposed to the *Be a Man* program are less likely to say that men should make the decisions about sex, that men need to have other women, that women who carry condoms are easy, and that there are times when a woman should be beaten.

about AIDS, disclosure of one's HIV status, and utilization of voluntary counseling and testing (Kelly et al. 2005).

APPLYING HEALTH COMMUNICATION TO POLICIES AND PRACTICES

Challenges remain ahead for the health communication community, including practitioners, academics, and policy makers.

Valuing and using different types of evidence

This selective research review illustrates how communication can be mobilized to influence individual behaviors, as well as shift power

CASE STUDY

Box A.3.11 Integrated Communication Campaigns Inspire Collective Action and Reduce Stigma in South Africa

Soul City, a South African NGO, employed national television and radio entertainment-education programs, complemented by newspaper supplements and a national advocacy strategy involving lobbying of government and decision makers, to address a wide range of issues from HIV/AIDS and youth sexuality, domestic violence, sexual harassment and hypertension, to small business development and personal finance. Evaluation data from two points in time (1999 and 2000) measured 80 percent reach among members of the intended audience. Public marches mobilized by Soul City helped support passage of anti–domestic violence legislation in 1999. Anecdotal evidence suggests increased collective empowerment and collective action as a result of community action modeled in an entertainment education series, including one case in which a township was inspired to fight back against economic exploitation and renamed itself "Soul City" in recognition of the source of their motivation (Scheepers et al. 2004).

The evaluation of another HIV/AIDS-related television serial, *Tsha Tsha,* produced by the South Africa Broadcasting Corporation, Curious Pictures, and another local NGO, the Centre for AIDS Development Research and Evaluation (CADRE), found large differences between viewers and nonviewers even after controlling for factors that predict access to and exposure to the drama. Viewers were more likely to have positive attitudes about HIV issues addressed in *Tsha Tsha,* including stigma toward people living with HIV/AIDS; were more likely to practice HIV preventive behaviors, such as abstaining from sex, being faithful to one partner, having sex less often, using a condom to prevent HIV; and were more likely to undergo voluntary counseling and testing to determine their HIV status. Viewers also reported an increased sense of responsibility for the well-being of others as *Tsha Tsha* portrayed the dynamics of living openly with HIV and the problems and challenges involved in sharing one's status with others. It provided strong, positive images of young people confronting their HIV positive status (Kelly et al. 2005).

relations, cultural practices and norms, policy frameworks, economic status, and other social and political realities affecting health. However, different kinds of evidence exist for different types of outcomes with the evidence for social structural change (for example, empowerment, equity, policy change) more likely to be anecdotal or qualitative and evidence for individual change (for example, behaviors including participation, efficacy/self-confidence, gender attitudes, and social norms) more likely to be quantitative. Both types of evidence are important and both support the conclusion that communication, properly employed, is a powerful force for social change. Anecdotal and qualitative evidence invite different kinds of inferences than quantitative evidence and may resonate with some audiences better than others. And while it is possible to quantify higher-order changes, such as cultural and structural shifts over time, to do so requires methodological approaches that few projects have the time, resources, or donor support to undertake.

Working across sectors

Complex health issues have forced health practitioners to address a number of issues that cut across different sectors. The HIV/AIDS component of the Danida health and education sector programs in Mozambique is an example of bisectoral collaboration that is now being expanded to include the agricultural sector.

Working within regions

Natural disasters and emergencies have demonstrated the need to design and implement regionwide strategies. The tsunami disaster showed lack of cooperation in both the immediate emergency and the subsequent responses. On the contrary, the international response to the potential avian flu pandemic suggests increasing coordination and cooperation to implement regional plans and strategies. Several international initiatives (for example, GAVI, PEPFAR, Roll Back Malaria) have provided strategic guidance for global and regional responses to health challenges such as immunization, HIV/AIDS, and malaria. However, the communication component within these regional and global strategies is often limited to dissemination efforts and it lacks specificity on the role of communication.

Addressing broad societal issues that affect health

Lifestyle and urban planning issues are two key entry points to public health in the modern world, whereby communication cuts across a number of issues that have societywide implications. The transformation of Colombia's capital, Bogotá, and its implications for health, are a good example of this. Through an intervention focused on three components—citizenship and culture, moral values, and a renewed regulatory framework—the city went from being a chaotic metropolis to the prime example of urban development in the region.

Monitoring, evaluation, and indicators

There has been an increased emphasis on moving from a focus on behavioral impact to a focus on process and how that affects both individual and population-level health outcomes. Increased focus on process will provide deeper understanding of the nuances and particularities of development and health, especially those that remain embedded in cultural practices. A focus on context and communities as units of analysis has emerged as critical to an understanding of the effectiveness of interventions in health promotion and communication. Unfortunately, the politics and economics of public health communication leave little room and resources for longitudinal approaches, particularly under the realization that health changes take time. Two initiatives that may help overcome this short-term perspective include (a) engaging universities to develop longitudinal and external monitoring and evaluation as an academic and scientific challenge and (b) encouraging donors to consider funding longer (5- to 10-year) initiatives rather than shorter (1- to 3-year) initiatives.

The discussion on monitoring and evaluation also has brought increasing attention to issues of indicators in health communication. The most significant change over time is the increased attention given to process indicators, such as the ones outlined in the Communication for Development and Social Change Framework, and to the role qualitative approaches could play in this context and move from impact to also include process and from effects to also assess leadership, accountability, and other dimensions.

Increasing the focus on human resources and capacity building

Over the past decade, many developing countries have moved toward increasing decentralization of their health systems; thus, availability of human resources at national, regional, and local levels has emerged as a central element to ensure effective health interventions, including health communication. The theme of the 2006 World Health Day highlighted this issue as it focused on human resources as its theme. Health communication capacity needs to be developed both in service and preservice settings as well as across disciplines in public health.

Developing health communication competencies

The discussion on human resources highlights the importance of focusing on competencies needed to develop effective health communication interventions. This is true both for practitioners originally trained as communicators, who, generally speaking, come to the field with little understanding of social mobilization, social and behavioral theories, and sustainable change, and for practitioners trained in public health and other areas, who come to the field with little understanding of communication issues. Training institutions, particularly universities, should play a central role in this effort. Efforts made in the past have aimed at identifying and operationalizing key competencies for development and health communication. These contributions might be brought more intensely before academic institutions in efforts to create training programs that could train a critical mass of practitioners with core competencies in health communication.

Refocusing funding priorities

A realistic approach dictates that the challenges could be met only if sufficient and adequate funding is available to implement necessary programs. While the international public health community has allocated significant resources to a variety of areas in public health, resources allocated to health communication are limited and/or earmarked for specific health themes, which complicate cross-sectoral or cross-cutting approaches. Increased funding should be aimed at assessing the value added by health communication to public health efforts (especially those linking health and social outcomes), exploring new methodologies to monitor and evaluate interventions, and strengthening long-term efforts for human resource development.

Making a distinction between typologies of health problems

Carefully tailored communication interventions emerge based on a profound understanding of the health problem encountered and, at the same time, draw on the generic options about individual behavior, policies, and environmental factors. For example, in the case of a communicable disease such as malaria versus a cardiovascular disease, malaria requires handling the problem of individual behavior vis-à-vis the risk of mosquito bites. However, it also requires attention to policies on access to both prevention (bed nets) and treatment. Malaria requires some attention given to the waters where mosquitoes breed, while cardiovascular diseases are linked to lifestyles acquired over time such as physical activity, smoking patterns, food patterns, and the like. However, cardiovascular diseases will also require attention both to individual behaviors, policy, and environmental factors.

Making a distinction between emergency diseases and development-oriented health problems

Emergency diseases such as SARS or avian flu require very different communication responses compared with the long-term development-oriented health challenges posed by HIV/AIDS. Typically, responses to emergency diseases are vertical and mass media borne, containing high proportions of information dissemination and social mobilization in response to the immediate needs demanded by the emergency. Participatory approaches take the form of social mobilization and less as longer-term empowerment strategies. HIV/AIDS contains both elements of urgency, due to the lethal dimension linked to each HIV transmission, and also to strong elements dealing with fundamental issues of poverty, gendered power imbalances, lack of voice of PLWHA, issues of stigma and denial, and so on. Despite all the differences, we see in both long-term and short-term responses the need to deal with a mix of individual behavioral patterns, policy issues, and environmental factors.

Making a distinction between a broad-based (horizontal) versus a narrow-based (vertical) definition of the health problem

Taking sexual and reproductive health and rights as an example, this is a crucial issue to be addressed in young nations and/or countries in transition. The broader-based definition of the issue would lead to a rights-based approach and move into issues of power and gender relations, socioeconomic determinants of the problem, and both collective and individually oriented responses. Furthermore, while vertical approaches focus on a specific health problem, the horizontal approach entails a cross-cutting view that may tackle tuberculosis, HIV/AIDS, malaria, and diabetes in one specific area. A good example of a communication vehicle with the necessary flexibility to cater to the breadth of a horizontal and vertical approach with each of the specific diseases is the Tanzanian FEMINA Health Information Project. It deals broadly with sexual and reproductive health and rights of young Tanzanians, while managing to treat the specificities of the individual diseases and contextual factors related to them. The distinctions in definition of a health problem result in the need to define differing strategies, which again reflect different criteria for strategy development.

Choosing the appropriate level of intervention

The strategic communication response may be defined not only in relation to both local community-based constituencies but also to national forum of either ordinary people or decision makers in parliament. Furthermore, the transnational, regional, and often global response mechanisms are gaining growing attention. For example, there has been, in recent years, increased recognition of HIV/AIDS not only being defined as a local or national problem but also requiring transnational response mechanisms, which have been developing over the last five years.

Choosing the appropriate thematic emphasis of intervention

This ranges from focus on individual behavioral determinants to a broader socioeconomic, cultural, and political focus. In the example of polio, there has been a significant change in focus from the grand vaccination campaigns focusing on social mobilization in the late 1980s to today's broader-based campaigns with strong advocacy components. Most often, however, many organizations remain focused on behavioral interventions. Lifestyle-related health problems, such as diabetes type II, call not just for addressing behavioral dimensions but also for considering the overall development process touching upon urbanization and the consequential changes this has upon everyday life.

Focusing on content, not channels

Strategic communication, as it is understood in behavior change communication, is embedded in the logic of producing messages directed at target audiences. However, as a consequence of focusing not only on behavior change communication but increasingly on advocacy communication, participatory communication, and communication for social change, it is resulting in altered communicative strategies. From a focus on messages, we now witness a growing emphasis on showing/representing social problems and situations, inviting the audience to engage in collective reflection and action. For example, sexual and reproductive health and rights have moved away from the narrow focus on messages of family planning to a broadly defined, rights-based strategy encompassing women's empowerment and gender roles.

Communication for Development in Governance

> *"The World Bank Group has come a long way in recent years in recognizing the power of communications as an integral development tool, but we have further to go. Communications must be part of everything that we do, from our operational work in projects, to our policy research, to our engagement with clients and other partners."*
>
> —Paul Wolfowitz, President, World Bank
> Remarks before the Global Communications Forum (2006)

APPROACHES, THEMES, AND LEVELS

The critical importance of a free and balanced flow of information to an engaged and active civil society, through an independent media and transparent government, has long been acknowledged. Article 19 of the Universal Declaration of Human Rights guarantees that "everyone has the right to freedom of opinion and expression; this right includes freedom to hold opinions without interference and to seek, receive, and impart information and ideas through any media, and regardless of frontiers."

Implied in Article 19 is the connotation that the media are potential champions of the poor, oppressed, and politically suppressed. However, in the 60 years since the Declaration of Human Rights was promulgated, reality has often been sadly at variance with these intentions. Now, in a 21st-century society where the means of communication have developed exponentially, possibilities for community empowerment and access to information have also expanded. The furtherance of media and communication processes in support of increased information flows, accountability of governmental authorities, transparency, anticorruption measures, and increased democratic reform that guarantees political participation for all citizens are all now firmly on the governance agenda.

Communication plays a pivotal role in improving governance in developing countries. Governance may be defined as (a) the process by which governments are selected, monitored, and replaced; (b) the capacity of the government to formulate and implement sound policies effectively; (c) the respect of citizens and the state for the institutions that govern economic, political, and social interactions among them; and (d) the capacity for active and informed economic, social, and political dialogue among citizens within a public sphere.

Communication also enhances public participation. Participation and monitoring mechanisms may be situated in national efforts to improve public sector performance, increase transparency, and reduce corruption. A system of checks and balances, in which communication is one of the key elements, is designed to achieve accountability among and within various agencies of government, to manage conflicts of interest in the public sector, to disperse power effectively through increasing public participation, and to limit situations conducive to corrupt behavior. The effective management within the public sector relies upon these systems of accountability (World Bank 2006b).

Governance also incorporates attention to the public sphere, in which informed citizens actively engage in dialogue on political matters. Communication enhances the potential for civil society to hold governmental authorities accountable as well as to engage in political decision making. Empowering citizens to demand accountability and participation in decision making is critical to good governance. Participatory communication can only foster in an environment of freedom from political, economic, and social pressures.

The governance theme may be further categorized in terms of the following issues: (a) public institution governance; (b) local government and communities; (c) anticorruption, accountability, and institutional transparency; (d) economic reforms and infrastructure for service delivery; and (e) role of the media in monitoring institutional governance.

Public institutions governance

Active participation of citizens and civil society groups in policy making is now widely considered a sound investment and a core element of good governance, as it allows governments to tap wider sources of information and improves the quality and participation of the decisions reached by institutions at all levels. Citizens' participation and civic engagement take several forms, but each of them has at its core interactive communication models.

According to a number of international organizations, including the OECD and the World Bank, governments, in strengthening their relations with citizens and their participation to policy making, should ensure that information flows and communication channels are complete, objective, reliable, and accessible. More importantly, consultation, participation and dialogue with citizens should foster active political participation.

Effective communication in public sector institutions is a primary function of institutional performance, as well as its leadership. It is through clear and consistent communication of the practices, values, and objectives of the various public sector bodies to staff, management, and external stakeholders that the public sector most effectively supports good governance outcomes and contributes to stakeholder confidence in the public sector. In particular, openness, integrity, and effective communication are vital prerequisites of good governance. These qualities contribute to, and are implicitly linked with, other principles such as disclosure, commitment, and integration to ensure accountability in the use of public assets in the quest to achieve stated goals and objectives and required performance levels.

Communication can significantly improve public sector performance and policy formulation when members of institutions convey information and engage in dialogue with citizen groups. Moreover, communication can play a vital role in facilitating new public sector dynamics such as cross-agency governance arrangements and policy design, which are becoming more common as public sector organizations and governments seek to address increasingly complex and/or wide-ranging policy issues. Such arrangements are also facilitated by the application of new information and communication technologies that enable the rapid formation of virtual organizations to perform specific policy or operational tasks.

Commitment to information technology, however, should be based on a critical assessment of local conditions and needs. It should be realistic and not intrusive so as to operate in harmony with existing communication channels in promoting popular participation.

Access to public sector information

Governance entails public debate and open, participatory decision making; hence, the organization of interest groups and the free exchange of ideas, opinions, and information are essential to good governance. Addressing the information and communication needs of the poor and other oppressed groups is also essential, particularly when basic information concerning human rights and entitlements, public services, health, education, employment, and the like, is lacking. These groups also lack visibility and defining policy priorities and accessing resources.

The public sector is the single biggest producer of information in the developing world. Examples are demographic data, economic statistics, geographic information, business information, and local-level government information. This information resource has a considerable social and economic potential, which is untapped most of the time. Public sector information is an important economic asset: it constitutes raw material for new services, improvement of already existing services, and facilitation of commerce and trading. The presence of readily available information products based on public sector information could greatly facilitate the functioning of society as a whole. There are, however, a number of barriers that hamper the realization of the full economic and social potential of public sector information in developing countries.

Local government and communities

There is a growing consensus among development agencies, NGOs, and development practitioners that good local governance creates the conditions for sustainable development and poverty reduction by increasing citizens' participation in the local development process. Local authorities and civic groups can be influential in delivering quality services to local citizens. If they are to fulfill these roles effectively, good communication is essential to manage and answer the most pressing questions of local development: Do these local government reforms offer new spaces and significantly increase popular participation in governance? Do local governments appreciate the potential embedded in local media? What are groups working on participation doing in relationship to governance? What participatory methods can be used? A growing body of literature demonstrates ways citizen input can be linked to policy-making processes and can improve perceptions of local government legitimacy (Renn, Webler, and Wiedemann 1995).

Local governments and citizen participation play a major role in this effort by ensuring more effective and accountable local infrastructure and service delivery for the poor and by improving dialogue among different entities, including the state, local communities, and the private sector. For the last 20 years, the concept of participation has been widely used in local development, referring primarily to community activities. This concept has now been enhanced to incorporate citizenship rights and local democratic governance. Nowhere is this seen more clearly than in the multitude of new programs for decentralized governance that are found in both Southern and Northern countries.

Part of the international donors' and NGOs' local development strategies involves building partnerships and communication channels with and between national institutions, local authorities, community organizations, civil society, the private sector, and citizens. These strategies also involve promoting policy and institutional reforms to enable the transfer of powers and financial resources to more effective and accountable local spheres of government. Popular education and communication activities methodologies are needed to strengthen citizens' awareness and responsibilities under new local governance legislation.

Monitoring and evaluation of the communication activities should be undertaken at multiple levels and particularly in local communities. Fortunately, local authorities have increased their monitoring and evaluation activities in recent years, although most of such work is still conducted in-house.

Anticorruption, accountability, and transparency

Civil society organizations (CSOs) and citizens play a key role in fighting corruption. In so doing, they constitute an effective self-governance tool. The OECD, World Bank, EU, Transparency International, and other bodies widely recognize the role that an informed civil society plays in fighting corruption and advocating for more accountability and transparency in government. But what does this mean from a communication standpoint?

CSOs and the general public have taken advantage of multiple communication channels, both to support the monitoring processes and to denounce corrupt government practices. They have done so through various practices, including the encouragement of ombudsmen and whistleblowers.

The EU placed communication as one of the linchpins of anticorruption efforts in countries seeking accession to EU. "Communication on a Comprehensive EU Policy against Corruption" ensures that independent media and the free flow of information are among the most important anticorruption efforts a country can make. Communication also helps the process of demystifying and depersonalizing government—opening up information, informing citizens of their legal rights in dealing with government, and publishing staff manuals that are easily accessible to department users, contractors, and think tanks. An increasing number of studies suggest that media prevalence can be linked to improved delivery of government services because media coverage creates pressure for accountability (Adsera, Boix, and Payne 2000; Besley and Burgess 2002).

Efforts to fight corruption and realize transparency, however, have concentrated mainly on economic transparency at the level of governments and projects. Of equal importance is attention to transparency at the policy formulation level of development goals and projects. Inasmuch as development goals are mostly determined by international agencies that are largely influenced by the North, the funding of development projects in countries of the global South are mainly based on Northern constructs of development. Development is primarily viewed within economic and political points of reference that are often in conflict with economic, social, cultural, or political points of reference of countries in the South. Transparency at the policy level requires the adoption of universal constructs of development that take into consideration cultural, as well as societal particularities.

Economic reforms and infrastructure for service delivery

Economic reforms and infrastructures constitute a significant part of the donors' lending and technical assistance programs to developing countries. Such reforms go to the core of the norms around which societies are organized, thus affecting the relationship and informal interactions between institutions and citizens. Such reforms, therefore, require all parties to accept a significant change in beliefs and perceptions about the nature of public goods and a new balance between government responsibility, public investment, and private sector activities.

Economic reforms require a shift in the rights and responsibilities of all players and call for national mobilization of civil servants, ministries, businesses, academics, media, unions, consumers, civil society, and NGOs to move the economic reforms and infrastructure-building programs forward.

In this highly complex sociopolitical environment, economic reforms and infrastructure projects are under increased public scrutiny. Performance of communication activities based on product outputs (for example, number of radio and TV spots, advertisements, and so on) is no longer sufficient to meet these new demands. Constituencies want to know more about how reforms can have a significant impact on poverty reduction and the economic participation well-being of all citizens. Traditionally, many infrastructure projects have often been accompanied by controversy. In this respect, a communication role has often been that of damage control. Within the current development context, however, communication is expected to anticipate and prevent problems, not just chronicle their efforts.

Role of the media in good governance

The role of the media is critical in promoting good governance through institutional monitoring. The media are a critical element in a country's institutional accountability and anticorruption efforts. They have a dual role to play: they not only raise public awareness about corruption, its causes, consequences, and possible remedies; they also investigate and report incidences of corruption. The effectiveness of the media, in turn, depends on access to information and freedom of expression, as well as a professional and ethical cadre of investigative journalists.

When the media are working well, they prevent corruption via their monitoring activities. Investigative journalism may reveal inequities and violations and, by doing so, reinforce social values. In a very practical sense, they may also reduce the incidence of corruption in both the public and private sector. By the same token, in an environment of free speech and a free press, the media perform a watchdog function and expose social injustices wherever they occur. In an open, pluralistic, and developed society, the media are a particularly effective tool for exposing and preventing corruption; they are successful at this, because corruption cases usually make the news.

In recent years, the word "governance" has been integrated into the language of development and social change. The term has a wide range of connotations and understandings, often depending upon the stance of the organization, body or authority involved.

In one example, Australia's overseas aid agency, AusAID (2000: 3–6), has a broad view of the subject:

> *Effective governance means competent management of a country's resources in a way that is fair, open, accountable, and responsive to people's needs.*
>
> *Good governance is the basic building block for development. It is the most effective investment that Australia can make in promoting sustained growth, improving living standards, and reducing poverty.*
>
> *Support for good governance is not restricted to central governments, but must be adopted by service delivery areas of partner governments, local administrations, civil society, and the private sector.*

In addressing the various constituencies and improving governance, AusAID has targeted five key areas:

- Improved economic and financial management
- Increased public sector effectiveness
- Strengthened law and justice
- Development of civil society
- Strengthened democratic systems

The World Bank has made governance its central plank in lending decision making, while some country programs consist entirely of funds for this sector. In 2005, World Bank lending for governance, public sector reform, and rule of law totaled some US$2.9 billion, constituting 13 percent of the bank's new lending for the year.

Apart from specific lending programs, governance and anticorruption measures are mainstreamed in all World Bank country strategies, especially in those countries prone to corruption. The Bank's work on governance covers anticorruption, administrative and civil service reform, decentralization, public financial management, tax policy, and legal and judicial reform. Demands for good governance are expressed through media development, participation, and social accountability measures.

The role of media in good governance initiatives is a relatively new area of concentration for international agencies and donors. In 1999, the World Bank's vice president for East Asia and the Pacific, Jean-Michel Severino, put it this way:

> *We have seen the need for clean, open, and effective institutions, and we recognize the corrosive effect of corruption, both on investor confidence and also on those institutions and investment decisions. A free press, informed, and well trained in the skills of analysis and investigation, may be one of the best resources a country can have in managing the challenges and taking advantage of the opportunities presented by the globalized economy.*

The difficulties facing international agencies, donors, and NGOs in assisting the strengthening of communication processes to better combat poor governance issues are manifold. The World Bank itself has admitted that it "does not have the authority to demand press freedoms in its borrowing countries" (Severino 1999: 2).

UNESCO is another international organization with an ongoing program supportive of press freedom and governance. Its 2005 World Press Freedom Day theme was devoted to the subject. The Final Declaration of the global conference stressed "independent and pluralistic media are essential for ensuring transparency, accountability, and participation as fundamental elements of good governance and human-rights based development." It also called on UNESCO's member states to "respect the function of the news media as an essential factor in good governance, vital to increasing both transparency and accountability in decision-making processes and to communicating the principles of good governance to society" (Matsuura 2005).

The dilemma facing the international community in this domain is in translating words into actions through a positive interface with national governments and in-country authorities and in combating attempts to derail the process and deny the citizenry access to the information needed to improve lives.

EVIDENCE AND VALUE ADDED BY GOVERNANCE AND DEVELOPMENT

Relative to other development themes, such as health, communication in support of good governance represents a relatively new field and one with a unique set of challenges. Further study will be required to provide evidence of successful practices in different development sectors. The following cases illustrate the promise and potential of development communication in the governance arena.

Voices on the Breeze: Communication for empowerment in Zambia

Until 2003 when Breeze FM came on the air, the people of Chipata in eastern Zambia had little involvement in the content of their local radio broadcasting. Information came from two main sources: government radio stations, which broadcast from the capital city, Lusaka, located some 600 kilometers away, and civil society and religious sources. The communication was largely one-way and was about issues that the government, civil society, and church organizations thought were important for the people. Two things were missing: relevant and localized information on the issues that most affected and most concerned people in the region and the opportunity to discuss and bring to public attention their concerns and perceptions.

When Breeze FM opened in the provincial town of Chipata in 2003, the situation changed. The commercial station prided itself on serving the community. It hired a retired school teacher who soon became known as "Gogo" (grandfather) Breeze. Gogo Breeze is pioneering a new type of journalism. Every day he travels on his bicycle from township to township and village to village, meeting and talking to people about their lives and problems. In addition to recording their long-ignored folklore and music, Gogo Breeze follows up on people's complaints and grievances. He covers distances of up to 70 kilometers responding to the requests from villagers to visit their areas. When at the station he spends a lot of time receiving ordinary folk who come into town.

Other programs include the most popular "Letters from Our Listeners," in which people, young and old, ask for his assistance in resolving issues ranging from family and community conflicts to poor governance and service delivery at central, provincial, local, and traditional levels. The government is slowly waking up to the fact that the local radio station is more effective in communicating important information to the public than its own national station and, as a result, it is beginning to work with the Breeze station on agricultural, education, environmental, and health issues (Jacobson 1997: 86, 88–89).

Not just radio: India and the rural newspaper revolution

India has undergone more dramatic and rapid change in its media landscape perhaps than any other country, characterized particularly by a dramatic liberalization and an explosion of satellite television. A less documented, but no less significant, revolution is taking place in its rural newspaper industry.

In many countries, people living in rural areas are considered to be a low priority for newspapers. Distribution is expensive, newsgathering difficult and advertisers are often uninterested in a population with so little purchasing power. In India, however, rural areas are increasingly important business for newspapers. In many Indian states, including Madhya Pradesh, Bihar, Jharkhand, Chhattisgarh, and Uttar Pradesh, newspapers have fine-tuned their publication and delivery schedules to deliver newspapers by 6 a.m. to villages (or at least those that are close to roads), in every district of the state. A market for newspapers has been created by growing literacy rates, improved roads and other communications, increased purchasing power, and increased hunger for information of all kinds. Newspapers, which have found their urban markets declining or stagnating, and advertising income leaching to television, have been forced to look for new markets.

Local newspaper editions are now important information channels for development agents at the village level. CSOs have been able to get community news, including women's news, as well as to publicly raise these issues in the wider society. This development has been reported to add transparency to the dynamics of political parties, generating discussion on given policy options. On the other hand, Sevanta Ninan, an Indian media researcher who has written extensively on this revolution, argues that the revolution has its drawbacks. "Rural scribes are loose cannons. They inform, but they also sensationalize and trivialize." The newspaper revolution has also tended to be driven by profit maximizing, rather than development concerns. The Indian government is resisting pressure to liberalize radio broadcasting and this in turn has prevented the emergence of a vibrant community radio sector. Rural newspapers are in some respects filling this gap, providing an obvious point of engagement for those working to improve governance.

Communication for empowerment in Peru: Citizens' Media Watch

Citizens' Media Watch brings together 11 CSOs to monitor the quality of the mass media in Peru. Founded in 2001 and hosted by the NGO, Calandria, it consists of the National Association of Advertisers (ANDA), UNICEF, communication faculties of several different universities, and a web of interested specialists and opinion leaders. There is also a group of volunteers from seven cities: Lima, Arequipa, Cusco, Puno, Iquitos, Trujillo, and Chimbote. The principal objectives of Citizens' Media Watch are to mobilize civil society institutions to work toward better-quality mass media content; make visible citizens' opinions regarding the media; educate and mobilize citizens to achieve the right to voice their opinions; and influence the authorities, entrepreneurs, and media themselves to see their responsibility in communicating with Peruvian audiences. Citizens' Media Watch claims that it is currently the only institution in Peru dedicated exclusively to monitoring media for better quality and to offering mechanisms for citizen participation. Through Media Watch, citizens can express their opinion about media.

Ter Yat: The Ugandan megaforum

Ter Yat is a weekly political talk show broadcast on Mega FM, a community-based radio station in Gulu, northern Uganda. It was established explicitly to increase dialogue and public understanding in order to defuse tensions. Supported by DFID, but run on a commercial basis, the station broadcasts 24 hours a day, and has a strong emphasis on development programming. Unlike most other radio stations accessible in the region, it broadcasts in Luo, the local language. Audience research suggests that it is listened to by more than half a million people. *Ter Yat* is one of the most popular programs on the station. It is broadcast on Saturday mornings. Political leaders and opinion makers discuss issues of regional and national importance. Ministers, members of parliament, religious leaders, politicians, and rebels talk in the studio or by phone and give their views on the way forward to peace and development.

THE POTENTIAL FOR DEVELOPMENT COMMUNICATION IN THE FIELD OF GOVERNANCE

Communication provides the foundation necessary for the facilitation of good governance, through promotion of effective government, accountability, and the active engagement of participants in civil society. The above examples illustrate how local radio and newspaper systems can engage citizens in relevant political dialogue and decision making.

It is important to note that good governance and good government are not the same. Good governance is based on the participation of all people concerned. Focusing on the operation of governmental institutions, such as decentralization, does not go far enough. Decentralization does not always signify democratization. In reality the motives for decentralization may hide a central authorities' desire to dispense with certain obligations while tightening their control in other areas.

In order to promote participation, it is important to reinforce independent and pluralistic media. For media to be able to offer a critical view of government, political and economic systems must enable the media to operate in as open a public sphere as possible. Press freedom is never guaranteed, particularly when media industries are commercialized—even in a democracy. Apart from creating the appropriate political and economic environments for a free press system, it is crucial to educate journalists to the highest ethical and professional standards possible.

These issues are relevant to all media systems, especially print and broadcasting. They also address ICTs' potential to promote governmental transparency and to engage civil society in yet to be defined ways. Discussions of relevant media systems must take into account the expectations and aspirations of the communities involved. For the media to provide a useful public sphere for political dialogue, technological systems, content, and language need to be accessible by local communities. In addition, although most of this discourse tends to focus on the importance of news and information systems, the critical role of popular culture in political socialization should not be overlooked.

The Role of ICTs in Communication for Development

> *"We, the representatives of the peoples of the world, assembled in Geneva from 10 to 12 December 2003 for the first phase of the World Summit on the Information Society, declare our common desire and commitment to build a people-centered, inclusive, and development-oriented Information Society, where everyone can create, access, utilize, and share information and knowledge, enabling individuals, communities, and peoples to achieve their full potential in promoting their sustainable development and improving their quality of life, premised on the purposes and principles of the Charter of the United Nations and respecting fully and upholding the Universal Declaration of Human Rights."*
>
> —Declaration of Principles: World Summit on the Information Society, 2003

ICTs can be vital tools in Communication for Development efforts to achieve the Millennium Development Goals in health, education, and community development and in a number of other initiatives. They can deliver a range of services, help capacity building, empower communities, and bridge social divides. For example, rural artisans in Thailand are now able to use the Internet to market their crafts to a global audience. Urban women in Senegal use the power of technology to advocate for gender policies on employment and to increase support for environments more conducive to entrepreneurial activities by women. Access to and use of affordable information are critical to human survival—

be it access to information on public services and the delivery of health services, the price of agricultural commodities, or the latest information on the weather. How to access and leverage information in the planning and execution of development remains a key issue that has been prioritized by governments, nongovernmental agencies, and civil society.

With the benefit of hindsight and based on evidence from the field, it is now clear that the success of ICT projects is conditioned by an integrated approach to development and social change. ICTs are not a panacea to all development problems and cannot by themselves contribute to sustainable development. ICTs require enabling political and cultural environments and supportive infrastructures in order to succeed.

Projects need uninterrupted supplies of electricity along with technical and logistical support, availability of technical know-how, and back-end services. The success of e-governance projects, for example, may rest on the availability of government information, adequate turnarounds of response, and the availability of accessible hardware and affordable services. In other words, ICT projects require an integrated approach, an enabling environment, and the required capital expenditures. All too often, ICT projects are standalone initiatives relying too much on the technological capacities of such tools, neglecting other crucial considerations.

While governments; nongovernmental agencies, such as the World Bank and the FAO; the private sector; and civil society continue to invest in ICT projects, there is also a vital need for comparative studies and assessments of the impact of ICT projects and their contribution to development and social change. This is essential—for without adequate benchmarks and an appreciation of successes and failures, the potential of ICT projects will remain a mystery. Agencies therefore need to continue to support ICT projects and the ancillary services they require, making sure to assess and prepare the needed environment for the effective use of these tools. The more participatory an ICT project is, the better the chances are that it will achieve its objectives. An enabling environment must include opportunities for women and marginalized sectors of society to use ICTs effectively for their development. Such involvement in the planning and delivery of ICT projects along with other stakeholders is a strategic choice that needs to be made by organizations involved in the sector.

THE PROLIFERATION AND PROMISE OF ICTS

In recent years, much of the world has experienced exponential growth in the distribution and use of advanced ICTs. Their diffusion has accelerated rapidly in recent decades due to the convergence of what were once distinct technologies (for example, the telephone, the radio, the television, and the computer). The appearance of cable and satellite transmission systems has also sped the diffusion of ICTs. In turn, such developments have spawned powerful media industries that now employ millions of people in an "information society" of global proportions.

Wireless telephone and Internet access have grown the most dramatically of all ICTs, with subscriber increases of over 15,000 percent and 8,300 percent, respectively, between 1991 and 2003 (see table A.3.1). In fact, mobile phones are now the preferred technology among communication planners intent on providing basic telephone service to neglected populations. China, for example, is modernizing and expanding its telecommunication sector by "leapfrogging" its established land-line phone systems in many areas.

In addition to the scientific and engineering innovations that have made ICTs affordable to increasing numbers of people worldwide, many governments have deregulated their telecom sectors and, in the process, privatized what were formerly state-run industries. As a result, urban consumers in wealthy nations are now connected to sources of information and entertainment that were once beyond their means and even their imaginations.

Although the connectivity and multimedia features of ICTs have increased access to information of all kinds, the provision and sharing

Table A.3.1 Global Access to ICTs, 1991–2003

	1991	2003	% increase
Main telephone lines	546 million	1.21 billion	222
Mobile cellular subscribers	16 million	1.33 billion	8,306
Personal computers	130 million	650 million	500
Internet users	4.4 million	665 million	15,045

Source: Data derived from ITU (2003) and cited by Hudson (2006).

of such information on a global scale remain major challenges. Copyright and censorship policies restrict the flow of information, both within and across national borders. Vested interests, public as well as private, seek control of ICTs for their own purposes. Fortunately, forces dedicated to expanding people's access to and use of ICTs have emerged. The "open-source movement" is one such force. It consists of a growing number of computer programmers, software designers, and content providers who wish to expand citizens' access to information of all kinds through online collaboration and sharing (DiBona, Cooper, and Stone 2006). Open-source advocates are dedicated to the proposition that media content should be made available to people everywhere through existing network-enabled distribution systems.

OVERCOMING OBSTACLES TO ICT ACCESS AND USE

Although ICTs and the information resources that accompany them are expanding at exponential rates throughout the world, they are doing so in uneven and discriminatory ways. Telecommunication and computer services still are restricted to the urban centers of most developing countries. Rural, poor, and disadvantaged persons in these nations are denied access to ICTs because they are poor and often marginalized, both geographically and politically. The fact is the vast majority of people in developing countries have never made a telephone call, much less used a computer. African nations are the most underserved by ICTs. Together, they have only 6 telephone subscribers per 100 people. Such density is less than one-tenth that found on other continents. As a result, while Africa is home to approximately 13.5 percent of the world's population, less than 2 percent of all Internet users reside there (ITU 2003).

In its 1997 Statement on Universal Access to Basic Communication and Information Services, the United Nations Administrative Committee on Coordination (ACC) concluded that most developing countries, especially the least developed countries (LDCs), are not reaping the benefits of the communications revolution since they lack the following basic services:

- Affordable access to core information sources, cutting-edge technology, and sophisticated telecommunications systems and infrastructure
- The capacity to build, operate, manage, and service the technologies involved

- Policies that promote equitable public participation in the information society as both producers and consumers of information and knowledge
- A workforce trained to develop, maintain, and provide the value added products and services required by the information economy (United Nations Administrative Committee on Coordination 1997, cited by Hudson 2006)

Whereas increasing numbers of people in North America, Europe, and parts of Asia are privileged to have telephones and computers in their homes and in their places of work, residents of poor countries are denied access to these technologies and, hence, the essential connectivity that they provide. To date, neither governments nor private companies have invested adequately in the infrastructure—trained personnel, reliable power supplies, and technical support systems—required for ICT networks to operate on a large scale. With the exception of radio, the costs associated with the installation, maintenance, and continuous upgrading of communication technologies are considered to be prohibitively high. They are likely to remain so for the foreseeable future. For this reason, the challenge of "mainstreaming" ICTs for the benefit of neglected and underserved populations in developing nations is viewed best from a community as opposed to an individual consumer or even household perspective.

ICTS AS CATALYSTS FOR COMMUNITY DEVELOPMENT AND SOCIAL CHANGE

For more than 40 years, the mass media—print, radio, and television—have been addressing development needs in education, health, agriculture, family planning, and the like. Customarily, such initiatives have relied on the mass media to inform, educate, and persuade large numbers of people. By the same token, such programs have often been criticized for being technocentric and "top-down" in their approaches to community development and social change. As a result, programs incorporating new and inherently more interactive ICTs are gaining favor insofar as they connect people and communities to one another and to previously unavailable information resources.

Unquestionably, wireless telephones and other ICTs are a promising means for meeting the information needs of rural people and other underserved populations. Cell phones typically are less costly to install and maintain than fixed-line technologies. They can be expanded incrementally, they can provide a range of voice and data services, and they can access open-source content. When planned in a coordinated way, they can also have a powerful multiplier effect on development. For example, within the past three years, the small nation of the former Yugoslav Republic of Macedonia succeeded in linking all of its 460 primary schools and all of its 100 secondary schools to the Internet. At the same time, it trained 80 master trainers and all 2,500 of the nation's secondary school teachers in Internet use (DOT-COM Alliance 2006).

On an international scale, ICTs are now used to supplement traditional classroom instruction by providing students and teachers with worldwide access to educational materials of all kinds. The networking of schools within and across regions via the Internet is also increasing rapidly. One such network, World Links, was founded by the World Bank in 2001. Now a private entity, it provides Internet access to over 1,000 school-based learning centers. Comparable Internet services have been supported in recent years by other regional and international consortia, including Schoolnet Africa, LearnLink, and the DOT-COM Alliance.

ICTs also are being deployed increasingly within the health sectors of many nations, both to extend coverage and to improve the quality of medical care in remote areas. Telemedicine services now include satellite-based emergency communications; training of medical personnel (doctors, paraprofessionals, and village health workers) via the Web; and remote diagnosis, the virtual treatment and monitoring of patients. In many respects, the communication protocols associated with these innovations are modeled on the two-way radio services established by Australia's "Flying Doctor" program, which began in 1928, and by Alaska's Rural Health Service, which was launched some 40 years later.

While ICTs are directly increasing people's access to education and health services, they also are enhancing the value of other communication media. For example, radio remains the most accessible mass medium in rural areas of many nations and is likely to remain so for years to come. Community radio stations are the prime source of information and entertainment for millions of rural listeners in Latin American countries. Stations affiliated with the *Asociación Latinoamerica de Educación Radiofónica* (ALER) and the World

Association of Community Radio Broadcasters (AMARC) have "reinvigorated" their service to village audiences by (a) providing local programmers access to Internet materials, (b) downloading audio files from portals with radio content, and (c) providing online training and other distance learning opportunities.

Telecenters have proven to be another popular means of supporting for development initiatives at the local level. They have done so by facilitating citizen access to ICT services. Telecenters typically are located in municipal buildings or in space purchased or leased from private owners. Depending on the way they are structured and the time of day, they may operate either as government and/or as commercial enterprises (that is, cybercafés). "Embellished" telecenters, in addition to fulfilling citizens' private information and communication needs, are community driven and frequently provide a range of services in education, health, and other sectors. For example, Mali's Community Learning and Information Centers (CLICs), operates 13 telecenters, which last year provided telecommunication services to over 25,000 paying customers and training to over 500 individuals in commercial and development-related subjects.

Unfortunately, the promise of community telecenters has not been fulfilled in many rural communities. Failure to establish adequate revenue streams is mostly to blame for their demise in most cases. Staff recruitment and retention, unreliable power supplies, problems with Internet connectivity, difficulties maintaining and replacing equipment, and lack of consumable materials, such as paper and toner for computer printers, have compounded the centers' precarious financial circumstances. To address such problems, partial government subsidies, perhaps derived from universal service funds or other funding mechanisms, will likely be required if telecenters are to survive in rural and other underserved areas. In other words, the local community is crucial in the running of both local radio stations and local telecenters, because they demand continuity in resources in order to become sustainable. Otherwise they end up being—as it has happened in several countries—kind of "relay stations" for substance produced outside the community.

The fate of telecenters illustrates the persistent temptation within many development agencies—both national and international—to regard the latest generation of ICTs as panaceas for deeply rooted social and economic problems. The power and pervasiveness of the media are such that they can and do promote wishful, even utopian thinking, among their advocates. When manifested in "build-it-and-they-will-come" pilot projects, such thinking produces costly and disappointing results. In order to avoid such outcomes, experience suggests that tough issues and questions must be posed at the outset of any ICT planning exercise. These include (a) the degree to which the presumed recipients of new information services are involved in their design and implementation; (b) the level of commitment, organization, training, and technical support present at different levels to sustain a program beyond its pilot phase; and (c) the ability and willingness of program participants to learn from their mistakes, to experiment with alternative funding schemes, and, when necessary, to adjust their goals and operations to meet changing circumstances.

For ICTs to have a positive and lasting effect on community development and social change, they must be controlled as much as possible at the local level. The planning of new services requires the articulation of a shared vision: one that is arrived at by negotiation among all potential stakeholders (for example, community representatives, service providers, and development sector officials). Such a vision should also set priorities on how new ICTs are going to be used—to increase access to the Internet and communication services, to provide instruction and/or training, to extend the reach of regional health clinics, and so on.

Once a new ICT network or service has been launched, the challenge is to integrate its technical and human components and to define the management, financial, and accounting procedures required to sustain it. Such arrangements and the training that accompanies them are crucial to any program's success. It also is true that programs rarely develop exactly as they were planned. For this reason, time and flexibility are required to modify ICTs to fit changing circumstances and to continue meeting community needs.

ICTS FOR DEVELOPMENT EVIDENCE AND VALUE ADDED

As noted above, ICTs are used in a wide variety of contexts around the world. These include education, job training, e-governance, e-commerce, capacity building, health care, business services, advocacy and networking, and agricultural development. Increasingly, ICTs are being used to accomplish a range of objectives—from behavioral change to education and advocacy. Projects vary in their aims and objectives and are based on different paradigms of communication and social change. Many are motivated by the need to bridge the "digital divides" existing in many societies.

The following examples of ICT-based projects illustrate different mixes of technologies and the various paradigms of Communication for Development, incorporating top-down as well as participatory models of social change.

HIV/AIDS prevention in cross-border areas of the Greater Mekong Subregion

An example of a current ICTs for development project delivering a range of objectives is UNESCO's *ICT and HIV/AIDS Prevention in Cross-Border Areas of the Greater Mekong Subregion*. Using ICTs, the project focuses on three areas: (a) high-risk behaviors, (b) trafficking of women, and (c) drug abuse among minorities.

This project uses both directed and participatory communication to achieve its objectives. While certain components of the project, the geographic information systems for example, facilitate the mapping of cross-border migration flows and are expert-led, the radio drama is produced within a participatory paradigm and involves sections of the community in the planning of story lines and the production of the radio dramas.

Expected outcomes

- Develop ICT learning materials for HIV/AIDS preventive education in the local languages of the GMS communities.
- Build the capacities of teachers, health workers, multimedia providers, and other stakeholders for HIV/AIDS preventive education.
- Expand the use of ICT interventions in HIV/AIDS preventive education.
- Deliver ICT-based interventions to isolated, marginalized, and vulnerable populations (UNESCO 2006).

The World Bank Institute's "Virtual Souk"

An example of ICTs in e-commerce is the Virtual Souk project for rural artisans in the Middle East and North Africa. The livelihoods of a variety of rural artisans are under threat from the lowering of demand for traditional arts and crafts. The Virtual Souk provides people with the opportunity to maintain their traditional livelihood as craftspeople. The Virtual Souk is a system of locally controlled Web e-commerce, which aims to provide artisans from the Middle East and North Africa (MENA), often isolated from the most lucrative national and international markets and constrained in their production mechanisms by the demands of the tourists, with access to a wider market and the chance to safeguard their traditional techniques of production (World Bank 2005a, 2005b). The Virtual Souk is based on a user-friendly and multilingual Web database catalogue of products and artisans. This has enabled artisans to sell their products to anybody over the Internet. ICTs are used to facilitate the following:

- International trade in traditional craft
- The livelihoods of traditional rural artisans
- The creation of awareness of traditional culture
- Capacity building
- Networking

The project is based on a partnership between multiple stakeholders, including NGOs, rural artisans, and ICT providers.

Outcomes

More than 1,000 artisans have benefited from this project. Despite this, the lack of infrastructural capacities, shortfalls in ICTs training, lack of NGO support, and availability of and access to technology remain key issues that are barriers to the regionwide implementation of the Virtual Souk (World Bank 2005a, 2005b).

The Gyan Ganga Telecentre Project, Gujarat, India

This project, jointly supported by the government of Gujarat and a private organization (n-Logue), is founded on 3,000 information kiosks used to fulfill multiple functions in a variety of locations in rural Gujarat. Using an indigenously manufactured WLL (local loop) technology, the project envisages the delivery of a range of services including economic information, e-education, e-governance, computer-mediated training, and public services information. The project is based on cooperation among three tiers: n-Logue—that is, the overall project implementer; the local Internet service provider; and the operator of the local ICTs kiosk. It is hoped that connectivity will lead to "wealth creation," increases in urban-rural skills and educational opportunities, better health through telemedicine, and e-governance enabled through the availability of a variety of online resources supportive of citizenship. The communication model used in this project is a combination of directed and participatory models.

Outcomes

While this project has definitely improved access to the use of ICTs and played a key role in bridging the digital divide, its implementation has been a learning experience for all concerned. The larger lessons from this project have universal validity and can be used to illustrate the strengths and weaknesses of contemporary telecenter projects. Such projects tend to be capital intensive and require infrastructural support, long-term political backing, investments in training, and the maintenance of technology, and most importantly the digitalization of back-end services. In other words, the success of ICTs projects, such as telecenters, is based on key investments in multiple support elements—from the technology itself to the software and in the "attitudes" of all stakeholders (Gupta and Agrawal 2006).

Women's Voices in Kenya

This project, which is supported by the Intermediate Technology Development Group (ITDG) and the Department for International Development (DFID), focuses on the use of ICTs for the empowerment of women in Kenya. It is part of a larger, three-nation (Peru, Zimbabwe, Kenya) project on women's representation and advocacy for social change. In Nairobi, the project is based in two shanty towns, Mathare and the Redeemed Village. In each of these villages, women have been trained (in scripting, shooting, and editing) to use video technology to record a variety of stories on issues and problems in their lives. These stories range from the plight of AIDS orphans to shelter, land tenure, alcohol, drug abuse, and crime. These 15-minute "Telling Our Story" features have been shown on national TV, on German TV, and on the BBC. The programs have also been used in the context of advocating for better government support schemes aimed at dealing with the issues faced by these women and the communities of which they are a part.

The communication paradigm used in this project is specifically oriented toward empowerment and advocacy for structural change. Changing the system and life opportunities are seen as essential to human development.

Outcomes

One of the major outcomes of this project has been the creation of self-confidence in women who are empowered to take hold of their lives, to realize the benefits of such control, to strengthen community, and to recenter their place at the heart of the family. Furthermore, the programs have directly led to government interventions aimed at rectifying some of the more obvious shortfalls of development in these two shanty towns in Nairobi (Women's Voices 2006).

Lessons Learned: Knowing How Much It Really Costs—Total Cost of Ownership

All projects with an ICT component should consider the total cost of ownership (TCO) to ensure that appropriate measures are taken to (a) budget necessary resources and (b) maximize the benefits of technology use. While TCO is not a new concept, it has not yet been integrated fully into project design and implementation (DOT-COM Alliance 2006).

Creating Enabling Environments for ICTs

Experience across a broad spectrum of development initiatives suggests that ICTs function best as catalysts for change when they are preceded by empirical research and needs assessments and accompanied by policy reforms and infrastructure investments at various levels. The latter include (a) the articulation of national development goals by sector that acknowledge and define the contributions ICTs are expected to make; (b) the enactment of regulatory reforms that facilitate the deployment of ICTs in cost-effective and sustainable ways, whether by public and/or private agencies; (c) the development of innovative financing and investment schemes, which recognize that the private sector is unlikely to expand services to rural and disadvantaged groups without appropriate incentives; and (d) the enhancement of communities' capacity over time so that they can assume prime responsibility for the design, maintenance, and expansion of ICT services and networks.

Conclusions

THE NEED FOR NEW THINKING

The collapse of the Soviet Union, coupled with the rise of U.S. power and globalization, necessitate rethinking the meaning of development. The breakdown of the demarcation of the First, Second, and Third Worlds and the presence of the Global North and Global South in every region of the world is a stark reality that simply cannot be ignored.

Consequently, here is a need for a new concept of development that emphasizes cultural identity and multidimensionality or multiplicity. The present-day "global" world, in general as well as in its distinct regional and national entities, is confronted with multifaceted crises. Apart from the obvious economic and financial crisis, we could also refer to social, ideological, moral, political, ethnic, ecological, and security crises. In other words, the previously held traditional modernization and dependency perspectives have become more difficult to support because of the growing interdependency of regions, nations, and communities in our globalized world.

From the criticisms of both the modernization and dependency paradigms, a new viewpoint is emerging which we have referred to in the past as "multiplicity." This perspective argues that considerations of communication needs to be explicitly built into development plans to ensure that a mutual sharing/learning process is facilitated. Such communicative sharing is deemed the best guarantee for creating successful transformative projects.

The new starting point is examining the processes of "bottom-up" change, focusing on self-development of local communities. The basic assumption is that there are no countries or communities that function completely autonomously and that are completely self-sufficient, nor are there any nations whose development is exclusively determined by external factors. Every society is dependent in one way or another, both in form and in degree. Thus, a framework is needed within which both the center and the periphery could be studied both separately and in their mutual relationship (at global, national, and local levels).

Attention is also needed to critically analyze the content of development agendas. An understanding of the way in which development projects both encounter and transform power relationships within (and between) the multiple stakeholders who are affected by such projects; and an understanding of the way in which communication plays a central part in building (or maintaining or changing) power relationships is needed.

NO SUSTAINABLE DEVELOPMENT WITHOUT COMMUNICATION

Communication for Development has become multifaceted, multidimensional, and participatory, and it should be seen in its sociopolitical, economic, and cultural contexts to be relevant for people.

In essence, Communication for Development is about the development of people. The MDGs and all other development initiatives should be addressed and assessed from a people's perspective. It is therefore essential to take into account the perspective of local communities and to cooperate with organizations (United Nations, governmental, NGOs, the public and the private sector, and civil society) that have developed a trust within a community.

In practice and in view of both globalizing and localizing pressures Communication for Development is becoming even more necessary within the context of the 21st century, bearing in mind the new political, economic, and communication landscapes.

This includes listing and defining its various domains, such as project-related and community communication, development journalism, development communication in the mainstream media, educational communication, health communication, environmental communication, social marketing, social mobilization, advocacy, and so on.

However, Communication for Development should not be technology driven. It should be based on social issues and concerns. Technology is at best a facilitator and a tool.

Instead, culture and social dialogue are central to development and deserve greater emphasis in Communication for Development programs.

MAIN CHALLENGES FOR THE FIELD OF COMMUNICATION FOR DEVELOPMENT

Main challenges for Communication for Development to be recognized as a field in its own right and to be adopted systematically in development initiatives are as follows:

1. Good governance, transparency, accountability, and development communication go hand in hand. Good governance and a good government are not the same. Good governance is based on the participation of all people concerned. Decentralization of governmental institutions does not necessarily imply people's participation. Decentralization does not always mean democratization. In reality the motives for decentralizing may hide a wish of central powers to get rid of certain responsibilities while tightening their control. This blurs the lines of accountability. For this reason, local media have a crucial role to play in facilitating a mutual understanding between those in power and the communities.
2. Participatory concepts in the context of Communication for Development can be complex and challenging. Communities consist of fluid interests and shifting relationships.
3. Participation can take place at different levels: (a) research/assessment, (b) decision making, (c) benefits, (d) evaluation, and (e) implementation. Participation is about changing power relations. While empowering one group, it may do the opposite to another. Meaningful participation requires organization around common interests and awareness on how to handle power relations.
4. Communication for Development can play a crucial role in assessing the feasibility of an initiative, in minimizing political risks, and in identifying opportunities for positive change. The value of this role should be made evident to policy and decision makers, indicating how by involving stakeholders from the start, Communication for Development is instrumental in assessing the situation, leading to better program and project design. It also strengthens local stakeholders' sense of ownership, increasing its sustainability.
5. It is important to reinforce independent and pluralistic media to foster good governance and transparency. Print media can play a special role in society as they are sometimes more independent

and pluralistic than radio and television. However, all media need to be sensitized and become more participatory; even better, they need a political environment compatible with, and conducive to, the requirements of free and participatory media systems. Currently there is often a gap between what media report and the realities of a country. Pure commercialism avoids tackling the crucial issues of a country because such issues do not sell. It undermines the role of media as watchdogs. Press freedom is never guaranteed, not even in a democracy.

6. Communication for Development has not made full use of the potential of radio, which in some regions could be the most effective participatory tool. Radio has the highest penetration in many rural areas in developing countries. It is not too late to rediscover radio. In particular community radio (often linked to the global world through the Internet) has proven its ability to make participation effective and sustainable. Therefore, ICTs are also an important tool to facilitate development programs and projects provided that application and operation systems are made available in local languages.
7. With respect to policies and resources, Communication for Development initiatives need to be properly enabled by concerted actions, and adequate policies and resources. These should consider longer timescales. It is essential to bridge the digital divide by supporting community access to relevant information in their own language and at an affordable cost, for example, through community telecenters/multimedia centers. This should also involve support for the production of content by the local communities. It is crucial to encourage the production of diverse local content in local languages for the media and ICTs, bearing in mind the potential of interactive technologies to carry multimedia content.
8. Build alliances. There is a need for effective linkages that give voices to the poorest and have the ability to engage with policy and influence decision making on sustainable development. To this end, special attention should be given to fostering local, national, and regional Communication for Development processes.
9. New global partnerships are necessary with the media, development agencies, universities, and governments. It is important to identify possibilities for convergence and for complementing

existing work and to coordinate and document such work via a truly independent scientific body.

Note

1. As stated previously, whereas the first three themes were part of the overall framework of the Congress, ICTs were not. They have been dealt in special sessions and within a cross-cutting thematic stream called Communication Labs.

Bibliography

Adsera, A., C. Boix, and M. Payne. 2000. "Are You Being Served? Political Accountability and Quality of Government." Research Department Working Papers Series 438, Inter-American Development Bank, Washington, DC.

Airhihenbuwa, Collins, and Rafael Obregón. 2000. "A Critical Assessment of Theories/Models Used in Health Communication for HIV/AIDS." *Journal of Health Communication* Vol. 5 (supplement): 5–15.

Airhihenbuwa, Collins, Bunmi Makinwa, and Rafael Obregón. 2000. "Toward a New Communications Framework for HIV/AIDS." *Journal of Health Communication* Vol. 5 (supplement): 5–15, 101–12.

Ajzen, I., and M. Fishbein. 1997. *Understanding Attitudes and Predicting Social Behavior*. New York: Prentice-Hall.

AusAID. 2000. *Good Governance: Guiding Principles for Implementation*. Canberra: AusAID.

Babalola, S. 2005. "Strategic Communication Changes Norms and Intentions Related to FGC in Nigeria." *Communication Impact* 18 (June). Baltimore, MD: Johns Hopkins Center for Communication Programs.

Balit, S. 1998. "Listening to Farmers: Communication for Participation and Change in Latin America." Rome: FAO. http://www.fao.org/sd/CDdirect/CDan0018.htm.

———. 2004. "Communication for Isolated and Marginalized Groups Blending the Old and the New." *Communication for Development Roundtable Report*. Rome: FAO.

Bandura, A. 1986. *Social Foundations of Thought and Action*. Englewood Cliffs, NJ: Prentice-Hall.

Beltrán, S. L. R. 1974. "Rural Development and Social Communication: Relationships and Strategies." Proceedings at the Corner-

CIAT International Symposium on Communication Strategies on Rural Development, Cali, Colombia, March 17–22. Ithaca, NY: Cornell University, 11–27.

Besley, T., and R. Burgess. 2002. "The Political Economy of Government Responsiveness: Theory and Evidence from India." *Quarterly Journal of Economics* November: 1415–51.

Boulay, M., J. D. Storey, and S. Sood. 2002. "Indirect Exposure to a Family Planning Mass Media Campaign in Nepal." *Journal of Health Communication* 7 (5): 379–99. Cambridge, MA: The MIT Press.

Center for Communication Programs. 2006a. "The Adolescent Reproductive Health Program in Bangladesh." http://www.hcpartnership.org/Programs/Asia/bangladesh/ARH.php.

———. 2006b. "Y.E.A.H. Launches 'Be a Man' Campaign in Uganda." http://www.hcpartnership.org/Press/press2006-06-21.php

Chemers, M. M. 2000. "Leadership Research and Theory: A Functional Integration." *Group Dynamics: Theory Research and Practice* 4: 27–43.

Deane, J., and T. Scalway. 2003. *Missing the Message? 20 Years of Learning from HIV/AIDS.* London: The Panos Institute.

DFID (UK Department for International Development). 2003. "Enabling Effective Support." DFID, London.

Díaz Bordenave, J. 1994. "Participative Communication as a Part of Building the Participative Society." In *Participatory Communication: Working for Change and Development,* ed. S. A. White and N. K. Sadanandan, 35–48. London: Sage.

DiBona, C., D. Cooper, and M. Stone, eds. 2006. *Open Sources 2.0: the Continuing Evolution.* Sebastapol, CA: Calpoly.

DOT-COM Alliance. 2006. *DOT-COMments e-Newsletter*19 (March). http://www.dot-com-alliance.org/newsletter/article.php?article_id=161.

Elliott, J. A. 1994. *An Introduction to Sustainable Development.* London: Routledge.

El-Zanaty, F., and A. Way. 2006. Egypt Demographic and Health Survey 2006. Cairo: Ministry of Health and Population, National Population Council, El-Zanaty and Associates, and ORC Macro.

Evans, R. G. and G. L. Stoddart. 1990. "Producing Health, Consuming Health Care." *Social Science Medicine* 31: 1347–63.

FAO (Food and Agriculture Organization of the UN). 1984. *Expert Consultation on Communication for Development.* Rome: FAO.

Feek, W. 2006. The Communication Initiative Web site. http://www.comminit.com.

Figueroa, M. E., D. L. Kincaid, M. Rani, and G. Lewis. 2002. *Communication for Social Change: A Framework for Measuring the Process and Its Outcomes.* New York: The Rockefeller Foundation and Johns Hopkins Center for Communication Programs.

Fraser, C., and S. Restrepo-Estrada. 1996. "Communication for Rural Development in Mexico: In Good Times and in Bad." FAO, Rome.

Fraser, C., and J. Villet. 1994. *Communication—A Key to Human Development.* Rome: FAO.

Freire, P. 1983. *Pedagogy of the Oppressed.* New York: Seaburg Press.

Fuglesang, M. 2005. "*SiMchezo!* Magazine: Community Media Making a Difference." In *Media, Communication, and Social Change: Rethinking Communication for Development,* ed. O. Hemer and T. Tufte, 385–403. Göteborg, Sweden: NORDICOM; Buenos Aires: CLACSO.

Gray-Felder, D. 1998. "Communication and Social Change: A Position Paper and Conference Report." http://www.communicationforsocialchange.org/pdf/socialchange.pdf.

Gumucio-Dagrón, A. 2001. *Making Waves: Stories of Participatory Communication for Social Change.* New York: The Rockefeller Foundation.

Gupta, P., and S. M. Agrawal. 2006. "Rural Telecom: A Case Study on Gyan Ganga project, Indian Institute of Management, Ahmedabad." http://www.iimahd.ernet.in/ctps/pdf/Gyan%20Ganga%20Report.pdf.

Hornik, R. 1989. "Channel Effectiveness in Development Communication Programs." In *Public Communication Campaigns,* 2nd ed., ed. R. E. Rice and C. K. Atkin, 309–30. Newbury Park, CA: Sage.

Hudson, H. E. 2006. *From Rural Village to Global Village: Telecommunications for Development in the Information Age.* Mahwah, NJ: Lawrence Erlbaum Associates.

IOM (Institute of Medicine). 2004. *Health Literacy: A Prescription to End Confusion.* Washington, DC: National Academies Press.

Irigoin, Maria, Paula Tarnapol, Dana Faulkner, and Gloria Coe, eds. 2002. "Mapping Competencies for Communication for Development and Social Change: Turning Knowledge, Skills, and Attitudes Into Action." The Change Project/Academy for Educational Development, Washington, DC.

ITU (International Telecommunication Union). 2003. *World Telecommunication Development Report*. Geneva: ITU.

Jacobson, J. 1997. "Changing Communication Strategies for Reproductive Health and Rights: An Overview." In *Working Group on Reproductive Health and Family Planning Report from the Meeting on Changing Communication Strategies for Reproductive Health and Rights* (December 10–11, 1997, Washington, DC). New York: Population Council.

Kawachi, I., B. P. Kennedy, and K. Lochner. 1997. "Long Live Community: Social Capital as Public Health." *The American Prospect* 8 (35): 56–59.

Kelly, K., W. Parker, H. Hajiyiannis, P. Natlabati, D. L. Kincaid, and M. Do. 2005. *Tsha-Tsha: Key Findings of the Evaluation of Episodes 1–26*. South Africa: CADRE.

Kemm, James. 2005. "The Limitations of Evidence-Based Public Health." *Journal of Evaluation in Clinical Practice* 12(3): 319–24.

Kincaid, D. L., and M. E. Figueroa. Forthcoming. "Communication for Participatory Development: Dialogue, Collective Action and Change." *Handbook of Applied Communication*, ed. L. Frey and L. Cissna. Mahwah, NJ: Lawrence Erlbaum Associates.

Lord, R. G., and D. J. Brown. 2004. *Leadership Processes and Follower Self-Identity*. Mahwah, NJ: Lawrence Erlbaum Associates.

MacBride, S. 1980. *Many Voices, One World*. London/UNESCO: Kogan Page.

Malhotra, A., S. Mathur, R. Pande, and E. Roca. 2005. "Do Participatory Programs Work? Improving Reproductive Health for Disadvantaged Youth in Nepal." *Development Outreach* May. http://www1.worldbank.org/devoutreach/may05/article.asp?id=303.

Malikhao, Patchanee. 2005. "HIV/AIDS Prevention Campaigns from a Thai Buddhist Perspective." *Media Development* 52 (2): 57–62.

Maticka-Tyndale, E., D. Elkins, M. Haswell-Elkins, D. Rujkarakorn, T. Kuyyakanond, and K. Stam. 2004. "Contexts and Patterns of Men's Commercial Sexual Partnerships in Northeastern Thailand: Implications for AIDS Prevention." *Qualitative Health Research* 14 (3): 328–44.

Matsuura, L. 2005. "World Press Freedom Day 2005: Media and Good Governance—Message by UNESCO Director-General." http://portal.unesco.org/ci/en/ev.phpURL, 2005.

McKee, N., E. Manoncourt, C. Yoon, and R. Carnegie, eds. 2000. *Involving People Evolving Behaviour*. Penang, Malaysia: Southbound.

McKinley, M., and L. Jensen. 2003. "In Our Own Voices: Reproductive Health Radio Programming in the Peruvian Amazon." *Critical Studies in Media Communication* 20 (2): 180–203.

Mefalopulos, P. 2005. "Communication for Sustainable Development: Applications and Challenges." In *Media, Communication, and Social Change: Rethinking Communication for Development*, ed. O. Hemer and T. Tufte, 247–60. Göteborg, Sweden: NORDICOM; Buenos Aires: CLACSO.

Moser, C. O. 1993. *Gender Planning and Development: Theory, Practice, and Training*. London and New York: Routledge.

Nutbeam, D. 2000. "Health Literacy as a Public Health Goal: A Challenge for Contemporary Health Education and Communication Strategies into the 21st Century." *Health Promotion International* 15: 259–67.

Panos. 2003. *Missing the Message? 20 Years of Learning from HIV/AIDS*. London: The Panos Institute.

Piotrow, P. T., D. L. Kincaid, J. G. Rimon, and W. Rinehart. 1997. *Health Communication: Lessons from Family Planning and Reproductive Health*. Westport, CT: Praeger.

Population Reference Bureau. 2006. "World Population Data Sheet." http://www.prb.org/pdf06/06WorldDataSheet.pdf.

Quebral, N. 1975. *The Making of a Development Communicator*. Laguna, Philippines: University of the Philippines–Los Baños.

Ramírez, R. 1997. "Understanding Farmers' Communication Networks: Combining PRA with Agricultural Knowledge Systems Analysis." Gatekeeper Series No. 66. IIED: London. http://www.iied.org/sarl/gatekeepers/gk_backissues/41_80.html; http://www.poptel.org.uk/iied/agri/66-farmerscommun.html.

Renn, O., T. Webler, and P. Wiedemann. 1995. *Fairness and Competence in Citizen Participation: Evaluating Models for Environmental Discourse*. Dordrecht, Netherlands: Kluwer.

Robinson, W., and F. El-Zanaty. 2006. *The Demographic Revolution in Modern Egypt*. Oxford, UK: Lexington Books.

Rockefeller Foundation. 1999. *Communication for Social Change: A Position Paper and Conference Report*. New York: Rockefeller Foundation. www.communicationforsocialchange.org/pdf/positionpaper.pdf.

Rodríguez, C. 2005. "From the Sandinista Revolution to Telenovelas: The Case of *Puntos de Encuentro*, Nicaragua." In *Media, Communication, and Social Change: Rethinking Communication for Development*, ed. O. Hemer and T. Tufte, 367–84. Göteborg, Sweden: NORDICOM; Buenos Aires: CLACSO.

Rogers, E. M. 1962. *Diffusion of Innovations*. New York: Free Press.

———. 1976. *Communication and Development: Critical Perspectives*. Beverly Hills, CA: Sage.

———. 2003. *Diffusion of Innovations*, 5th ed. New York: Free Press.

Salamanca, H. 2004. "Evaluation of the *Puye* Vaccination Campaign in Colombia." http://www.comminit.com/evaluations/eval2005/evaluations-88.html.

Sandfort, T. 1998. "Homosexual and Bisexual Behaviors in European Countries." In *Sexual Behavior and HIV/AIDS in Europe*, ed. M. Hubert, N. Bajos, and T. Sanford, 68–105. London: UCL Press.

Scheepers, E., N. J. Christofides, S. Goldstein, S. Usdin, D. S. Patel, J. Garth. 2004. "Evaluating Health Communication: A Holistic Overview of the Impact of *Soul City* IV." *Health Promotion Journal of Australia* 15 (2): 121–33.

Senge, P. M. 1994. *The Fifth Discipline: The Art and Practice of the Learning Organization*. New York: Currency Doubleday.

Servaes, J. 1999. *Communication for Development: One World, Multiple Cultures*. Creskill, NJ: Hampton Press.

———, ed. 2003. *Approaches to Development: Studies on Communication for Development*. Paris: UNESCO.

Servaes, J. and P. Malikhao. 2004. *Communication and Sustainable Development*. Rome: FAO.

Severino, J.-M. 1999. "Free Press the Key to Asia." *Australian Financial Review* (April 5): 2.

Simonds, S. K. 1974. "Health Education as Social Policy." *Health Education Monographs* 2: 1–25.

Stogill, R. G. 1948. "Personal Factors Associated with Leadership. A Survey of the Literature." *Journal of Psychology* 25: 35–71.

Sukda, S. 2000. "Sexual Values and Risk Behavior of Students in State University." Chulalongkorn University, Bangkok.

Terry, D. J., C. Gallois, and M. McCamish. 1993. *The Theory of Reasoned Action: Its Application to AIDS-Preventive Behavior*. New York: Pergamon Press.

Tirmizi, S. A. 2002. "The 6-L Framework: A Model for Leadership Research and Development [electronic version]." *Leadership and Organization Development Journal* 23: 269–79.

UNAIDS (Joint United Nations Program on HIV/AIDS). 1998. *Connecting Lower HIV Infection Rates with Changes in Sexual Behavior in Thailand: Data Collection and Comparison*.

———. 1999. *Reducing Girls' Vulnerability to HIV/AIDS: The Thai Approach* (case study). Geneva: UNAIDS.

———. 2000. *HIV and Health-Care Reform in Phayao: From Crisis to Opportunity*. Geneva: UNAIDS.

———. 2006 *Report on the Global AIDS Epidemic: Executive Summary*. Geneva: UNAIDS.

UNAIDS, UNICEF (United Nations Children's Fund), and WHO (World Health Organization). 2002. "Epidemiological Fact Sheets on HIV/AIDS and Sexually Transmitted Infections in Thailand." http://www.unaids.org.

UNAIDS, USAID (U.S. Agency for International Development), and IMPACT. 1998. "Meeting the Behavioral Data Collection Needs of National HIV/AIDS and STD Programs." Report of workshop conclusions.

UNDP (United Nations Development Programme). 2004. *Thailand's Response to HIV/AIDS: Progress and Challenges*. Bangkok: UNDP.

———. 2006. "Communication for Empowerment: Developing Media Strategies in Support of Vulnerable Groups." Oslo. http://www.worldbank.org/wbi/news/docs/Severinoon freepress.htm.

UNESCO (United Nations Educational, Scientific, and Cultural Organization). 2005. "Media and Good Governance." http://www.unesco.org.

———. 2006. Trafficking and HIV/AIDS Project. Bangkok. http://www.unescobkk.org/index.php?id=475.

USAID. 2001. Draft concept paper: Communication activity approval document. Office of Population and Health, United States Agency for International Development, Washington, DC.

United Nations Administrative Committee on Coordination. 1997. "Statement on Universal Access to Basic Communication Services." April.

Vincent, Robert. 2003. "Communication for Social Change Indicators: Background Reading for the Exchange Discussion on Communication for Social Change, Exchange." London.

Waldick, Lisa. 2001. "Staking a Claim in Cambodia's Highlands." Reports: Science from the Developing World. International Development Research Centre March 30, 2001. http://www.comminit.com/strategicthinking/stfaocommnrm/sld-1701.html.

White, S. A. 1994. *The Concept of Participation: Transforming Rhetoric to Reality. Participatory Communication: Working for Change and Development*. Newbury Park, CA: Sage.

WHO. 1958. Constitution of the World Health Organization. Geneva: World Health Organization.

———. 2003. *Global Health Sector Strategy for HIV/AIDS 2003–2007*. Geneva: WHO.

———. 2004. *The World Health Report 2004: Changing History*. Geneva: World Health Organization.

Witte, K., G. Meyer, and D. Martell. 2001. *Effective Health Risk Messages: A Step-by-Step Guide*. Newbury Park, CA: Sage.

World Bank. 2005a. "Artisan as Entrepreneur." http://www1.worldbank.org/artisan/mideast.htm.

———. 2005b. "Virtual Souk: E-Commerce for Unprivileged Artisans." http://unpan1.un.org/intradoc/groups/public/documents/Other/UNPAN022138.pdf.

———. 2006a. "Development Communication." http://web.worldbank.org/WBSITE/EXTERNAL/TOPICS/EXTDEVCOMMENG/0,,menuPK:34000201~pagePK:34000189~piPK:34000199~theSitePK:423815,00.html.

———. 2006b. *Global Monitoring Report 2006*. Washington, DC: World Bank.

Women's Voices. 2006. "Case Study: Women's Voices in Nairobi." http://www.itdg.org/?id=womens_voices2.

Yasarekomo. 2004. *Una Experiencia de Comunicación Indigena en Bolivia*. Rome: FAO.

APPENDIX 4

Papers Selected by the Scientific Committee for the World Congress on Communication for Development

The World Congress on Communication for Development launched a call for papers in July 2005, which resulted in the submission of 559 abstracts from 88 countries. These were reviewed by a scientific committee composed of 23 leading professors and practitioners of Communication for Development from 18 academic and research institutions. After a thorough review of all abstracts, the committee invited 290 authors to submit a full paper to the Congress. Of the 213 papers submitted, 137 (from 43 countries) were accepted and their authors were invited to participate in the WCCD.

The majority of the papers accepted came from Canada and the United States (24 percent), and the Asia and Pacific region (24 percent). Next came Europe (19 percent), Africa (18 percent), and Central and South America (13 percent). The Middle East and North Africa was the least represented region, with only 2 percent of the papers selected. The most represented countries, with four or more papers accepted, were Australia, Canada, India, Peru, the Philippines, South Africa, the United Kingdom, and the United States. Together those countries accounted for 56 percent of the papers accepted.

Regarding the types of organizations that proposed papers, academia—mainly universities—were responsible for 48 percent of those accepted, and civil society—predominantly NGOs—was responsible for 30 percent. The private sector—mainly independent consultants—and governments were the next most represented categories, with 5 percent of papers each.

The papers selected were recommended for thematic and poster sessions. A few authors, however, did not accept the invitation to present their papers in the venue recommended.

The papers were integrated into the WCCD program as follows:

Health Sessions

Aubel, Judi. "Using a Neglected Cultural Resource in Development Programs: Grandmother Networks and Participatory Communication."

Bamezai, Gita. "Grassroots Communication Innovations to Make Rural Health More Pragmatic and Scope for Community Ownership."

Chitnis, Ketan. "Scaling Up Communication for Social Change: Implications of the Community-Based Health and Development Model in Jamkhed, India."

Goldstein, Susan, and Esca Scheepers. "Using Edutainment for Social Change—Evidence from Soul City over 6 Years."

Gray-Felder, Denise, Ailish Byrne, James Hunt, Afework Ayele, and Mirgissa Kaba. "CFSC and Youth Clubs Tackle HIV/AIDS in Ethiopia: Using and Evaluating Youth-Focused Dialogue."

Hegazi, Sahar. "Making a Difference: The Success Story of Social Communication in the Battle against Polio in Egypt."

Ogden, Ellyn, Silvio Waisbord, Lora Shimp, and Shan Thomas. "Communication for Disease Eradication: Using Social and Epidemiological Data to Increase Immunity."

Vega, Jair. "Project: Joven Habla Joven (Young People Speak)—A Communication Intervention for Social Change to Improve Sexual Responsibility."

Yahaya, Mohammed. "The Influence of Parent-Child Communication Pattern in Risky Behaviour Reduction among Vulnerable Groups in Nigeria."

Governance Sessions

Adam, Gordon. "News Based or Needs Based? Can Journalism and Advertising Paradigms Be Replaced by Development-Driven Broadcasting Initiatives?"

Alfaro Moreno, Rosa María. "El Desarrollo en la Agenda Pública."

Islam, K M Baharul. "National Information and Communication Infrastructure Policies and Plans towards Poverty Reduction: Emerging Trends and Issues in Africa."

Knippel, Steffen, and Sandra Jackson. "Empowering the Tataskweyak Cree Nation—A Case Study in Effective Communication and Consultation."

Misuraca, Gianluca C. "ICTs for Local Governance in Africa."

Moreno, José Manuel, and Francisco Sierra. "The Experience of Participatory Budgets in the City of Seville: Methodology for Planning Communication Patterns and Constructing Citizenship."

Quarry, Wendy. "Decision Makers DO Want Communication—What They May Not Want Is Participation."

Salazar García, Lina María. "Policy Advocacy Effectiveness and Knowledge Assets: A Case Study about U.K. and Colombian Non-governmental Organisations."

Schippner, Beatriz, and Andrés Quispe Martínez. "Building a Private-Public and Social Partnership to Change Water and Sanitation Management Models in Small Towns."

Walker, Gregg, Steven Daniels, Susan Senecah, Tarla Peterson, Anthony Cheng, and Jens Emborg. "Pluralistic Public Participation: Case Studies in Collaborative Learning."

Sustainable Development Sessions

Barroso, Monica. "Waves in the Forest—Radio Communication and Livelihoods in Brazilian Amazonia."

Bessette, Guy. "Participation, Bananas, and Desertification."

Bossi, Richard, Elizabeth Booth, Tito Coleman, and Roberta Hilbruner. "GreenCOM: 12 Years of Innovation in Strategic Communication for Environmentally Sustainable Development."

Jallov, Birgitte. "Assessing Community Change: Development of a 'Bare Foot' Impact Assessment Methodology for Community Radio."

Odoi, Nora Naiboka, Dezi Ngambeki, and Wilberforce Tushemereirwe. "Communication for Environment and Natural Resource Management."

Ogawa, Yoshiko. "Unsaid Messages: Power Relations within Agricultural Extension Training."

Papania, Patrick, Elizabeth Booth, Karabi Acharya, Tito Coleman, and Shera Bender. "Strategic Communication for System-wide Change: Experience and Results from the Medicinal and Aromatic Plant Sector in Morocco."

Ruiz, Jorge Martínez, Pablo C. Hernández, and José Luis M. Ruiz. "¿Hacemos de la Comunicación una Mercancía?"

Uwamariya, Josephine Irene. "Community Participation in Monitoring the Rwanda PRSP Implementation."

Vyakaranam, V. L. V. Kameswari. "Communication in Environmental Projects: Experiences from Madhya Pradesh Forestry Project."

Poster Sessions

The poster sessions involved the following presentations:

HEALTH

Alakonya, Chrys. "Radio-Based Health Communications on Sexual and Reproductive Health for Somali Speaking Horn of Africa."

Aubel, Judi. "Using a Neglected Cultural Resource in Development Programs: Grandmother Networks and Participatory Communication."

Bamezai, Gita. "Grassroots Communication Innovations to Make Rural Health More Pragmatic and Scope for Community Ownership."

Brazier, Ellen. "Skilled Care during Childbirth: Applying a Behavior Change Approach."

Chitnis, Ketan. "Scaling Up Communication for Social Change: Implications of the Community-Based Health and Development Model in Jamkhed, India."

Claasen-Veldsman, Retha, and Mirtha Snyman. "Audiocassettes: An Alternative Medium for HIV/AIDS Awareness in South Africa."

Concha, Maritza, Maria Elena Villar, Mikele Aboitiz Earle, and Sherri Porcelain."Establishing Best Practices: Assessment of Communication and Participation within a Community Partnership to Support Community Health Workers."

Davidson, Rochelle. "Media for Development: News Media Coverage of Women's Health within the Realm of PMTCT of HIV/AIDS in South Africa."

De Wet, Gideon. "Communication for Sustainable Development Challenges: Local AIDS Councils' Role in the HIV and AIDS Pandemic in South Africa."

Fanelli, Carolyn. "Zimbabwe's Child-Friendly National Plan of Action for Orphans and Other Vulnerable Children."

Garg, Bishan. "Communicating for Health Action in Rural Areas in India."

Haq, Zaeem. "Reaching the Hard to Reach: Therapeutic Communication with Depressed Women in a Poor Rural Area."

Kalisa, Narcisse. "Addressing Sexual and Reproductive Health Related Taboos in Mass Media Communications: Experience in Rwanda."

Malan, Mia, and Elizabeth Gold. "Radio Content Analysis in Kenya Shows Improved News Coverage of HIV/AIDS."

Malikhao, Patchanee. "A Comparative Study of Two Thai Communities with Differing Buddhist versus Christian Participatory Approaches to HIV/AIDS Prevention."

Mayer, Doe. "Women Connect! Using Communication Strategies to Strengthen Women NGOs in Africa."

McArthur, Lisa. "Njoo Tuzungumze! Come, Let's Talk! Behavior Change Communications and VCT in Tanzania."

Micevska, Maja. "Telecommunications, Public Health, and Demand for Health-Related Information and Infrastructure."

Milton, Viola. "Combating HIV/AIDS on the SABC: Public Service Broadcasting, Rainbowism, and Media Advocacy."

Mody, Bella. "Embedding Communication into Development Initiatives: Examples from HIV/AIDS."

Muturi, Nancy. "Approaches and Methods for HIV/AIDS Communication: Best Practice and Lessons Learned from the Caribbean."

Nugent, Rachel, and Sonbol Shahid-Salles. "How Much Health Improvement Can Be Bought for a Million Dollars? Communicating Health Priorities to Different Policy Audiences."

Shahjahan, Mohammad, C. Jacoby, N. McKee, and M. Boulay. "The Know Yourself Program: Taking Adolescent Reproductive Health to Scale in Bangladesh."

Storey, Douglas, D. Lawrence Kincaid, Maria Elena Figueroa, and Carol Underwood. "Communication, Ideation, and Contraceptive Use: The Relationship Observed in Five Countries."

Vértiz, Vanessa. "La Educación Entretenimiento en el Medio Radial en el Marco de un Modelo de Comunicación para el Cambio Social en la Amazonía Peruana."

Vor der Bruegge, Ellen, and Bobbi Gray. "Microfinance—A Vehicle for Sustainable Public Health Communication."

GOVERNANCE

Adkins-Blanch, Sara. "Communication for Development: Bridging the Research-to-Policy Gap."

Barroso, Monica. "Waves in the Forest—Radio Communication and Livelihoods in Brazilian Amazonia."

Colombi, Alice, and Giuliana Frugone. "Interculturality in the Feminine: For a Sustainable Citizenship."

Croce-Galis, Melanie. "Putting the RAPID Framework into Action to Keep Research Off the Shelf and in Practice."

Eribo, Festus. "Transparency and Development Communication: A Content Analysis of Nigerian Press Coverage."

Guo, Qin. "Internet and Participatory Communication in China."

Hartenberger, Lisa. "Promoting Elections in Afghanistan: A Comparison of Two Radio Formats."

Machicado, Rosmery. "El rol de la sociedad civil sobre el control de los medios de información en los nuevos escenarios de conflictos sociales: El caso de Bolivia."

McAnany, Emile. "Incentives and Participation in Development Communication: Evidence from Sixty-Four Recent Projects."

Milan, Stefania. "Community Media and Regulation: Re-writing Media Policy from a Communication for Development Perspective."

Salazar Garcia, Lina Maria. "Policy Advocacy Effectiveness and Knowledge Assets: A Case Study about U.K. and Colombian Non-governmental Organizations."

Schippner, Beatriz, and Andrés Quispe Martínez. "Building a Private-Public and Social Partnership to Change Water and Sanitation Management Models in Small Towns."

Sharmin, Arifa S. "Communicating with Impact: Reducing Vulnerability to Climate Change."

Skjerdal, Terje. "Developing a Journalism Programme in the South."
Solórzano, Irela, Sarah Bradshaw, and Amy Bank. "The Changing Nature of Change: A Nicaraguan Feminist Experience."
Spurk, Christoph. "Evaluating the Quality of Journalistic Reporting."
Uwamariya, Josephine Irene. "Community Participation in Monitoring the Rwanda PRSP Implementation."
Venkatram, Shree. "Equipping Youth from Socially and Economically Disadvantaged Communities in Using the Wall Newspaper for Communication and Change."
Walker, Gregg, Stephen Daniels, Susan Senecah, Tarla Peterson, Anthony Cheng, and Jens Emborg. "Pluralistic Public Participation: Case Studies in Collaborative Learning."

SUSTAINABLE DEVELOPMENT

Antonopoulos, Antonia. "Know Thyself: Conscious Inter-cultural Communication for Western Development Workers."
Aqrabawi, Tamara, Sawsan Zaidah, and Daoud Kuttab. "Community Radio for Development in Jordan."
Bossi, Richard, Elizabeth Booth, Tito Coleman, and Roberta Hilbruner. "GreenCOM: 12 Years of Innovation in Communication for Environmentally Sustainable Development."
Camacho, Carlos. "América Latina, En el Reto de Construir Puentes con y entre las Ciudadanías."
Castillo Tzab, Delfina de los Angeles, and Jannet Valero. "Políticas de Protección Civil vs. Estrategias de Comunicación ante Desastres Naturales."
Czuczman, Kate. "A Networked Research Approach."
de Jong, Dick, Jaap Pels, and Peter McIntyre. "Giving Local Partners and the Poor a Voice in Development."
Genilo, Jude William. "Community-Based Communication in Thai Rice Farming Villages: The Construction of Local Knowledge and Practices."
Hambly Odame, Helen. "Masculinity in the Movement—Gender Dimensions of Communication for Development."
Jackson, Sandra, and Steffen Knippel. "Empowering the Tataskweyak Cree Nation—A Case Study in Effective Communication and Consultation."

Jallov, Birgitte. "Assessing Community Change: Development of a 'Bare Foot' Impact Assessment Methodology for Community Radio."

Kaun, Karen. "ICT and Development in Tanzania: A Matter of Priorities."

Kranz, Johannes, Georg Gruenberg, and Juliana Stroebele-Gregor. "When Difference Matters: Communication and Development with Indigenous Peoples in Latin America."

Mark-Adeyemi, Adedayo. "Strategic Communications in Development: A Case Study of Lagos Water Corporation Private Sector Participation Communication Strategy."

Marsh, Deyna, and Steve Menzies. "Using Communications to Improve the Management of Water Resources in the Cook Islands."

McKee, Neill, M. A. Salas, N. Shahzadi, and H. J. Tillmann. "Visualisation in Participatory Programmes (VIPP): Taking Stock of Its Diffusion and Impact."

Moreno, José Manuel, and Francisco Sierra. "The Experience of Participatory Budgets in the City of Seville: Methodology for Planning Communication Patterns and Constructing Citizenship."

Moreno, Marisol, and Javier Moreno. "Group D: Rural Education, Media, and Empowerment of Communities in the Colombian Andean Area."

Moumouni, Charles. "From Modernization Theories to Participatory Leadership Communication: A New Model for Sustainable Development."

Odoi, Nora Naiboka, Dezi Ngambeki, and Wilberforce Tushemereirwe. "Communication for Environment and Natural Resource Management."

Pojman, April. "A Case Study in Communication for Social Change: Strengthening Municipal Capacity in Water and Sanitation."

Prabakar, Neeraja. "Science for Women."

Protz, Maria. "Towards an 'Archaeology' of Communications for Development: A Foucauldian Analysis of Theory and Practice over 40+ Years."

Reyes, Donna. "Participatory Development Communications: Its Role in Enhancing Protected Area Management in the Philippines."

Sengupta, Ami. "Enacting an Alternative Vision of Communication for Social Change: Minga's Approach in the Perúvian Amazon and Its Implications for Theory and Practice."

Yahaya, Mohammed. "The Influence of Parent-Child Communication Pattern in Risky Behavior Reduction among Vulnerable Groups in Nigeria."

Zhao, Jinqiu. "The Internet and Rural Development: Case Studies of ICT Projects in China."

Other Papers Accepted

The following papers were also accepted by the Scientific Committee:

Agunga, Robert, and Chike Anyaegbunam. "Towards a Discipline and Profession of Communication for Development—Improving Project Implementation as the Key to Poverty Reduction."

Arain, Imran, Nayab A. Burney, and Sajida Parveen. "Investing in Adolescents: An Informed Effort for Information, Education and Communication."

Bakineti, Ritia, and Steve Menzies. "Using Communications to Improve Waste Management in the Pacific Island Nation of Kiribati."

Beardon, Hannah. "Participatory Planning for Rural Communications Systems."

Cardey, Sarah. "The Importance of Integration: The Role of Communication in an Integrated Framework for HIV/AIDS Care, Support, Treatment and Prevention."

Chetley, Andrew. "The Use of ICTs in the Health Sector in Developing Countries: Can ICTs Make a Difference in Health Communication?"

Correa, Mirtha. "Congreso de la República: La Representación Política y la Participación Ciudadana."

De Aguilera, Miguel. "Un Enfoque en Comunicación para la Salud: Jóvenes, Estilos de Vida y Culturas del Riesgo."

Enghel, Florencia. "Participatory Documentary-Making with Indigenous Communities in Argentina: Lessons Learnt."

Faka'osi, Sione. "Improving Waste Management in Tonga: Communication for Behavioural and Institutional Changes."

Fernando, Sheryl. "Development Communication: A Tool in Attaining the Millennium Development Goals in the Cordillera Administrative Region."

Fiona, Otway. "Breaking The Silence: Behind the Scenes of a Video-Based Participatory Communication Project in HIV Prevention."

Gadala, Carmen. "Fortalecimiento de la Labor Periodística en los Temas de los Acuerdos de Paz a Estudiantes y Catedráticos de Comunicación y Periodistas Guatemaltecos."

Giffard, C. Anthony, and Nancy Van Leuven. "Five Views of Development: How News Agencies Cover the Millennium Development Goals."

Goyal, R. S. "Meeting Reproductive and Sexual Health Information Needs of Adolescents in a Community Setting."

Griffiths, Patrick, and Nick Crofts. "Communication for Social Change Supports Harm Reduction Advocacy."

Hadland, Adrian. "Community Television for Sustainable Development: A South African Case Study."

Ileleji, Poncelet. "Communication as a Catalyst to Development (The Gambia YMCAs Experience)."

Ishmael-Perkins, Nick. "Understanding Community Radio Programming: Lessons for Localising Development."

Joshi, Deependra. "Mainstreaming Communications into Conservation Policies and Practices in Nepal."

Kabole, Ibrahim, Barbara Pose, and Ayeta Anne Wangusa. "Tuwasiliane—'Let Us Communicate' In Swahili. Catalyzing the Creation and Exchange of Local Content in Tanzania."

Kema, Koronel, Joseph Komwihangiro, Satiel Kimaro, Vumilia Ngandango, and Barbara Pose. "A Multisectoral Participatory Approach to Turning a Water and Sanitation Intervention into a Motor for Community Development."

Kēpa, Mere and Linitā Manu'atu. "Speak and Speak: Tongan People Talking Our 'Voice' in the National Diploma in Teaching Early Childhood Education (Pasifika)."

Kumar, Manish. "Participatory Message Development on Anemia—A Case Study from Uttaranchal, India."

Lalli, Pina, Ajna Galicic, and Giulia Minoia. "Communication for Development: New Paradigms?"

Lehnert, Andreas. "Asocars: Educación para el Desarrollo Sostenible en la Asociación de Corporaciones en Colombia: Metodología de Trabajo y Teorías Básicas."

Linden, Ank. "Human Rights, Communication Development and National Development Plans."

Loose, Ana Maria. "Espécies Introducidas en Galápagos: De la Indiferencia Social a la Conciencia y Participación Pública."

Lopes, Cristiano. "The Brazilian Model of Digital Inclusion—What We Can (and What We Can Not) Learn with It."

Mannell, Jenevièeve. "Working to Reduce Poverty among the Ultra Poor of Bangladesh through Social Communication."

Marcus, Jerry, and Claudia Velasquez. "Communication Efforts Strengthen Informed Choice in Bolivia, Ecuador and the Democratic Republic of the Congo."

Marietjie, Myburg. "Free the Conversation—Strengthening Media and Advocacy Capacity to Build a Habit of Participative and Informed HIV and AIDS Communication between Citizens and Government."

Martínez Ruiz, José Luis, and Jorge Martínez Ruiz. "La Comunicación: Un Activo Potencial para la Sustentabilidad en Las Comunidades Campesinas."

Menzies, Steve, Leah Nimoho, and Ritia Bakineti. "Using Communications to Strengthen National Environmental Management in the Pacific Islands."

Mhando, Martin. "Participatory Video Production in Tanzania: An Ideal or Wishful Thinking?"

Nascimbeni, Fabio. "The @Lis International Stakeholders Network: How to Build Sustainable Cooperation Links between Europe and Latin America."

Nimoho, Leah, and Steve Menzies. "Using Communications to Promote Sustainable Coastal Fisheries Management in Vanuatu."

Pereira, Claudia. "La Experiencia de Comunicación Estrategica en Nicaragua."

Perlman, Harriet, and Esca Scheepers. "Across Borders—Health and Development Communication: The Importance of Working Regionally (Challenges, Outputs and Assessing Impact)."

Razzak, Sultan Muhammad. "Participatory Theatre: An Effective Behavior Change Communication (Bcc) for Sustainable Development."

Ruiz, Jorge Martínez, and José Luís Martínez Ruiz. "Clotilde Cob, un Paradigma de la Comunicación Rural."

Shinar, Dov. "Democratic Media and Peace Journalism: Essential Requirements for Effective Development Communication."

Shrivastava, K. M. "Communication for Development: Some Policy Considerations."

Singh, Sandeep, and Steve Menzies. "Using Communications to Promote Community-Based Waste Management in Fiji's Rural Communities."

Srivastava, Sanjay. "Environmental Security, Communication Levels and Conservation Attitudes in Rural India—Opportunity Assessment and Policy Recommendations."

Tossy, Titus. "ICTs Training for Improving Health Care of Rural Populations."

Tufte, Thomas. "Is There Only an A, B And C in HIV/AIDS Communication?"

Van De Fliert, Elske. "Assessing the Impact of Communication in Sustainable Rural Development: Reporting Change for Inducing Change."

Vishnu, Prabhir. "The Increasing Leverage of a 'Media-Class Combine' in Policy Dialogues in India."

The complete database of all the 137 papers selected for WCCD is available in the DVD-ROM attached to this publication and on the WCCD Web site at http://www.devcomm.org. The database is searchable by author, title, and country.

References

Aubel, Judi. 2006. "Using a Neglected Cultural Resource in Development Programs: Grandmother Networks and Participatory Communication." Paper prepared for World Congress on Communication for Development.

Chitnis, Ketan. 2006. "Scaling Up Communication for Social Change: Implications of the Community-Based Health and Development Model in Jamkhed, India." Paper prepared for the World Congress on Communication for Development.

Davies, Rick, and Jess Dart. 2005. "The 'Most Significant Change' (MSC) Technique—A Guide to Its Use." http://www.mande.co.uk/docs/MSCGuide.pdf

Communication Initiative. 2006. "Health in a Time of Poverty: A Background Note." Background paper prepared for the WCCD—http://www.devcomm.org/devcomm/Sessions/tabid/81/Default.aspx?macroId=3&microId=302.

DFID (UK Department for International Development) and World Bank. 2006. "Background Note on Communication in Governance." Background paper prepared for the WCCD—http://www.devcomm.org/devcomm/Sessions/tabid/81/Default.aspx?macroId=3&microId=302.

FAO. 2006. "Communication for Sustainable Development." Background paper prepared for the WCCD—http://www.devcomm.org/devcomm/Sessions/tabid/81/Default.aspx?macroId=3&microId=302.

Goldstein, Susan, and Esca Sheepers. 2006. "Using Edutainment for Social Change—Evidence from Soul City over 6 Series." Paper prepared for the World Congress on Communication for Development.

Gray-Felder, Denise, Ailish Byrne, James Hunt, Afework Ayele, and Mirgissa Kaba. 2006. "CFSC and Youth Clubs Tackle HIV/AIDS in Ethiopia: Using and Evaluating Youth-Focused Dialogue." Paper prepared for the World Congress on Communication for Development.

Healthlink. 2006. "Communicating Health Research: How Should Evidence Affect Policy and Practice?" *Findings* 5 (April): 1–6.

Jacobson, J. 1997. "Changing Communication Strategies for Reproductive Health and Rights: An Overview." In *Report from the Meeting on Changing Communication Strategies for Reproductive Health and Rights, Washington, DC, December 10–11, 1997*, ed. Working Group on Reproductive Health and Family Planning, 1–2. New York: Population Council.

Mazzei, Leonardo, Colin Fraser, and Sonia Restrepo Estrada with Silvia Balit and Lucia Grenna. "What Do They Think? Policy Makers and the Role of Communication for Development: A Perception Study Conducted in 2005–2006." Development Communication Division, External Affairs and United Nations Relations Vice Presidency, World Bank, Washington, DC.

Mazzei, Leonardo, and Donal O'Leary. 2006. "Setting Standards for Communication and Governance: The Example of Infrastructure Projects." Presentation at the World Congress on Communication for Development.

McKenna, Maryn. 2006. Presentation at the workshop on avian influenza, at the World Congress on Communication for Development.

Odoi, Nora Naiboka, Dezi Ngambeki, and Wilberforce Tushemereirwe. 2006. "Communication for Environment and Natural Resource Management." Paper prepared for the World Congress on Communication for Development.

Panos. 2006. "Implementing Communication for Development Thinking in Southern Realities—Negotiating Politics, Profit, and Poverty towards Social Inclusion." Paper prepared for the World Congress on Communication for Development." http://www.panos.org.uk/files/icts_conceptnote.pdf.

Quarry, Wendy. 2006. "Decision Makers DO Want Communication—What They May Not Want Is Participation." Paper prepared for the World Congress on Communication for Development.

Quarry, Wendy, and Ricardo Ramírez. 2005. "Analysing How Decision Makers Perceive Communication for Social Change." *MAZI: The Communication for Social Change Report* 3 (May).

Ramírez, Ricardo. 1997. "Understanding Farmers' Communication Networks: Combining PRA with Agricultural Knowledge Systems Analysis." Gatekeeper 66, International Institute for Environment and Development, London.

Reinikka, Ritva, and Jakob Svensson. 2004. "Power of Information: Evidence from a Newspaper Campaign to Reduce Capture." Policy Research Working Paper 3239, World Bank, Washington, DC.

Sandman, Peter M., and Jody Lanard. 2005. "Bird Flu: Communicating the Risk." *Perspectives in Health* 10 (2): 1–6. http://www.paho.org/English/DD/PIN/Number22_article1.htm.

Schippner, Beatriz, and Andrés Quispe Martínez. 2006. "Building a Private-Public and Social Partnership to Change Water and Sanitation Management Models in Small Towns." Paper prepared for the World Congress on Communication for Development.

Solórzano, Irela, Sarah Bradshaw, and Amy Bank. 2006. "The Changing Nature of Change: A Nicaraguan Feminist Experience." Paper prepared for the World Congress on Communication for Development.

———. 2006. "A Compendium of Regional Perspectives in Communication for Development." Paper prepared in collaboration with the Communication for Development Group, Sustainable Development Department.

UN (United Nations) General Assembly. 2006. "Convention on the Rights of Persons with Disabilities." http://www.un.org/esa/socdev/enable/rights/convtexte.htm#convtext.

Usubiaga, Cristina, Steffen Knippel, and Sandra Jackson. 2006. "Empowering the Tataskweyak Cree Nation—A Case Study in Effective Communication and Consultation." Paper prepared for the World Congress on Communication for Development.

Eco-Audit

Environmental Benefits Statement

The World Bank is committed to preserving endangered forests and natural resources. The Office of the Publisher has chosen to print *World Congress on Communication for Development* on 25 percent postconsumer recycled paper, FSC certified, in accordance with the recommended standards for paper usage set by Green Press Initiative—a nonprofit program supporting publishers in using fiber that is not sourced from endangered forests. For more information, visit www.greenpressinitiative.org.

Saved:

Trees*	Solid Waste	Water	Net Greenhouse Gases	Electricity
18	1,102	6,659	2,031	13
*40' in height and 6–8" in diameter	Pounds	Gallons	Pounds	Million BTUs

green press INITIATIVE